Black Cowl
in the American West

Black Cowboys in the American West

On the Range, on the Stage, behind the Badge

Edited by Bruce A. Glasrud and Michael N. Searles

Foreword by Albert S. Broussard

UNIVERSITY OF OKLAHOMA PRESS : NORMAN

Also by Bruce A. Glasrud and Michael N. Searles
Buffalo Soldiers in the West: A Black Soldiers Anthology
(College Station, Texas, 2007)

Library of Congress Cataloging-in-Publication Data

Names: Glasrud, Bruce A., editor. | Searles, Michael N., 1942– editor.
Title: Black cowboys in the American West: on the range, on the stage, behind the
  badge / edited by Bruce A. Glasrud and Michael N. Searles; foreword by Albert S.
  Broussard.
Description: Norman, OK : University of Oklahoma Press, [2016] | Includes
  bibliographical references and index.
Identifiers: LCCN 2016007239 | ISBN 978-0-8061-5406-0 (pbk. : alk. paper)
Subjects: LCSH: African American cowboy—West (U.S.)—Biography. | African
  American cowboys—West (U.S.)—History—19th century. | Cowboys—West
  (U.S.)—History—19th century. | Cowboys—West (U.S.)—Biography.
Classification: LCC F596 .B565 2016 | DDC 978/.00496073—dc23
LC record available at http://lccn.loc.gov/2016007239

The paper in this book meets the guidelines for permanence and durability of the
Committee on Production Guidelines for Book Longevity of the Council on Library
Resources, Inc. ∞

Contents

Foreword

The American cowboy remains one of the most iconic figures in American history. Indeed, in an era of global communication, thanks in large measure to the prevalence of the World Wide Web and access to the Internet, the cowboy's image and iconography have crossed national and international boundaries. Commonly depicted in popular media, dime novels, and best-selling fiction such as Larry McMurtry's *Lonesome Dove* or James Michener's *Centennial* as bold, courageous, fiercely independent, and occasionally prone to violence, the cowboy serves as an endearing figure in the American imagination.

Yet African American cowboys remained largely absent from these fictitious portrayals, although they made brief appearances as cooks, domestics, body guards, prostitutes, and trail hands. The American public slowly began to reevaluate the role of African American cowboys as part of an avalanche of new scholarship that appeared during the civil rights movement in the 1960s. Although Philip Durham and Everett L. Jones were not the first scholars to note the significance of black cowboys, their path-breaking book *The Negro Cowboys* (1965), published a half-century ago, did more than any single publication to advance the argument that African American cowboys played significant and multifaceted roles in the nineteenth-century West. Rather than representing only a minute percentage of American cowboys and relegating them to the margins of western history, Durham and Jones maintained that black cowboys constituted about one-quarter of all cowboys, or more than five thousand individuals. Moreover, they argued convincingly that black cowboys had been prominent in the history of the cattle industry from its beginning in the 1850s until its demise in the late nineteenth century. Thus black cowboys helped to shape and develop the American West as both slaves and freedmen, but they had gained the majority of their experience with cattle after the vast herds had escaped or migrated into West Texas. Here, African American cowboys became expert riders, ropers, and herdsmen and learned to follow the Spanish longhorn cattle that were expanding on the West Texas plains. Other black cowboys such as Bill Pickett, Nat Love, and Jim Beckwourth became highly respected among cowboys of all races and nationalities, serving as lawmen, rodeo performers, and scouts.

Black Cowboys in the American West, edited by Bruce Glasrud and Michael Searles, an excellent collection of both previously published and original essays, builds upon the work of Durham and Jones, to be sure, but it advances many new arguments as well. In addition to the intensive work in archives, special collections, newspapers, and periodicals, this important collection also brings the secondary literature up to date, for the contributors have mined an impressive array of secondary sources that will prove useful to scholars as well as the general public. The collection's primary strength lies in illuminating the great diversity in the black cowboy experience. Although these men and women helped to settle and build black communities, interacted and occasionally intermarried with all of the peoples in the American West, and forged meaningful careers, they remain an understudied area in this literature. Living in the nineteenth-century West did not provide an escape from either racism or racial violence, but black cowboys were permitted greater autonomy and freedom than many of their counterparts experienced in either rural or urban western communities. They also appear to have escaped the brutal violence and terrorism that visited African Americans in many southern communities and northern cities.

Each section of this book describes the role of black cowboys as they attempted to navigate the delicate racial etiquette and expectations of white Americans in the nineteenth-century West. Readers may find part II, "Performing Cowboys," especially intriguing, for it discusses the role of black cowboys in the rodeo circuit but also examines the music of black cowboys, a topic that folklorist Alan Govenar and other cultural historians have examined in the past two decades. Readers will also find the breadth of this collection refreshing. Sara R. Massey's excellent *Black Cowboys of Texas* (College Station, 2000), which contains twenty essays on African American cowboys, is limited to the Lone Star State. *Black Cowboys in the American West* bridges this gap and contains important material on the African American cowboy experience throughout the entire West. Thus, in much the same manner that Philip Durham and Everett Jones forced us to reimagine the American West from an entirely different perspective in 1965, a West where an African American cowboy was almost as likely to tend a cattle herd or ride in a cattle drive as a white cowboy, *Black Cowboys in the American West* will also challenge its readers to reexamine some long-established areas of western history.

ALBERT S. BROUSSARD

Acknowledgments

Like any authors or editors, we have incurred a number of debts. In particular we wish to thank the authors who wrote the chapters used in this book. Four of them prepared original essays for us: thanks, Deborah M. Liles, Cecilia Gutierrez Venable, Miantae Metcalf McConnell, and coeditor Michael N. Searles. Texas A&M University history professor Albert S. Broussard graciously agreed to write the foreword; many thanks, Al. Two of the chapters derive from books published by Texas A&M University Press and two others from Texas Tech University Press studies; these publishers kindly allowed us to use the works. The Texas Folklore Society granted us permission to use an enjoyable article by Alan Govenar. Editors at the *Chronicles of Oklahoma*, *Persimmon Hill*, and *Western Historical Quarterly* answered our inquiries and supported our quest. Even though *American Visions* is now out of circulation, its publisher Gary A. Puckrein and editor Joanne Harris enabled us to use an informative article. San Antonian Kristine Robb scanned and then edited the original copies; we appreciated your work, Kristine. Beginning with our initial inquiry, University of Oklahoma Press editor Chuck Rankin provided encouragement. Editor Kathleen Kelly of that press carefully took our manuscript through the editorial review process. Also at the University of Oklahoma Press, Emily Jerman Schuster produced a book from the manuscript. Copyeditor John Thomas's thorough review enabled a collection of articles to become a whole. Pearlene Vestal Glasrud read the manuscript and helped polish writing glitches. Thanks, Pearlene. We have minimally edited the previous publications for volume consistency. Any errors remain our own responsibility.

BRUCE A. GLASRUD

MICHAEL N. SEARLES

Black Cowboys
in the American West

Introduction

"Don't Leave Out the Cowboys!"

BRUCE A. GLASRUD

"Don't leave out the cowboys," African American writer and poet Langston Hughes cautioned historian William Loren Katz in 1967 as Katz prepared his opus, *The Black West* (1971). Katz followed suit and included a chapter in his book titled "The Cowboys." Though Hughes likely used the word "cowboy" in its broadest sense—as the people who traversed, settled in, and established communities in the United States West—his focus on black cowboys was telling. To that point in time cowboys were assumed to be white. The significance, Katz reminded us, was "that the real cast of characters had to be revealed. Black men and women had to ride across the pages of textbooks just as they rode across the western plains."[1] Thanks to Hughes, Katz, and an increasing number of scholars, we now know that black cowboys have not been left out and that they were a part of the growth of the West.

With that recognition, and given the above-mentioned efforts as well as additional publications, why a new book on the black cowboys? There are reasons to offer a new look at the contributions of blacks to this storied occupation. It is now fifty years since a scholarly, single-volume work has been published on the general topic of black cowboys in the West. Though a wide range of articles about black cowboys and the western communities have been published over the ensuing years, much of that literature is scattered in journals and books not readily available to readers or even known by scholars or lay people. Moreover, exciting new research has been completed, and we have included much of that work in our book. It is important to recognize that a few women were black cowboys, though they were neglected in earlier studies, and to acknowledge, as Art T. Burton has done so well, that lawmen and criminals are also part of the black western experience. We emphasize that black slaves were used through-

3

out the South to tend livestock but point out that black cowboys are most often associated with Texas and Mexico. The black cowboys roamed, worked in, and settled the entire West and existed, as late as the twenty-first century, as riders, ranch workers and owners, rodeo performers, and characters in fiction and movies. Not only do black cowboys appear in books and articles, they are featured in song, in poems, in stories, in novels, and, of course, in movies—hence this broad-based and inclusive book.

Fifty years ago (1965) two UCLA professors of English published a path-breaking, informative, well-researched, and exciting book, *The Negro Cowboys*.[2] With this study Philip Durham and Everett L. Jones ignited a new chapter in the study of the history of the western portion of the United States—exploring the role African Americans played in its settling, formation, and community building. Ten years earlier, in 1955, Durham had set the stage for their book with the publication of two articles, "The Lost Cowboy" in the *Midwest Journal* and "The Negro Cowboy" in *American Quarterly*. In 1964, prior to publication of their book, the duo coauthored two articles, "Slaves on Horseback" in the *Pacific Historical Review* and "Negro Cowboys" for the *American West*. The year following publication of *The Negro Cowboys*, in 1966, they published a young adult's version of their work as *The Adventures of the Negro Cowboys*.[3] Over the past fifty years the publications of Durham and Jones have successfully entertained and informed scholars, lay persons, and youth about black cowboys in the western United States.

In *The Negro Cowboys*, Durham and Jones covered the life and adventures of the hitherto ignored black cowboys. In the first seven chapters they explained the movement to the West by black Americans, how blacks learned cattle work during slavery, and then in chronological and geographical chapters the development of the cattle industry in the late nineteenth century and the roles played by African Americans in that growth. That was not all, the authors reminded us, and they discussed blacks as mustangers, as outlaws and lawmen, and as performers. The book ended with three intriguing studies of Deadwood Dick (Nat Love), blacks and show business, and "the West as fiction." A thorough and convincing book-length study, it held up for years and remains as a solid, though dated work, in print yet today. Although criticized as exaggerated, and perhaps it was somewhat in order to override disbelievers, their book, along with William H. Leckie's *The Buffalo Soldiers* (1967), encouraged other studies of the role and experience of African Americans in the West.[4] Due to the efforts of these and numerous other authors about the black experience in the West, there exist today three general histories of African Americans in the western United States—one, and the first, by Quintard Taylor, *In Search of the Racial Frontier: African Americans in the American West*; and two others, one by Albert S. Broussard, *Expectations of Equality: A History of Black Westerners*, and one by Douglas Flamming, *African Americans in the West*.[5]

Four years after publication of *The Negro Cowboys*, in 1969, one of the pioneering historians of the black western experience, University of Oregon history professor Kenneth Wiggins Porter, published the results of years of research as "Negro Labor in the Western Cattle Industry, 1866–1900" in an article for *Labor History*. In his study Porter portrayed the numerous and challenging aspects of the black cowboys' jobs. Porter's comprehensive investigation alerted us to the black men (about eight to nine thousand) who served as cowboys during the late nineteenth century. As Porter concluded, "That a degree of discrimination and segregation existed in the cattle country should not obscure the fact that, during the halcyon days of the cattle range, blacks there frequently enjoyed greater opportunities for a dignified life than anywhere else in the United States."[6]

Two years later (1971) Porter's article, together with others from his lifelong research into African American western history, was published in *The Negro on the American Frontier* by Arno Press—a publication that had been solicited by William Loren Katz.[7] That same year Katz's own book, *The Black West*, appeared with his chapter "The Cowboys," in which Katz wrote about quite well known black westerners such as Nat Love, Cherokee Bill, Mary Fields, and Isom Dart.[8] In 1972, Bruce A. Glasrud wrote the first of his publications, *Promises to Keep: A Portrayal of Nonwhites in the United States*; it focused on the experiences over time of various peoples of color in United States history—included was an article by Kenneth Wiggins Porter.[9]

Even before publication of *The Negro Cowboys* and "Negro Labor," an African American scholar at Lincoln University had published pioneering articles on black westerners, including black cowboys. W. Sherman Savage produced "Negroes on the Cattleman's Frontier" for *Midwest Journal* (1954–55) and "The Negro Cowboys on the Texas Plains" for the *Negro History Bulletin* (1961). Not until 1976, however, when he was eighty-five years old, was Savage able to publish his signal contribution, *Blacks in the West*. That book, which covered the years 1830–90, included a section on the cattle industry. In one riveting paragraph he focused on Emanuel Organ, who Savage referred to as "Texas's greatest black cowboy of the 1870s."[10] Unfortunately, black American scholar W. Sherman Savage's contributions to the study of black cowboys were not included in the bibliography compiled by Durham and Jones, though they did cite two of his other articles. Kenneth Wiggins Porter, in his aforementioned article, neglected to cite or mention Savage's studies at all.

Since the publications by Durham and Jones, Porter, and Savage, a plethora of other authors and their studies have added to our knowledge of black cowboys in the West. General works include Sara R. Massey's *Black Cowboys of Texas*, which carries more than twenty scholarly portrayals of African American cowboys in and from the Lone Star State. *Black Cowboys*, edited by Paul W. Stewart and Wallace Yvonne Ponce, offers photographs and short vignettes of at least eighty African Americans who worked with cattle from the 1830s through the 1950s. Gina De Angelis gave us *The Black Cowboys*, a book for young adults, and more recently Tricia Martineau Wagner completed a work that focuses on ten black western cowboys, *Black Cowboys of the Old West*.[11] Although each of these books made important contributions, Massey's was the most scholarly and informative, but none rivaled Durham and Jones's insightful and complete regional book on black cowboys. For a succinct article-length overview of the black cowboys, turn to Roger D. Hardaway, "African American Cowboys on the Western Frontier," published originally in *Negro History Bulletin*.[12]

When discussing and evaluating the existence of black cowboys in the West and their work-related efforts, we must not overlook the extensive African background of the cattle industry. A recent book, Andrew Sluyter's *Black Ranching Frontiers: African Cattle Herders of the Atlantic World, 1500–1900*, thoroughly relates the experiences and work-related knowledge of African workers as they expanded across the Atlantic world from the sixteenth to the twentieth century. Sluyter takes his account all the way to Louisiana in the United States, although not to what became the western United States.[13]

There is one additional outstanding and thoroughly engaging book to be mentioned: Michael K. Johnson's *Hoo-Doo Cowboys and Bronze Buckaroos: Conceptions of the African American West*. Johnson, a professor of English, has focused on cultural representations of the black cowboys and African Americans in the West in general. His title was taken from a novel by Ishmael Reed and the western films starring black cowboy actor and singer Herb Jeffries. There is nothing not to like and admire in Johnson's study, whether he addresses literature, films, science fiction, or black characters and authors. In the process, we learn much about black cowboys and their mystique as well as other African American inhabitants of the American West.[14]

Additional authors have focused their books on individual African American cowboy biography; most covered Bill Pickett, Nat Love, Daniel W. "80 John" Wallace, George McJunkin, or Mathew "Bones" Hooks. Pickett appears to be the favorite, perhaps because more information about his life is available. Two works worth reviewing are Cecil Johnson, *Guts: Legendary Black Rodeo Cowboy Bill Pickett*, and Colonel Bailey C. Hanes, *Bill Pickett, Bulldogger: The Biography of a Black Cowboy*. On New Mexican McJunkin, see Franklin Folsom, *Black Cowboy: The Life and Legend of George McJunkin*; for a good study of West Texas fixture Bones Hooks, check Bruce G. Todd, *Bones Hooks: Pioneer Negro Cowboy*. Texas cowboy and rancher "80 John" Wallace is depicted in Hettye Wallace Branch, *The Story of "80 John": A Biography of One of the Most Respected Negro Ranchmen in the Old West*.[15]

Last, but not least, is "Deadwood Dick," or Nat Love, who self-published his own autobiography in 1907. This work has been republished with a first-rate introductory essay, "Nat Love Rides into the Sunset of Slavery and Racism," by editor Brackette F. Williams. The title of Love's marvelous, though partially exaggerated autobiography is *The Life and Adventures of Nat Love, Better Known in the Cattle Country as "Deadwood Dick."* Somewhat surprisingly, no one has tackled the task of writing a book-length scholarly biography of Nat Love. A few young adult books have been produced on Love's life, including Harold W. Felton, *Nat Love: Negro Cowboy*; Holly Cefrey, *From Slave to Cowboy: The Nat Love Story*; and Patricia C. McKissack and Frederick L. McKissack, *Best Shot in the West: The Adventures of Nat Love*.[16]

Although we do not include any pieces of fiction in this anthology on black cowboys, black and white novelists too wrote about and featured black cowboys in the West. African American filmmaker, novelist, and Dakota homesteader Oscar Micheaux wrote two early autobiographical novels—*The Conquest* and *The Homesteader*—about his life in the Dakotas; however, he was not a cowboy but peripheral to them. Other black novelists include Oregonian Percival Everett, who in *God's Country*, *Watershed*, and *Wounded* wrote about the black western experience. In *God's Country* the lead character is Bubba, a black cowboy and scout. Ishmael Reed's *Yellow Back Radio Broke Down* is a fascinating tale of the Loop Garoo Kid, or the Hoo Doo Cowboy. In David Anthony

Durham's *Gabriel's Story*, a black youth leaves his home in Kansas to seek a better life and traverses the West looking; he has an exciting and eventful journey.[17]

White novelists have also depicted black westerners. In Paulette Jiles, *The Color of Lightning*, one prominent character is Texas slave Britt Johnson. Elmer Kelton's *Wagontongue*, about a cowboy strike in late nineteenth-century Texas, is a great read by a literary icon; Jack Ravage, in *Singletree*, provides interesting scenarios of a black life in the West; Patrick Dearen, in *The Big Drift*, tells a story set in West Texas in the mid-1880s when a white cowboy is rescued during a blizzard by a former slave. Novelist Joe Lansdale's main character is Nat Love in *Paradise Sky*.[18] On fiction short stories about the black West, read Bruce A. Glasrud and Laurie Champion's *The African American West: A Century of Short Stories*, an informative review of the black West through literature.[19]

Overall, then, who were the black cowboys? What did they do? Perhaps Tricia Wagner put it best when she wrote, "These cowboys worked with horses and cattle as wranglers, riders, ropers, bulldoggers, broncobusters, and mustangers. They were drovers, foremen, cowpunchers, cattle rustlers, brand readers, cattlemen, cooks, singers, and fiddlers." Some, she asserted, "were legends in their own time; others lived lives of relative obscurity."[20] They came from varied backgrounds; most were male; some grew up in slavery, some as freedmen and women after the Civil War. Many started in Texas and Mexico; others came, as did trail driver Jean Spence Perrault, from other states. Perrault started life in Louisiana, then moved to southeast Texas. Mississippian Holt Collier spent a year as a black cowboy in Texas soon after the Civil War before returning to Mississippi. He ultimately became a noted bear hunter whose name is entwined with Theodore Roosevelt and the "teddy bear."[21] Black cowboys settled in and enabled the development of communities throughout the American West.

As we have learned, not all black cowboys resided in Texas. Charlie Glass grew up in Indian Territory (Oklahoma) and eventually accepted work in southeastern and later western Colorado. In 1917 he moved to the Utah-Colorado border. Glass became fearful of and disliked by sheepherders and had a number of fights with them, one in which he killed a man in 1921. Glass lived until 1937, when he died of a broken neck in a fall from a pick-up truck driven by his sheepherder enemies. He was referred to as a good rider and a top-notch man with a lariat. Walker D. Wyman and John D. Hart have provided us with an informative account in "The Legend of Charlie Glass."[22] Jim Kelly, "The Ebony Gun," served as chief enforcer and cowhand for the Print Olive ranch in

Texas. In 1876, because of the passing of free range, rustlers, and legal troubles, Olive moved his ranching business to central Nebraska. Kelly went along, once more as enforcer, but the Olives were a little too free with the use of their pistols, and Print Olive spent some time in prison. By 1880, Kelly and the Olives had moved back to Texas.[23]

Black cowboys scattered and moved with or to jobs where their skills could be utilized. A prominent African American cowboy in western South Dakota was Bunk White. Jessie Stahl settled in California in the early twentieth century, where he became a prominent rodeo rider; he pioneered riding his horse backwards. One Colorado cowboy, Willie Kennard, applied for and became the marshal in central Colorado. Kennard was a former member of the Ninth Cavalry of buffalo soldiers. Born in Washington, D.C., Charles J. Rhone moved to Wyoming, where he became "a most skillful cowboy."[24] According to Walter Dean Myers, Joshua Loper rode from Texas to Montana in 1871, a long and hard journey trailing a herd of cattle. He followed that with at least six more drives to and through the Plains in the 1870s. In a chapter titled "Cattle and Ranching," Thomas P. Newgard and William C. Sherman mentioned a number of black men in the late nineteenth and early twentieth centuries who worked as cowhands in North Dakota. In Colorado, John Henry Harris became well known as a "singing cowboy." Black cowboys in the late nineteenth century also were featured in dime novels; one such man was "Arizona Joe," a sidekick of Anglo hero "Texas Jack."[25]

The migration of southern blacks north and west did not stop at the U.S. border; some former black slaves became cowboys and ranchers in Canada. One such, John Ware, was raised as a slave in South Carolina, then at the Civil War's end moved to Texas, and on to Alberta, Canada, in 1882. While working for the Bar U Ranch he became legendary for his cowboy skills and his ability to survive stampedes, bucking broncs, blizzards, rustlers, and racism. He later established his own ranch near Red Deer River. Ware died in 1905. As a black cowboy Ware, known as "the Negro Cowboy," was part of the western experience shared with his compatriots south of the Canadian border. His life has been depicted by Grant MacEwan, *John Ware's Cow Country*; Ian Hundey, *John Ware: Cowboy*; and in a novel by Bill Gallaher, *High Rider*.[26]

Even though much information about black cowboys can be discovered, the question of the number of black cowboys is open. How many were there? There is no easy answer. For example, Porter claimed that eight or nine thousand black cowboys worked in the late nineteenth century, and Durham and Jones concluded that five thousand black cowboys operated in the West from the end of the Civil War to the mid-eighties. Both of those numbers have been challenged from two directions. A few authors report that the number should be from nine to twelve thousand but provide no specific evidence for their numbers. On the other hand, a few recent historians have suggested that five thousand is also an inaccurate number, that it is too high—but once more, as the U.S. Supreme Court remarked in a recent court decision (albeit on a different topic), there is no evidence to the contrary.[27] As a result, in this volume we assume that at least five thousand African Americans worked and operated as black cowboys in the years beginning with 1866 (the number might even be closer to the estimate of Porter). The number might even be greater; we doubt very much that black female cowhand Johana July and her counterparts were listed by the U.S. Census as cowboys or cattle workers, if they were even counted for the census.

Modern-day researchers recognize that black cowhands were not all male. As far as we know, almost all, if not all, who worked on the long trail drives were men, but black women were present on the ranches and farms in the West, doing jobs of cattle and horse raising and tending. Former slave Julia Blanks and her husband worked on the Adams Ranch in the Frio Valley of Texas. She served as cook for the roundups, carried a sixty-pound can of water from the river on her head, and when her help was needed rode with her husband attending the cattle. Later her oldest daughter followed suit. Two additional South Texas black women cowhands were Johana July and Henrietta Williams Foster, or "Aunt Rittie," as she was known. Aunt Rittie, who owned her own home and cattle, thrived in her cattle- and horse-raising environment. Johana July is discussed in an original essay in this volume.[28]

This book is meant to be an inclusive study of black cowboys in the western United States from before the Civil War to at least 1886, a year that signaled the end of the great trail drives. We go beyond those years with articles included from studies on twentieth-century rodeos, music, people, and films and extend the study even beyond 1966, when the previous inclusive work on black cowboys in the West was published. At the same time, we do not mean to imply that the only group left out of previous discussions was the black cowboys.

As Arnoldo De Leon pointed out so well in his recent article for the *Journal of South Texas*, "*Vamose Pa'Kiansis*: Tejanos in the Nineteenth-Century Cattle Drives," persons of Mexican descent have seldom been recognized despite the fact that they were approximately 15 percent of the trail-riding cowboys in the late nineteenth century. Two other studies of cowboys of Mexican descent are Martin W. Sandler, *Vaqueros: America's First Cowmen*, and Russell Freedman, *In the Days of the Vaqueros: America's First True Cowboys*. S. Kay Gandy also tells us about Native Americans who were cowboys.[29]

Black Cowboys in the American West comprises a foreword written by Texas A&M University scholar Albert S. Broussard, this introduction by Glasrud, basic article compilations divided into three parts that include four or five articles each, an overview, and a bibliography. In part I, "Cowboys on the Range," we devote attention to the African Americans who could be referred to as cowboys, both before and after the Civil War, and their work-related experiences. We emphasize the varied opportunities open to black cowboys who were adept at riding, taming, and working with cattle; this section includes discussion of both male and female cowhands and concludes with a visit to the life and career of the well-known black cowboy icon Nat Love.[30] Part II, "Performing Cowboys," looks at the cultural side of the cowboy experience, focusing on rodeos in Texas and Oklahoma as well as songs, films, movies, and writings. Mentioned are black performers such as Herb Jeffries and Bill Pickett. Part III, "Outriders of the Black Cowboys," considers three African Americans who performed duties similar in nature to that of the black cowboys, such as lawman Bass Reeves, postal carrier Mary Fields, and Charley Willis, the "singing cowboy."[31] After a tiring journey at the end of a long trail, black cowboys, like their white counterparts, relaxed for a short duration in cattle towns on the great north and westward cattle trail. A well-researched article by C. Robert Haywood focuses on one of those communities, Dodge City, Kansas. The book ends with Michael Searles's article titled "In Search of the Black Cowboy," which serves as the concluding overview to the book.

Black cowboys in the West have not been forgotten. The aftermath of the Civil War offered a trail to the West for blacks in the South and East. Not only was there a long line and tradition of African Americans serving as cowhands immediately after that war, some in the South were doing this work even before the war (Afro-Mexican Pedro Ramirez worked on ranches near San Antonio prior to Texas independence), and others continue to do so in the twenty-first century. The cattle industry provided adventurous people with economic incentives as well as open spaces in the American West. Perhaps Texas A&M University historian Albert S. Broussard summarized their motives best: "Working as a cowboy or ranch hand afforded a black man [or woman] a higher degree of freedom and autonomy than enjoyed by the typical tenant farmer or sharecropper."[32]

Former African American slaves were familiar with raising and herding cattle, and after the war some five to eight thousand herded cattle in long trail drives until the late 1880s. After that through the twentieth century thousands of blacks worked as cowboys, participated in rodeos, ranched, and were featured in books, movies, and television. Their lives may sound romantic to outside observers, but their work was difficult and intensive. They faced discrimination, but less than in the South from which many came. Service as black cowhands continues into the twenty-first century. These black cowboys, as other African Americans who either ventured west or grew up there, helped settle and establish black communities and agencies in the western United States. Many individuals and writers heeded the call of Langston Hughes to not forget the cowboys.

Notes

1. William Loren Katz, *The Black West: A Documentary and Pictorial History of the African American Role in the Westward Expansion of the United States* ([1971] Garden City, N.Y.: Doubleday Anchor Books, 1973), xi–xii; for "The Cowboys" chapter, 143–66.

2. Philip Durham and Everett L. Jones, *The Negro Cowboys* ([1965] Lincoln: University of Nebraska Press, 1983).

3. Philip Durham, "The Lost Cowboy," *Midwest Journal* 7 (1955): 176–82; Philip Durham, "The Negro Cowboy," *American Quarterly* 7 (Fall 1955): 291–302; Philip Durham and Everett L. Jones, "Slaves on Horseback," *Pacific Historical Review* 33 (1964): 405–409; Philip Durham and Everett L. Jones, "Negro Cowboys," *American West* 1 (Fall 1964): 26–31, 87; Philip Durham and Everett L. Jones, *The Adventures of the Negro Cowboys* (New York: Dodd, Mead, 1966).

4. Durham and Jones, *Negro Cowboys*; William H. Leckie, *The Buffalo Soldiers: A Narrative of the Negro Cavalry in the West* (Norman: University of Oklahoma Press, 1967). On the black soldiers, see also Bruce A. Glasrud and Michael N. Searles, eds.,

Buffalo Soldiers in the West: A Black Soldiers Anthology (College Station: Texas A&M University Press, 2007).

5. Quintard Taylor, *In Search of the Racial Frontier: African Americans in the American West, 1528–1990* (New York: W. W. Norton, 1998); Albert S. Broussard, *Expectations of Equality: A History of Black Westerners* (Wheeling, Ill.: Harlan Davidson, 2012); Douglas Flamming, *African Americans in the West* (Santa Barbara, Calif.: ABC-CLIO, 2009).

6. Kenneth Wiggins Porter, "Negro Labor in the Western Cattle Industry, 1866–1900," *Labor History* 10 (Summer 1969): 346–74, quote on 367.

7. Kenneth Wiggins Porter, *The Negro on the American Frontier* (New York: Arno Press, 1971).

8. William Loren Katz, *The Black West: A Documentary and Pictorial History of the African American Role in the Westward Expansion of the United States* (New York: Doubleday and Company, 1971).

9. Kenneth W. Porter, "Florida Slaves and Free Negroes in the Seminole War, 1835–1842," in *Promises to Keep: A Portrayal of Nonwhites in the United States*, ed. Bruce A. Glasrud and Alan M. Smith, 114–28 (Chicago: Rand McNally, 1972).

10. W. Sherman Savage, "Negroes on the Cattleman's Frontier," *Midwest Journal* 6 (1954–1955): 35–48; W. Sherman Savage, "The Negro Cowboys on the Texas Plains," *Negro History Bulletin* 24 (April 1961): 157–58, 163; W. Sherman Savage, *Blacks in the West* (Westport, Conn.: Greenwood Press, 1976): 86–95, 115–16, quote on 89.

11. Sara R. Massey, ed., *Black Cowboys of Texas* (College Station: Texas A&M University Press, 2000); Paul W. Stewart and Wallace Yvonne Ponce, *Black Cowboys* (Broomfield, Colo.: Phillips, 1986); Gina De Angelis, *The Black Cowboys* (Philadelphia: Chelsea House, 1998); Tricia Martineau Wagner, *Black Cowboys of the Old West* (Guilford, Conn.: Globe Pequot Press, 2011).

12. Roger D. Hardaway, "African American Cowboys on the Western Frontier," *Negro History Bulletin* 64 (January/December, 2001): 27–32.

13. Andrew Sluyter, *Black Ranching Frontiers: African Cattle Herders of the Atlantic World, 1500–1900* (New Haven: Yale University Press, 2012).

14. Michael K. Johnson, *Hoo-Doo Cowboys and Bronze Buckaroos: Conceptions of the African American West* (Jackson: University Press of Mississippi, 2014).

15. Colonel Bailey C. Hanes, *Bill Pickett, Bulldogger: The Biography of a Black Cowboy* (Norman: University of Oklahoma Press, 1977); Cecil Johnson, *Guts: Legendary Black Rodeo Cowboy Bill Pickett* (Fort Worth, Tex.: Summit Group, 1994); Franklin Folsom, *Black Cowboy: The Life and Legend of George McJunkin* (Niwot, Colo.: Roberts Rinehart, 1992); Bruce G. Todd, *Bones Hooks: Pioneer Negro Cowboy* (Gretna, La.: Pelican, 2005).

16. Brackette F. Williams, "Nat Love Rides into the Sunset of Slavery and Racism," in

Nat Love, *The Life and Adventures of Nat Love, Better Known in the Cattle Country as "Deadwood Dick"* ([1907] Lincoln: University of Nebraska Press, 1995): vii–xviii; Harold W. Felton, *Nat Love: Negro Cowboy* (New York: Dodd, Mead, 1969); Patricia C. McKissack and Frederick L. McKissack, *Best Shot in the West: The Adventures of Nat Love* (New York: Chronicle Books, 2012; Holly Cefrey, *From Slave to Cowboy: The Nat Love Story* (Buffalo, N.Y.: Rosen, 2003).

17. On Micheaux, see Betti Carol Van Epps-Taylor, *Oscar Micheaux: A Biography* (Rapid City, S.Dak.: Dakota West, 1999). Johnson, *Hoo-Doo Cowboys,* 7, 9; 13; Ishmael Reed, *Yellow Back Radio Broke-Down* (New York: Doubleday, 1969); David Anthony Durham, *Gabriel's Story* (New York: Doubleday, 2001); Percival Everett, *God's Country* (Boston: Beacon Press, 2003); Percival Everett, *Wounded* (St. Paul, Minn.: Graywolf, 2005).

18. Paulette Jiles, *The Color of Lightning: A Novel* (New York: William Morrow, 2009); Elmer Kelton, *Wagontongue* (New York: Bantam Books, 1972); Jack Ravage, *Singletree* (Laramie, Wyo.: Jelm Mountain, 1990); Patrick Dearen, *The Big Drift* (Fort Worth: Texas Christian University Press, 2014); Joe Lansdale, *Paradise Sky* (Boston: Little, Brown, 2015).

19. Bruce A. Glasrud and Laurie Champion, eds., *The African American West: A Century of Short Stories* (Boulder: University Press of Colorado, 2000).

20. Wagner, *Black Cowboys,* xiii.

21. Wesley Norton, "Negro Trail-Driver, Jean Spence Perrault, and His Beaumont Descendants," *Texas Gulf Historical and Biographical Record* 19 (November 1983): 35–50; Minor Ferris Buchanan, *Holt Collier: His Life, His Roosevelt Hunts, and the Origin of the Teddy Bear* (Jackson: Centennial Press of Mississippi, 2002).

22. Walker D. Wyman and John D. Hart, "The Legend of Charlie Glass," *Colorado Magazine* 46 (1969): 40–54. They also published their work in a booklet format, *The Legend of Charlie Glass* (River Falls, Wisc.: River Falls State University Press, 1970).

23. James M. Smallwood, "James Kelly: The Ebony Gun," in Massey, *Black Cowboys of Texas,* 143–53.

24. Betti VanEpps-Taylor, *African Americans in South Dakota* (Pierre: South Dakota State Historical Society, 2008), 119–21; Stewart and Ponce, *Black Cowboys,* 10, 24, 72–73, 180, quote at 73.

25. Walter Dean Myers, *The Journal of Joshua Loper: A Black Cowboy* (New York: Scholastic, 1999), 48–52; Thomas P. Newgard, William C. Sherman, and John Guerrero, eds., *African Americans in North Dakota* (Bismarck, N.Dak.: University of Mary Press, 1994), 48–52; Stewart and Ponce, *Black Cowboys,* 115, 180–82.

26. Grant MacEwan, *John Ware's Cow Country* (Edmonton, Alb.: Greystone, 1995); Ian Hundey, *John Ware: Cowboy* (Markham, Ont.: Fitzhenry and Whiteside, 2005); Bill Gallaher, *High Rider* (Victoria, B.C.: TouchWood, 2015). I thank my Canadian cousin, Ray Glasrud, for alerting me to the life and import of John Ware.

27. Porter, "Negro Labor"; Durham and Jones, *Negro Cowboys*; Quintard Taylor, *In Search of the Racial Frontier: African Americans in the American West, 1528–1990* (New York: W. W. Norton, 1998), 156–63, 341–42; William W. Savage Jr., *The Cowboy Hero: His Image in American History and Culture* (Norman: University of Oklahoma Press, 1985). On the number of black cowboys, see also Massey, *Black Cowboys of Texas*, xiii–xv.

28. T. Lindsay Baker, "Remembrances: Black Cowboy Life in Texas," in Massey, *Black Cowboys of Texas*, 23–38; Louise S. O'Connor, "Henrietta Williams Foster, 'Aunt Rittie': A Cowgirl of the Texas Coastal Bend," in Massey, *Black Cowboys of Texas*, 67–72. On Johana/Johanna July, see Jim Coffey, "Johanna July: A Horse-Breaking Woman," in Massey, *Black Cowboys of Texas*, 73–82.

29. Arnoldo De Leon, "*Vamos Pa' Kiansis:* Tejanos in the Nineteenth-Century Cattle Drives," *Journal of South Texas* 27, no. 2 (Fall 2014): 6–21; Martin W. Sandler, *Vaqueros: America's First Cowmen* (New York: H. Holt, 2000); Russell Freedman, *In the Days of the Vaqueros: America's First True Cowboys* (New York: Clarion Books, 2001); S. Kay Gandy, "Indian Cowboys, Black Cowboys, and Vaqueros," *Social Education* 72, no. 4 (2008): 189–93. See also Lawrence Clayton, Jim Hoy, and Jerald Underwood, *Vaqueros, Cowboys, and Buckaroos* (Austin: University of Texas Press, 2001).

30. On Nat Love, review Blake Allmendinger, "Deadwood Dick: The Black Cowboy as Cultural Timber," *Journal of American Culture* 16, no. 4 (Winter 1993): 79–89; Kenneth Speirs, "Writing Self (Effacingly): E-Race-D Presences in *The Life and Adventures of Nat Love*," *Western American Literature* 40, no. 3 (Fall 2005): 301–20; Susan Scheckel, "Home on the Train: Race and Mobility in the *Life and Adventures of Nat Love*," *American Literature* 74, no. 2 (June 2002): 219–50; Charity Fox, "Cowboys, Porters, and the Mythic West: Satire and Frontier Masculinity in *The Life and Adventures of Nat Love*," in *Fathers, Preachers, Rebels, Men*, ed. Peter Caster, 184–202 (Columbus: Ohio State University Press, 2011). See also Douglas Flamming's perceptive comments in Flamming, *African Americans in the West*, 63–70.

31. On Mary Fields, check Tricia Martineau Wagner, "A Force to Be Dealt With: Mary Fields," in *African American Women of the Old West* (Helena, Mont.: TwoDot, 2007), 13–25; a good depiction of Fields's life is Dee Garceau-Hagen, "Finding Mary Fields: Race, Gender, and the Construction of Memory," in *Portraits of Women in the American West*, ed. Dee Garceau-Hagen, 121–55 (New York: Routledge, 2005). Some information on Fields can be garnered in Gary Cooper, "Stagecoach Mary," *Ebony* 14 (October 1959): 97–100.

32. Alwyn Barr, *Black Texans: A History of African Americans in Texas, 1528–1995*, 2nd ed. (Norman: University of Oklahoma Press, 1996), 3; Broussard, *Expectations of Equality*, 46.

PART I

❧

Cowboys on the Range

I

Before Emancipation

Black Cowboys and the Livestock Industry

DEBORAH M. LILES

In this chapter, University of North Texas historian Deborah M. Liles argues that enslaved African Americans were used and trained in the livestock industry years before they rode up the trails as freedmen. This use of antebellum black labor is one that is generally overlooked, but it is important when considering the history of black cowboys. Liles has authored another significant piece on this topic, "Slavery and Cattle in the East and West," for the *East Texas Historical Journal*. She is also working on a critical and exhaustive study titled *Southern Roots, Western Foundations: The Peculiar Institution and the Livestock Industry on the Northwestern Frontier of Texas, 1846–1864*, forthcoming from Louisiana State University Press.

Had historians paid more attention to the cattle industry of the cis-Mississippi [trans-Appalachia] West, nothing would have appeared more logical [than black cowboys]. Mounted slaves, in their roles as "cattle hunters," displayed considerable skill as horsemen on the Carolina frontier, and generations of their descendants watched over cattle as the culture of their masters spread across the Deep South until it crossed the Sabine.[1]

As historian John D. W. Guice stated so well, many enslaved African Americans were known for their abilities as cowhands. This happened throughout the Old South and Indian Territory, not just in cattle-rich Texas. Some early scholars have discounted the ability of slaves in the livestock industry, but others have acknowledged the significant evidence that confirms the use of their labor. Slave narratives, letters, and journals preserve a history of slaves hunting, tending, rounding up, and branding cattle. These sources describe a use of chattel labor distinct from cash-crop agriculture and illustrate how those men, women, and children used these valuable skills after emancipation in the era of the great cattle drives. The years of bondage are not traditionally thought of as the foundational era of black cowboys in North America, but they were integral for many black Americans who went up the trails in the years after the Civil War.

When writing about overseers, owners, and their herders, Terry Jordan made the interesting observation that they were all "variously called 'cowpen-keepers,' 'cowkeepers,' . . . 'hands,' 'rangers,' and, in the case of African slaves, perhaps even 'cowboys.'"[2] Historian Peter H. Wood wrote that the unique knowledge slaves brought with them from Africa was a necessary component in the success of the industry in the Carolinas. He also observed that many white settlers requested slaves from the Gambia River area of Africa, for they were valued for their knowledge and ability to handle cattle. Even when their owners were present, "the care of their livestock often fell to a black. The slave would build a small 'cowpen' in some remote region, attend the calves, and guard the grazing stock at night."[3] Guice made many observations about slaves being used in the livestock industry, not least of all that "a 1770 regulation concerning land grants in Louisiana leaves little doubt concerning the use of slaves in this capacity. In order to become a grantee, applicants had to be 'the possessor of one hundred head of tame cattle, some horses and sheep, and two slaves to look after them.'"[4] Historian Edward Pearson noted that male slaves were generally used as ranch hands in the South Carolina low country when settlers realized the value of the livestock industry, and cattle owners such as James Joyner and Bernard Schenkingh used their slaves to manage several hundred head; other owners sold their livestock with slaves to new speculators.[5] This is just a smattering of the many examples by noteworthy academics that show black slaves participating in the livestock industry throughout the South.

"Cowboy" is a word that immediately conjures up an image, but one that may not be historically accurate. William W. Savage Jr. wrote that progress was being made back in 1979, when people were finally realizing that "cowboys came in colors other than white," but the word seldom rouses images of black heritage.[6] During slavery, and even today, however, the word "boy" was used to demean black men.[7] Wood suggested that "cowboy" was originated by absentee cattlemen referring to slaves who had been left in charge of the herds in the Carolinas. An added footnote makes the astute observation, "Might not the continued predominance of 'cowboy' over alternative terms such as 'cattleman' represent a strange holdover reflective of early and persistent black involvement in the cattle trade?" Along with that is the comment that "young Negroes with livestock responsibilities were still being designated as 'cow boys' (two words) in the plantation records of the Southeast" in 1865.[8] It must also be said that white men who worked cattle referred to themselves as drovers, traders, or stock raisers and keepers, as did census takers.[9]

Despite the work of these fine scholars, the notion that cattlemen who owned slaves were overwhelmingly more successful than those who did not has been overlooked until recently. Rather than examine the successful connection between stock raisers and low numbers of slaves in frontier counties, historians have erroneously concluded that the presence of a few slaves represented a lack of support or need for the institution west of the 98th meridian. Additionally, it is not uncommon to see variations of Eugene D. Genovese's opinion that slaves were inept cattle handlers who abused or neglected their masters' stock. The two most repeated incidents in Texas support the incompatibility. One concerns Joe, Samuel Maverick's slave who neglected to brand the cattle, which led to people calling unbranded cattle mavericks. The second example—which tells that Shanghai Pierce, a white cowboy, should ride the bad horses, because "those Negroes are worth a thousand dollars apiece [and] one might get killed!"—implies that slaves were far too expensive, and perhaps unskilled, to use for breaking horses.[10]

Although the frontier is most commonly associated with the livestock trade, it was not the only location where horses, cattle, sheep, and swine were kept. Plantation owners were not in the habit of keeping large herds, but some did. James Boyd Hawkins, whose various holdings of 40–105 slaves produced sugar, molasses, and cotton in Matagorda County, Texas, reported one thousand head of cattle in his 1853 property taxes, up from a total of one hundred in 1847.[11] Historian Kenneth Stamp wrote that most planters relied on drovers to supply meat, since they used their land for their cash crops.[12] This claim is supported with statistics gathered by Randolph B. Campbell from the 1850 and 1860 agricultural censuses, which show that slaves who lived in groups of ten to forty-nine resided on farms where the least amount of cattle was slaughtered, whereas the category that contained groups of nine or fewer slaves recorded the highest. Though Campbell's statistics support the generalization for most of the plantations, Hawkins's property tax records show that the cattle trade held a universal appeal. By using his slaves to tend his cattle, raise cotton and sugar, produce molasses, and run a mill, Hawkins demonstrated the multiple ways in which diversification of slave labor was beneficial to slaveholders. And he was by no means the only planter who raised and sold livestock as well as grew a cash crop. Guice noted that cattle supplied funds when cash crops did not provide adequate money, and that enough evidence "suggests that southern historians must reassess the planter's role as stockman and determine the inter-relationship between planters and herdsmen, decade by decade, throughout the antebellum period."[13]

It is safe to say that slaves on plantations experienced different living condi-tions from those who worked with owners who mainly participated in the live-stock industry. Testimonies of ex-slaves in the Works Progress Administration's Slave Narratives project confirm the different lifestyles many slaves experi-enced.[14] Many whose masters were involved in the livestock industry noted that they were well fed and seldom lacked for beef or bacon, whereas those who were in a plantation environment generally stated that there was little beef and other rations. It can also be concluded that slaves who belonged to cattlemen often experienced a different level of bondage. Much of their time was spent in conditions that offered opportunities for freedom. They were often armed, on horseback, or both, and many times they were without supervision in remote areas. This begs the question of why they did not escape. Historian James Smallwood suggested that the skill set employed by the cowboy slaves removed many of the restrictions faced by others. Slaves who worked stock ranked higher in the social hierarchy than those who worked in the fields, possibly because they often worked alongside their owners. Smallwood wrote that "Texas cattlemen treated some slaves with the same consideration that they gave white hands. Ranchers regarded some bondsmen as so indispens-able—not to mention trusted—that they used blacks in cattle drives to Mexico [where slavery was illegal]."[15] It is also important to note that, on cattle drives after the war, black cowboys were often treated with respect and paid the equiv-alent of white wages. This kind of working environment existed because they were acknowledged for their skills, not their color, and the fact that it existed in the years directly after the war all but confirms that this respect existed before as well.[16]

Campbell's main focus was on the lives of slaves who engaged in crop agri-culture, but he included information about slaves in the cattle industry. He addressed the seasonal work of branding and hog killing and noted that slaves who fed the livestock were up an hour earlier than their counterparts through-out the year. He wrote that Willis, one of Gov. Francis R. Lubbock's slaves and cowboys, bought his freedom with cattle proceeds, and that the first noted cattle baron in Texas, James Taylor White, "used black drovers and handlers for the thousands of head of cattle he owned in the Atascosito District." He also included the 1854 court case of the widowed Amanda Wildly in Jackson County, Texas, who did not wish to sell any slaves or horses to pay debts because it would "require the service of the principal part of the horses and negroes to take care of and manage the stock of cattle."[17]

Campbell's examples can be added to others. The Slave Narratives, which were seemingly geared toward asking slaves about their lives as they related to plantation agriculture, become valuable testimonials for slaves engaged in other industries besides cash-crop cultivation. Taken seven decades after slavery legally ended, the recollections of those who experienced the institution firsthand are sometimes viewed with skepticism. Common complaints are that memories often change with time, that the interviews were not always conducted in the most desirable ways, and that the questions were often leading. Despite their flaws, these collective memories provide a wealth of information about the lives of slaves before and after emancipation.[18]

Many testimonies provide a lens on slavery in the livestock industry. William Green was twelve when he was brought to La Vernia, Wilson County, where his new master "raised and trained wild horses" and he was "a buckerman . . . yes *buckerman.* . . . By the time I was twelve, I could break horses alongside the best of 'em. They wasn't as mean to us as they was to a lot of slaves, but we got our share of suffering. They whipped us with straps and not black bull-whips, like they used in Mississippi. Our food was better. We had meat—bacon, and sometimes beef. And we always had cornbread."[19]

Green's was by no means the only narrative that recounted working as a livestock slave. Austin Johnson was purchased in Louisiana and brought to Texas to work his new owner's cattle. Johnson trained horses for races in Hot Springs, Arkansas, and Louisville, Kentucky, which provided him with valuable knowledge. Purchasing a slave who knew how to handle horses was undoubtedly a calculated investment by his new owner.[20] Another slave, James Cape, was trained as a young child to ride horses and tend cattle. He and four other men went from southeastern Texas into Mexico get horses while he was still a slave. At one point he was the "leader" of a two-hundred-horse drive when a hailstorm erupted. His actions to stop the horses from "scatterment" were rewarded with a new saddle from his master. When the war began, Cape's master sent him into the army, as a substitute for a Dr. Carroll, to tend horses; while there he was shot in the shoulder. After the war, Cape worked as a cowboy for several different men in Texas and Missouri using the skills he acquired while he was enslaved.[21]

Monroe Brackins belonged to George Reedes, who owned a stock business on the Hondo River. Outfitted with homespun clothes, shoes, and "rawhide legin's," he learned how to break horses and work cattle. Like other livestock slaves, he remembered plenty of meat to eat, wild game and beef. Brackins and his parents stayed and worked with Reedes for a few years after the end of the war and then moved on. One of the cattlemen Brackins worked with as a freedman was William Wallace, a.k.a. Bigfoot Wallace.[22]

Other testimonies add to the bigger picture. Jacob Branch lived with his master in Double Bayou, Texas, where he and other slaves "tend de cattle and feed hosses and hawgs."[23] Jack Bess belonged to a rancher near Goliad, Texas, where he worked with the cattle and horses; Bess was another who remembered fair treatment from his owner and plenty of meat and vegetables to eat.[24] Henry Lewis was owned by Bob Code in Jefferson County, Texas. He stated: "When I six or seven year old dey 'cides I's big 'nough to start ridin' hosses. Dey have de big cattle ranche and I ride all over dis territory. I's too li'l to git on de hoss and dey lift me up, and dey have de real saddle for me, too. I couldn't git up, I sho' could stay up when I git dere. I's jis' like a hoss-fly." Lewis also stated that they branded cattle from March 1 to December 15, an observation that is fully supported by journals that record multiple trips of cattlemen as they cow-hunted throughout the year. Again, like the many others, Lewis remembered plenty of beef and bacon to eat.[25]

These stories are just a sampling of slaves' memories in the livestock industry. Exploring these narratives with the specific intent of looking for connections to the livestock industry changes the perception of what slaves did in Texas and other states. They challenge the notion that all slave owners wanted to be engaged in the cotton business. In his narrative, Felix Grundy Sadler recounted that his master, Jimmy Sadler, intentionally passed through rich Blackland Prairie soil and on to Bosque County to raise cattle.[26]

In addition to the Slave Narratives, property tax records show that many of the most, and least, known cattlemen owned slaves. Uniformity laws in Texas, and in other southern states, meant that all property was taxed at the same rate, no matter how valuable, to keep the balance of power between slave and nonslave owners. So, although a slave was without debate the most valuable property, he or she was taxed at the same rate as cattle or land, possibly the least valuable property. Thus, the slave owners did not pay a higher rate for their property than did the yeoman farmer for his.[27] Slave values varied according to age, gender, and ability, but what is strikingly similar is that a large number of men who became legends in the postwar cattle era were slave owners. Daniel Waggoner, Oliver Loving, John Simpson Chisum, to name but a few, owned large herds of cattle and were successful stock raisers and drovers at least a decade before the main drives began. Though many of these men owned more than enough land to raise cash crops and seemingly had the means to purchase larger numbers of slaves, they chose to engage in the livestock industry with fewer slaves than their planter contemporaries.

A well-known cowboy on the postwar cattle trail was "Nigger Frank." Frank belonged to John S. Chisum of Denton County long before he was praised by a white man as "the best line rider and horse wrangler" he had ever seen. When assessing the ability and contributions of slaves in the livestock industry, it is natural to assume that older men did the work, but Frank is an excellent counterexample. In August 1866, Frank accompanied Chisum, Charles Goodnight, Loving, and several other cattlemen on a drive from Trickham, Coleman County, to the Bosque Redondo Indian Reservation in New Mexico. Frank was approximately eight years old at that time and was considered old enough to "wrangle horses and go along on the cattle drive."[28] Using information from the Slave Narratives, journals, and other sources, there is plenty of evidence that slaves participated from the time they reached five years old. Much like young slaves in the crop industry, those in the livestock business were expected to earn their keep and produce profits for their owners as soon as possible.

Much like Savage's observation that "cowboys came in colors other than white," so did slave owners. The largest free black family in Texas were the Ashworths, led by brothers William, Aaron, Abner, and Moses. A "triracial" family (African, American Indian, and European), they moved from South Carolina to Texas in the first half of the 1830s and during the antebellum years owned a large amount of land and cattle. The brothers and a dozen or more members of their family raised cattle, and many of them owned slaves. Abner was the only one who raised a cash crop in 1849: 900 pounds of rice. That same year Aaron declared $14,000 in cattle, making him the largest cattle owner in the county. The Ashworth men owned few slaves, from two to nine, following the pattern of other successful cattlemen throughout the state. From Thornton, a seventeen- or eighteen-year-old man purchased to clear land and tend cattle, to a fourteen-year-old slave traded for a hundred head of cattle, slaves were used in all aspects of their business. Property tax records from Orange, Jefferson, Bell, and Angelina Counties record a correlation between the Ashworth slaves and their livestock that is similar to that of white slave-holding stockmen throughout the state.[29]

The Ashworths were not the only people who traded their slaves for cattle. Though it does not reflect the direct involvement of slaves in the industry, trading slave property for livestock says something about the mentality of the masters and of the value of the slaves. When George T. Reynolds returned to Texas with a medical discharge from the Confederate army, he reputedly had a "wounded soldier's bonus of $300 in Confederate money . . . the sum total of his worldly possessions."[30] Sometime before the end of the war, he purchased an unspecified number of cattle from local rancher John Robert Baylor, and he used a "negro girl," valued at $1,000, as part of the payment. Farther south, in Liberty County, William B. Duncan recorded the trade of thirty-one head of cattle for a slave while on a drive to Natchez.[31] And in Parker County, Milton Ikard, owner and probable father of famed black cowboy Bose Ikard, traded a mulatto woman to Oliver Loving for $1,000 worth of cattle.[32]

Another man who traded for one of his slaves was Daniel Waggoner. Sometime before 1854, he "partly bought and partly traded for a Negro boy about twelve years old." Within a couple of years, the young slave and his master drove cattle from the Sulphur River, south of Clarksville, to their new home in Wise County. During the war, Waggoner and his "Negro helper" kept the cattle herds together by riding "on the outskirts of the property and keeping the animals pushed back on the home range." When Waggoner drove three hundred steers to Shreveport, Louisiana, in 1861, the slave and an extended family member were left to tend the herd in Wise County. Waggoner made several other drives during the war years, undoubtedly repeating this same arrangement.[33]

The idea of using slaves to help raise cattle was alive and well all the way to the last moments of legal bondage. On June 12, 1865, just seven days before Juneteenth, Pleasant B. Watson and his brother-in-law, James Cartmell, left Washington-on-the-Brazos heading west with "two black boys and two black girls" to raise cattle. Their plans, however, were foiled when the slaves stole two of the mules and ran away to San Marcos, indicating that they were adept at handling the mules. The mention of the "two black girls" possibly leads to the assumption that they were taken for the "black boys," or that they were to provide for and serve the men. That could well be a false assumption. Harriett Robinson's testimony verifies that females also worked livestock: "Women broke in mules, throwed 'em down and roped 'em. They's do it better'n men."[34] As in cash-crop agriculture, slave men, women, and children all participated in their owners' financial pursuits.

Former slave owners hired freedmen to work their stock when slavery ended, and other cattlemen recognized the skills and value of black cowboys. Many Slave Narrative interviews recount some freedmen remaining with their former masters to work livestock and others being employed by different cattlemen. From Bose Ikard, whose gravestone bears the undying appreciation of Charles Goodnight, to the unnamed thousands who blazed a new trail in the history of black cowboys, the skills acquired during the years of slavery made former bondsmen and their children integral in the postwar cattle drives.[35] The role of slaves in the livestock industry is vastly underappreciated and rarely acknowledged, as is their participation in the postwar years. This volume shows that their place in cowboy history was no less valuable than that of their white contemporaries.

Notes

1. John D. W. Guice, "Cattle Raisers of the Old Southwest: A Reinterpretation," *Western Historical Quarterly* 8, no. 2 (April 1977), 184.

2. Terry G. Jordan, *North American Cattle-Ranching Frontiers: Origins, Diffusion, and Differentiation* (Albuquerque: University of New Mexico Press, 1993), 117.

3. Peter H. Wood, *Black Majority: Negroes in Colonial South Carolina* (New York: W. W. Norton, 1974), 28–33, quote from 31.

4. Guice, "Cattle Raisers," 185.

5. Edward A. Pearson, "'A Countryside Full of Flames': A Reconsideration of the Stono Rebellion and Slave Rebelliousness in the Early Eighteenth-Century South Carolina Lowcountry," in *The Slavery Reader*, ed. Gad Heuman and James Walvin, 569–93 (London: Routledge, 2003).

6. William W. Savage, *The Cowboy Hero: His Image in American History and Culture*

(Norman: University of Oklahoma Press, 1979), 4.

7. Kenneth Porter told of a fight that occurred in 1879, when Ira Olive, trail boss for the Olive brothers, picked a fight with Jim Kelly, a black cowboy. Olive knocked out two of Kelly's teeth with his gun, which is when a nineteen-year-old white cowboy stated, "If you hit that boy again . . . I'll shoot your damn eyes out." As Porter noted, Kelly was not a "boy"; he was a forty-year-old man. Kenneth W. Porter, "Negro Labor in the Western Cattle Industry, 1866–1900," in *The Negro on the American Frontier* (New York: Arno Press, 1971), 369–70.

8. Wood, *Black Majority*, 30–32, quotes from 31n, 32n.

9. Delphine Dawson Wilson, *John Barkley Dawson: Pioneer, Cattleman, Rancher* (n.p., 1997), 9–10.

10. Deborah M. Liles, "Southern Roots, Western Foundations: The Peculiar Institution and the Livestock Industry on the Northwestern Frontier of Texas, 1846–1864" (Ph.D. dissertation, University of North Texas, Denton, August 2013); Eugene D. Genovese, *The Political Economy of Slavery: Studies in the Economy Society of the Slave South* (New York: Pantheon Books, 1961), 117; Philip Durham and Everett L. Jones, *The Negro Cowboys* (Lincoln: University of Nebraska Press, 1965), 13, 17, quote from 17.

11. Margaret Lewis Furse, *The Hawkins Ranch in Texas: From Plantation Times to the Present* (College Station: Texas A&M University Press, 2014), 27, 35; Matagorda County Property Taxes, 1846–1910 (microfilm, Willis Library, University of North Texas, Denton, Texas). Hawkins's lowest number of declared slaves from 1847 through 1864 was thirty-nine (1847), highest was 105 (1858); lowest number of horses was six (1847), highest was eighty (1853); lowest number of cattle was zero (1858–60), highest was 1,000 (1853).

12. Kenneth Stamp, *The Peculiar Institution: Slavery and the Ante-Bellum South* ([1956] New York: Alfred A. Knopf, 1968), 50.

13. Randolph B. Campbell, *An Empire for Slavery: The Peculiar Institution in Texas, 1821–1865* (Baton Rouge: Louisiana State University Press, 1989), 80; Guice, "Cattle Raisers," 184.

14. The Slave Narratives are now available online from the Library of Congress: *Born in Slavery: Slave Narratives from the Federal Writers' Project, 1936–1938*, http://memory.loc.gov/ammem/snhtml/snhome.html.

15. James M. Smallwood, "Black Texans during Reconstruction, 1865–1874" (Ph.D. dissertation, Texas Tech University, Lubbock, December 1974), quote from 40.

16. This does not mean that the black cowboys were treated with the same respect when they arrived at their destination, or that some black cowboys did not have to tolerate racial confrontations. See Porter, "Negro Labor" for a description of the life and labor of black cowboys in the postwar era. See Jack Bailey, *A Texas Cowboy's Journal: Up the Trail to Kansas in 1868*, ed. David Dary (Norman: University of Oklahoma

Press, 2006), for a view of how blacks were sometimes viewed by white cowboys who had been slaveholders. It must be noted that negative comments made by Bailey were not about the quality of work done by black trail hands; C. Allen Jones, *Texas Roots, Agriculture and Rural Life before the Civil war* (College Station: Texas A&M University Press, 2005), 165.

17. Campbell, *Empire for Slavery*, 118–24, quotes from 124; Liberty County Property Taxes, 1837–1910 (microfilm, Willis Library, University of North Texas, Denton, Texas), show that White reported forty slaves worth $12,000, eighty horses worth $800 [low value], and three thousand cattle worth $10,500.

18. James West Davidson and Mark Hamilton Lytle, *After the Fact: the Art of Historical Detection*, Vol. 2 (Boston: McGraw-Hill, 2005), 177–206.

19. George P. Rawick, ed., *The American Slave: A Composite Autobiography* Supplement, Series 2, Vol. 5, *Texas Narratives* Part 4 (Westport, Conn.: Greenwood Press, 1979), 1594–95.

20. Ibid., 1459–62.

21. Statement of James Cape, "Slave Narratives," http://memory.loc.gov/ammem/snhtml/snvoices05.html (accessed November 12, 2014).

22. Statement of Monroe Brackins, "Slave Narratives," http://memory.loc.gov/mss/mesn/161/161.1.txt (accessed November 12, 2014).

23. Statement of Jacob Branch, "Texas Slavery Narratives 15," http://genealogytrails.com/tex/state/slavenarra15.htm (accessed November 15, 2014).

24. Works Project Administration, *Slave Narratives: A Folk History of Slavery in the United States from Interviews with Former Slaves, Texas Narratives*, Part 1 (Project Gutenberg Ebook, 2009), 72, www.gutenberg.org/files/30576/30576-h/30576-h.htm (accessed November 12, 2014).

25. Henry Lewis, "Texas Slave Narrative," http://freepages.genealogy.rootsweb.ancestry.com/~ewyatt/_borders/Texas%20Slave%20Narratives/Texas%20L/Lewis,%20Henry.html (accessed November 15, 2014).

26. Felix Grundy Sadler, "Slave Narrative," http://freepages.genealogy.rootsweb.ancestry.com/~ewyatt/_borders/Texas%20Slave%20Narratives/Texas%20S/Sadler,%20Felix%20Grundy.html (accessed August 7, 2012). It is important to mention that, even though these narratives are from Texas, many of the other states' slave narratives contain many of the same memories of slaves in the livestock industry.

27. Robin Einhorn, *American Taxation: American Slavery* (Chicago: University of Chicago Press, 2006), 206.

28. Seymour V. Conner, *The Peters Colony of Texas: A History and Biographical Sketches of the Early Settlers* (Austin: Texas State Historical Association, 1959), 234; Eighth Census of the United States, Denton County, Schedule II (Slave Inhabitants) (microfilm, Willis Library, University of North Texas, Denton, Texas); Denton

County Property Taxes, 1846–1910 (microfilm, Willis Library, University of North Texas, Denton, Texas); Clifford R. Caldwell, *John Simpson Chisum: Cattle King of the Pecos Revisited* (Santa Fe, N.Mex.: Sunstone Press, 2010), 54.

29. Quintard Taylor, *In Search of the Racial Frontier: African Americans in the American West* (New York: W. W. Norton, 1998), 38; Jason Gillmore, "Shades of Gray: The Life and Times of a Free Family of Color on the Texas Frontier," *Law and Inequality* 29 (2011): 81–85. See also Andrew Forest Muir, "The Free Negro in Jefferson and Orange Counties, Texas," *Journal of Negro History* 35, no. 2 (April 1950): 183–206. The Ashworths' early influence reached throughout Texas with the passage of the Ashworth Act of December 12, 1840, which exempted their family and freed black residents who were living in Texas on March 2, 1836, from the Texas Congressional Act of February 5, 1840. The February 5 act "ordered all free blacks residing in the Republic of Texas without the permission of congress to leave within two years or else be sold into slavery." See Randolph B. Campbell, ed., *The Laws of Slavery in Texas* (Austin: University of Texas Press, 2010), quote from 115.

30. Frances Mayhugh Holden, "Reynolds, George Thomas," *Handbook of Texas Online*, www.tshaonline.org/handbook/online/articles/fre31 (accessed January 30, 2013); Sallie Reynolds Matthews, *Interwoven: A Pioneer Chronicle* (College Station: Texas A&M University Press, 1982), 11.

31. Debbie Liles, "Slavery and Cattle in East and West Texas," *East Texas Historical Journal* 52, no. 2 (Fall 2014): 29–38.

32. Bruce Shackelford, "Bose Ikard, Splendid Behavior," in *Black Cowboys of Texas*, ed. Sara R. Massey, 134 (College Station: Texas A&M University Press, 2000). In the years that both Milton and Isabella Ikard reported ownership of cattle, they did not declare $1,000 worth of cattle in their Parker or Stephens County property taxes. It is possible that Loving sold some of those cattle for the Ikards, since that was his business.

33. William Curry Holden, *A Ranching Saga: The Lives of William Electious Halsell and Ewing Halsell* (San Antonio, Tex.: Trinity University Press, 1976), 27, 37–38; Wise County Property Taxes, 1857–1910 (microfilm, Willis Library, University of North Texas, Denton, Texas).

34. Harriett Robinson, *The Slave Narrative Collection*, www.okgenweb.org/collection/narrative/robinson_harriett.htm (accessed November 12, 2014).

35. Michael N. Searles, "In Search of the Black Cowboy in Texas," in *The African American Experience in Texas: An Anthology*, ed. Bruce A. Glasrud and James M. Smallwood, 86–101 (Lubbock: Texas Tech University Press, 2007); "Bose Ikard served with me four years on the Goodnight-Loving Trail, never shirked a duty or disobeyed an order, rode with me in many stampedes, participated in three engagements with Comanches, splendid behavior. Charles Goodnight."

2

Mathew "Bones" Hooks

A Pioneer of Honor

ANA CAROLINA CASTILLO CRIMM

West Texan Mathew Hooks emerged as a leading component of the community in and around Amarillo. Born in 1867, two years after the close of the war that ended slavery, Hooks learned to ride and break horses early in life. His knowledge of horses led him to become a wrangler, with duties to care for the horses. In 1884, while yet a teenager, Hooks joined men from the JR Morris ranch in West Texas. He moved to Clarendon in the Panhandle in 1886, where he worked as a cowhand until 1900, when he served as a porter in a hotel. In 1909 or 1910 he secured employment as a porter with the Santa Fe Railroad, a position he held until 1930. During his life, Hooks invested in real estate and emerged as a civic and social leader as well as a leader of his people. After retiring from the railroad, he counted numerous accomplishments, including creating an-all black community near Amarillo. As Ana Carolina Castillo Crimm summarizes Hooks's life, we can appreciate his legacy: "Hooks grew up with the Panhandle," Crimm writes, "as he developed from wrangler and cook, to bronc buster and horse trainer, to hotel and railroad porter, and finally to town builder and civic leader for the black community of Amarillo."

Dear Sir:

I wish to pay tribute to you on the occasion of the banquet given to you by the members of your Church, for it is men of your kind and spirit who make this world a better place in which to live. I wish tonight to present you with a lone white flower, a guerdon of honor, that I have been sending for the past fifty-two years in honor of the pioneer men and women who have helped to make this Panhandle County of ours one of the "white" spots of the nation, for it is one of the traditions of the Panhandle to give honor to whom honor is due. With heartfelt greetings to you and yours, and God bless you.

—Mathew Bones Hooks

Originally published as Ana Carolina Castillo Crimm, "Mathew 'Bones' Hooks," in *Black Cowboys of Texas*, edited by Sara R. Massey (College Station: Texas A&M University Press, 2000), 219–45. Reprinted with permission of Texas A&M University Press and the author.

Mathew Hooks, one of the first black horse wranglers and bronc busters in the Texas Panhandle, is probably best known for honoring the early pioneers with a white flower, a symbol that he later extended to others of equal courage and merit. Hooks grew up with the Panhandle, watching it change over a period of seventy-five years as he developed from wrangler and cook, to bronc buster and horse trainer, to hotel and railroad porter, and finally to town builder and civic leader for the black community of Amarillo. He had a true sense of history and a love of the early settlers that he shared, through his prodigious memory, with journalists, writers, and scholars, as well as school children, college students, and anyone who was interested in listening. His homespun philosophies entertained and engaged his audiences as he told the tales of the old days, of the early pioneers of the Panhandle. He actively preserved the history of the area and joined half a dozen old-timers organizations. With other pioneers, he helped found the Panhandle-Plains Museum, where his scrapbooks and papers are preserved.[1]

Mathew Hooks refused to be cowed by a society grown increasingly racist in the years after the Civil War. The black communities that he founded, first in Clarendon and later at North Heights in Amarillo, became havens where blacks could live in comfort and safety with their own businesses and their own homes. He recognized the contributions of his white friends, but Mathew Hooks had to fight his own battles for his rights and the rights of his people. In the end, his dedication, his drive, and his ambition personified the courage and grit of the Panhandle people whom he honored with his white flowers.

Mathew Hooks was born November 3, 1867, in the small community of Orangeville in Robertson County, Texas, to Alex and Annie Hooks.[2] The couple had received their freedom two years earlier, from Warren (or perhaps Cullen) Hooks, a plantation owner in Bowie County, northeast Texas.[3] The plantation, which employed as many as sixty-six slaves, was located near the present community of Hooks, on Highway 82, twenty-five miles west of Texarkana. Alex Hooks, while still a slave, was gifted with a native ability and a will to improve. He learned to read and write from "Old Man" Hooks, who broke the law to teach the bright young slave. Instead of hiring a white clerk, Warren Hooks put Alex in control of the plantation bookkeeping.[4]

With the end of the Civil War in 1865, the South was struggling to fit free blacks into its structure. Alex and Annie, who needed to find jobs and make decisions that had long been made for them, moved to Orangeville, where Alex became a community leader, something that may have later inspired his son. Alex, by putting his gifts of reading and writing to work, led the way in education, in Christian concepts, and in furthering the growth and development of his people. He willingly shared his talents as a teacher and preacher with the rapidly growing black communities.[5]

Their son Mathew was the first of their eight children. As Mathew said, he was the first thing they had ever owned. If the first five years of a child are the formative years, Mathew Hooks was blessed with a head start. From his family, he learned courage, determination, and strong Christian concepts. His home life, as he said later, made him what he was. "I can see young men," he said, "and see right away the effect their home has had on them. ... Men are just grown up boys and they act just the same when they grow up as when they were boys."[6] He benefited from his parents' biblical teachings and their strict moral code. He never smoked or drank and avoided conflict whenever he could. Mathew's father taught his young son to read and write, and Mathew, supported by his own cheerful personality and inveterate good humor, learned quickly to work hard and to follow through with whatever he started. "When I get an impulse to do something," he said, "I stick to it 'til I get it done. ... If I have to wait two hours to see a man I want to see, I wait. When the time is ripe to do a thing, it's right, and that's the time to do it." He also developed a sense of responsibility at an early age. As the eldest of eight children, it was often Mathew's duty to care for his four younger brothers and three sisters. "They made me rock the cradle for my brothers, and I've been rockin' somebody's cradle ever since."[7]

As a youngster, Mathew was thin and wiry, which earned him the nickname "Bones." He was also energetic, and by the time he was seven he could do a man's job. He worked to help his parents by driving the butcher's wagon around town and learned to harness and handle oxen and mules. Two years later, in 1874, D. Steve Donald, a cattleman from Denton County along the Red River north of Dallas, traveled to Robertson County on a cattle-buying trip. He needed someone to drive the camp wagon back to Denton, and Warren Hooks, Alex's old boss, assured Donald that young Mathew could handle the job. Mathew, on his first trip away from home, drove the camp wagon hitched to two oxen, Buck and Jerry, back to Denton with Donald and the herd of cattle. Donald, who paid for Mathew's return home, was impressed with the young boy's willingness and skill. The following summer, on another cattle-buying trip, Donald once again hired Mathew, only this time he provided him with his own mule, named Dinamite, on which Mathew made the return trip. For the next four years, Mathew continued to work for Donald and finally remained in Denton, because he was "old enough to make a hand."[8]

It was while Mathew worked for Steve Donald that he learned to ride and break horses. The cowboys on the DSD Ranch, as Hooks said, "made me the best bronc rider in the country. But they weren't trying to make me a rider, they were trying to get me throwed."[9] The teasing cowboys would put young Mathew on any horse that looked like it would buck him off. According to J. Frank Dobie, bucking was not usually a vicious act, but a natural instinctive response by horses to get rid of any clawed and fanged animal on their backs. Dobie, in his book on mustangs, described a story told to him by a cowboy: "That dun struck out pitching right through the middle of the herd. He pitched for half a mile right and left, backwards and forwards. There was no getting his motion. He pitched till we were both broke down and I was bleeding at nose, mouth, and ears."[10]

Such bucking was not uncommon, and riders such as Mathew Hooks had to put up with broncs who might buck, jump, or rear. The worst were the broncs with the "belly full of bedsprings." A horse like that tried everything to get rid of a cowboy on its back, "pawing for the moon, breaking in two half way up, sun-fishing on the way down, and then hitting the earth hard enough to crack open his rider's liver."[11] Some horses never did quit fighting and remained unbroken outlaws. Others might become killers, throwing themselves over backward on a rider or rolling on a rider to crush him. Horses and their pitching ability were frequently judged by their color. According to Hooks, "A sorrel steel dust is a hard pitcher; a bay hondo hasn't much pitch in him."[12] Most horses, however, found out quickly that the rider, especially when it was Mathew, could not be removed by any gyrations, regardless of their force, and the horse might as well give in and accept the burden.

After an uncounted numbers of falls, Mathew learned to hang onto the horse by whatever means was necessary. There were no predetermined rules such as those that bind modern rodeo cowboys to keep their spurs above the shoulders of the horse or not grab the horn (pulling leather). Mathew's light weight, his long legs, and his wiry frame were perfectly suited to bronc riding. He was sometimes put on the horses bareback or without a bridle. "One day the boys got me on a big gray horse, and turned him out of the corral, him pitching and running, and me without a bridle or any way to hold or guide him."[13] Through grit and determination, Mathew stayed on for twelve miles until the cowboys finally herded Mathew and his mount into camp. Mathew also learned that there were only four directions a horse could jump, and it did not take him long to judge the horses and outguess their movements. "We used to say that if you could ride a horse as far as three jumps, you could usually ride him, but you were usually thrown by the second jump."[14] Within a few years, Mathew, like a persistent tick, could hang onto a horse until it gave up pitching and accepted him in the saddle.

By the time he had become a teenager, he was confident that he could stay on any horse alive. An outlaw horse belonging to the DSD Ranch called "Old Bill" had been written off as unridable and was in use as a wagon horse. One Sunday, Mathew determined he would ride Old Bill while the family was at church. He saddled the horse in the barn so if the horse did buck him off it would not take off with the boss's saddle. When he climbed on, the horse exploded, broke through the barn door, "knocked over the stile block at the gate and took out up the road with me in the saddle." Several miles later, Mathew met the family, coming back from church in the buckboard, and managed to pull Old Bill to a stop. The astounded family asked him what made him think he could ride the outlaw. Mathew replied that the horse was made like all other horses, and if the cowboys could ride them, "I figured Old Bill could be rode, too."[15]

Mathew learned to love horses and willingly rode whatever was available. The demand for horses was great. Cowboys needed horses to work the cattle, and money was good in the cattle industry, which was booming during the late 1870s and early 1880s. Both cowboys and horses were needed to supply cattle to the ever-growing market—Mathew's skills were in demand. By the time he turned fourteen, he broke and trained horses as well as working as a horse wrangler. When a new horse was brought in, Mathew rode him daily, earning the horse's trust, until the horse was bridlewise. He was paid between $3 and $5 per horse or $25 per month with board. This money was as good as cowboys got, although it was not an easy job. While riding the horses, Mathew developed a friendship with each of the animals. As friends, he named the horses after anything and everything. "I gave them every name I could think of . . . after the people I knew, what they looked like, any peculiarity they had like Fox Trot or Run Away . . . after the bosses, the hands . . . after owls, hawks and coyotes. I even named one Miss Sally Chisum after Mr. Chisum's daughter."[16]

After Mathew had broken the horses to ride, the cowboys would take one or two of the newly broken horses to add to their string. Each cowboy had between seven and ten horses, most of them smaller Spanish mustangs, weighing around nine hundred pounds. Each cowboy might have a pet pony, but he also had "a cutting horse, a bridle horse, a night horse, a roping horse, a saddle horse and a packing horse." The night horses had to be the safest and most dependable, because, in an emergency such as a cattle stampede, a cowboy would have to jump on the horse without saddle or bridle, and the horse would carry him out of danger with nothing but his headstall and rope. These horses were often smart enough to bring a man back to camp if he were lost. The saddle horses were used for the daily duty of the roundup and were worked hard all morning for four to five hours in search of the elusive cattle. At lunch, the cowboys rode in and changed their exhausted, sweating mount for a second horse out of their string and rode out for a long, hot afternoon of gathering more cattle. Once the cattle were herded together, cowboys switched to their roping or cutting horses for separating the cattle to be branded. Some horses, like one Mathew called Chubby, were natural cow ponies and would follow a steer without being guided. "If you did not catch the steer that he was after, he got mad and shook his head from side to side and backed his ears." Once, a cowboy who was riding Chubby failed to rope a cow. The horse began to shake his head angrily, and Mathew commented, to the embarrassment of the cowboy and the glee of his companions, "That's the first time that Chubby has been disappointed that bad in a long time!"

As a horse wrangler, it was Mathew's duty to feed, doctor, and care for all of the horses. If there were twenty to twenty-five men on a roundup and each one had seven to ten horses, the remuda, or horse herd, might number from 140 to 250 horses. In the morning, the men would saddle their horses and, while they were at breakfast, Mathew rode the kinks out of each horse until it had quit bucking. Sometimes, on a cold morning, the spirited horses would give the young boy a considerable workout. Mathew accepted the job, because, as he noted, "The only thing I have found that a white man was afraid of was a rattlesnake and a pitching horse. I do not know why, but they were." After the cowboys had left to begin scouring the gullies and draws for hidden cattle, Mathew took the herd of horses to graze on nearby grass pastures.

When Mr. Donald began driving cattle into Oklahoma Indian Territory just across the Red River, Mathew worried about Indian raids. The cowboys had assured him that Indians could steal a horse right out from under a man, even with the horse tied to him, and he'd never know it. One afternoon while grazing the horses, Mathew lay down to take a nap and tied his mule, Dinamite, to his arm. The cowboys, finding him asleep, untied the mule and began to whoop like all the Indians in the world. Mathew recounted, "I awoke to see my mule gone and thought the Indians had me sho'. I left there fast and the boys had to head me off on their horses."[17]

By the time Mathew turned sixteen in 1884, Steve Donald had moved his operations west to Henrietta, near Wichita Falls. One afternoon, Mathew, on Dinamite, noticed a group of cowboys with a remuda and wagon coming across the prairies. It was J. R. Norris and his men returning to the JRE Ranch on the Pecos River in West Texas. Young Mathew rode Dinamite out to investigate the group, and, when asked if he were a cowboy, the tall, gangly black boy answered that he was. The cowboys began teasing him about his mule, telling him that no cowboy rode a mule. At the insult, Mathew challenged them to a race against Dinamite. They let him choose the horse he would run against, and, much to the chagrin of the cowboys, Mathew and Dinamite beat their horse and rider. Mr. Norris, evidently impressed with the courage of the young boy, invited him to come out west and become a real cowboy. Norris offered Mathew a new pair of boots and five horses for Dinamite if Mathew would go with them. Mathew answered, "Right here's where you get traded off, old mule." He turned Dinamite loose on the range and joined the JRE outfit for his first trip to West Texas. From then on, he rode horses.[18]

Few people, in 1850, would have guessed that the Panhandle of Texas would ever amount to much. Captain R. B. Marcy of the U.S. Cavalry, who was searching for Indians at the time across the dry grasslands and rolling hills, stated, "This country is, and must remain, uninhabited forever." Joseph McCoy, who opened Abilene, Kansas, and began the shipment of cattle to the East Coast, had examined the Panhandle and declared the seven million acres were absolute desert. For those who finally took the chance on settling the Panhandle, the greatest problems would not be the desert-like conditions, the dried grass, or the lack of water, but the over-abundance of buffalo and Indians. During the 1870s and 1880s, those problems were being solved by American military troops who were removing the latter, while buffalo hunters massacred the former. By 1876, reconstruction ended, and the cattle boom began. Charles Goodnight, familiar with the Panhandle, which he had traversed on his way to Colorado, and certain he could rid the area of the few remaining buffalo, brought sixteen thousand head of cattle from Colorado into the protected Palo Duro Canyon. With capital from John G. Adair, the English lord, Goodnight and Adair formed the JA Ranch and began the development of the Panhandle.[19]

The two earliest towns in the area were Mobeetie and Tascosa, both of unsavory character, and towns that Mathew did not enjoy visiting on the annual trail drives. Mobeetie, some eighty miles northeast of present-day Amarillo, had developed in 1874 as a supply store for buffalo skinners on Sweetwater Creek. It later became the southern terminus of the Jones-Plummer Trail and as such was inundated periodically with cowboys either coming or going from the railheads in Kansas. Mobeetie also served Fort Elliott, established in 1874 to remove the Plains Indians. Several troops of black soldiers, also known as Buffalo Soldiers, were stationed at the fort and their families made up the small community of blacks in Mobeetie. The town consisted of a supply store, owned by Charles Rath and Bob Wright, and numerous saloons. A scattering of homes made of buffalo skins gave the town its first name, Hidetown, which the city fathers changed in 1879 to the Indian word Mobeetie, which may have meant sweet water.[20]

Tascosa, the second major settlement in the Panhandle, lay approximately forty miles northwest of present-day Amarillo, on the Canadian River. Tascosa, from the Spanish word *atascosa*, meaning boggy or swampy, was at the beginning of the Dodge City Trail and, like Mobeetie, was periodically overrun with rowdy cowboys looking for a drink, a poker game, and a fight, usually in that order. Founded in 1876 by Spanish sheepherders, Tascosa was soon taken over by Charles Goodnight and his cowboys. Saloons flourished, along with general stores, which freighted in as much as fifty thousand pounds of merchandise monthly from Dodge City for the local cattlemen, including the XIT Syndicate, Goodnight's JA Ranch, and numerous smaller ranchers. Tascosa, like Mobeetie, was considered a den of iniquity and, therefore, not a place where Mathew Hooks liked to go.[21]

Mathew Hooks, brought up in a Christian tradition, preferred the town of Clarendon, established in 1878 just fifty miles southeast of Amarillo. Founded as a "Christian community" by the Reverend Lewis Henry Carhart, a Methodist minister, and his brother-in-law, Alfred Sully of New York, it was once again the backing of English investors that made the town possible. The town leaders carefully controlled the few saloons and prohibited any rowdy behavior from the cowboys who wandered through. One saloon owner refused to serve liquor to any young boys, and the town's citizens were so honest that bags of money could be safely left behind the saloon counter while a ranch owner transacted business in town. Their jail, although they built one, soon fell down from disuse. The boisterous, thrill-seeking cowboys wanted little to do with a town that they dubbed "Saints' Roost." Mathew, as a religious man who neither smoked nor drank, liked the God-fearing town. "Clarendon," he said, "was the white spot of civilization. Prohibition started there; colleges started there; everything good got its start in Clarendon."[22]

Claiming to be a Christian town, however, did not necessarily mean that the town accepted black citizens. Mathew was told that Negroes were not allowed in town. "But," he said, "I did not believe that, and that is the very reason why I am here today; I still don't believe it." He was determined to be part of the Christian town, and by quiet perseverance he made friends with the citizens, many of whom were small ranchers who used his services to break or train horses. It took several years and several persistent attempts, but he was eventually accepted by the residents and allowed to buy a small plot of land and build a home. "Friendship," he told a class of students in 1933, "can be more useful to you than anything else."[23]

Settlers, still wary of Indian raids in the 1870s, did not rush to the area, and only the hardiest of souls remained. Mathew Hooks was amazed by the ability of the early settlers to survive. Water was their greatest need, and they learned to find water holes by following birds to water in the mornings and to backtrack by following the birds' path from the water in the evening. They also learned to avoid areas where there were neither trails nor animals, which meant an absence of water. Mathew described the trail drive from Portales, New Mexico, to Texico, a stretch of some sixty miles where there was no water: "When you knew you couldn't get water, it was awful. You would just moan and grunt. The cook sometimes saved dish water from one meal to another. We also had a barrel of clean water that we kept for the coffee. One night I felt that I just had to have some water, so I got a little rubber hose and after everybody had gone to bed, I slipped up and stuck my hose in the first water I came to. It was the dishwater. I just fell back and groaned."[24]

Life was hard for those scratching out a living in the Panhandle. Settlers on the caprock—the flat plains that seem to stretch forever from the Canadian River in the north to the Pecos River in the south—built homes of sun-dried adobe bricks or stacked sod, which made cool, comfortable homes, although

they might not be the most civilized-looking buildings. Mathew recalled that
he could always tell where a settler lived from the kind of fuel they used. For
those who lived on top of the caprock, today known as the Edwards Plateau
west of Post, fuel was dried cow dung, or cow chips. Those below the caprock,
in the rolling, hump-backed hills west of Abilene, used scrub wood. Mathew
also noted that settlers found their directions on the unmarked plains by knowing that the wind usually blew from the southwest. In one instance he was riding from Mobeetie back to Clarendon and ran into two of the ranchers, Mr.
Tom Turner and Judge Wilson, but the wind was blowing so badly that they
could hardly see. "They asked me where Mobeetie was and I told them it was in
the direction of the wind, if it was not covered up."[25]

Mathew Hooks particularly admired the tenacity of the women. "Credit
for the advancement on the Plains belongs to the pioneer mothers. . . . When
the men brought their wives to the Plains the women demanded milk cows,
chickens, schools, churches and all the other attributes of civilization and culture." The men, he recalled, were satisfied with camping in tents and accepted
the saloons and gambling in Tascosa and Mobeetie. It was the women who
demanded civilization, worked for churches, and finally achieved the stability
that encouraged other settlers to come. Women such as Mrs. Goodnight, Mrs.
Bugbee (wife of Thomas S. Bugbee, the second man to establish a ranch in the
Panhandle), and Mrs. Patrick were, as viewed by Mathew, "the very strongest of
characters . . . who have seen all the modern things come." When the women
determined to vote Clarendon dry, Mathew said, "I thought it would be just as
easy to bring the Canadian River in and vote it dry. But those women got to
working, and after a while Clarendon was dry."[26]

Often alone, the women suffered the births and deaths of their children,
sacrificing for the success of their husband's ranches. They also defended
the lonely young black cowboy from the teasing or harassing that he often
endured. One woman stopped a group of cowboys who were firing blanks at
Mathew's feet. Another pioneer housewife, when a cowboy objected to eating with Mathew at the same table, replied, "Everyone is treated alike at my
table." Mathew responded in kind, caring for their children, as he had his own
brothers and sisters. Mothers trusted him with their young sons, knowing that
Mathew would teach them the horse skills that he knew so well. The mothers
also treated him as a son. One mother was concerned over her young son picking up Mathew's only curse word, "'y God," short for "By God." The mother

offered to buy Mathew a Sunday suit if he would stop the habit, which Mathew immediately did. Mathew knew that for the mothers, as it was for him, the hardships were the worst and the need for courage the greatest.[27]

The people of the Panhandle were, from Mathew's point of view, different from settlers elsewhere. "The climate and conditions here make them different.... I have seen one kind of man come here and stay awhile, and he just can't stand it, he just breaks down." But another kind, much like Mathew himself, did not let the country faze him, and that was the kind who remained. "One was a pioneer," he said, "and the other was just pioneering." It took the pioneers to settle the Panhandle, and Mathew always admired them for their strength, for he, too, knew what it took to survive in the Panhandle.[28]

By the time Mathew Hooks arrived in West Texas, there were already a number of successful ranches. The cattle boom had been going strong for almost ten years, and with the removal of both the Indians and the buffalo from the Panhandle plains the land was perfect for cattle, despite the earlier concerns of people such as Captain Marcy. Among the early ranches were the Frying Pan north of Amarillo, the T-Anchor near what would become Amarillo, the Two Buckle and Matador at the bottom of the Panhandle, and the Bar CC, the 777, the Turkey Track, and the Bar T along the Red River in the north; along the New Mexico border were the XIT, the LX and the 6666, the Quarter Circle T, and the Laurel Leaf; and along the Oklahoma line were the Diamond Tail and the Rocking Chair.[29]

Mathew's skill at horse breaking and training was in demand by all of the ranchers. He worked for almost all of them, including the XIT, the largest of the ranches, which would not outlast the century. In 1882, Texas lawmakers traded three million acres of Panhandle land to Matthias Schnell and A. R. Birck for the construction of the Texas state capitol. A Chicago firm, Taylor, Babcock and Co., bought out the Schnell-Birck contract and chose the land for the XIT in the ten counties along the New Mexico border, north and west of present-day Amarillo. The ranch was run by a syndicate made up of English investors who intended to subdivide the land for farming and sell it off. Until the population in the area increased, however, the investors ordered the huge acreage fenced using the newly invented barbed wire. By 1886, over 781 miles of land had been fenced and the ranch had imported over 150,000 head of high-grade, purebred cattle, worth over a million dollars.

Mathew continued to work part time for the JRE Ranch during his first years in the area, as well as hiring out to other outfits when they needed a horse trainer or a wrangler. He made friends with owners of the smaller as well as the larger ranches and soon became a popular and well-liked worker. His friendships sometimes got him into trouble. Once, Mathew hired out as a wrangler to two cowboys who were illegally gathering cattle. When the ranch owner and his cowboys surrounded the group, justice was swift and merciless. The two cowboys were hung and the rope had dropped over Mathew's neck. "Skillety" Bill, an acquaintance from the Frying Pan Ranch (hence his name) and member of the vigilante group, intervened. While the group waited, he questioned Mathew and, convinced that Hooks had been unaware of the intentions of the two cattle thieves, Skillety Bill let him go and told him to clear out of the country quick.[30]

After his narrow escape, Hooks left the Panhandle and returned to Henrietta in North Texas. He worked horses in Oklahoma until the threat of the hanging had passed, and then he returned to the Panhandle. During the summers he worked for most of the local ranchers. At different times he worked for Mr. George Brookshire of the Hashknife outfit, Billie Johnson of the "W" Ranch, Mr. Nash of the 7D range, Mr. Perry Autman of the PX outfit, the Cowan Ranch, which was located around the Davis and Guadalupe Mountains, the LX ranch, whose headquarters were near Dalhart, and the Chicago "C" outfit, which tried and failed to raise polled Angus cattle. Not all land was owned outright. The large ranches controlled the ranges wherever their cattle grazed, usually to a natural boundary such as a river or mountain range. "One fellow would be northeast of the mountains and that would be his range, then some other fellow would be located to the southeast of the mountains and that would be his range." Between five hundred and one thousand cattle might graze on any given range, some belonging to the big ranch, and others to the smaller ranches. "When a man bought a brand and the cattle, that gave him the right to the range. When he bought the brand and cattle of another range, the boys would gather up all the cattle they could find and turn them over to the buyer. When he bought the remnant, he got the range which included a section or two of land."[31]

Hooks remembered the ranches and their owners. The Hashknife was bought by Bill Ross, who moved the ranch to Arizona. T. J. McElroy, whose range extended from south of the Pecos to El Paso, bought the last remnants of the 7D, which had existed around Fort Stockton.[32] Other outfits, such as the LX, had never established a headquarters but only maintained a chuck wagon with thirty or forty men.

Not all of the ranches were large outfits. "When the big outfits began to dwindle down as the country became more settled, sometimes the cowboys would branch off and start a little outfit of their own," Hooks explained. "Then they would grow into big ranches." The smaller outfits were allowed to run their cattle on the same ranges as the big ranchers as long as the roundups were done jointly. According to Hooks, the ranchers, both large and small, were good neighbors and got along well.

When roundup time came, all the cattle owners would combine their forces to collect the cattle. Calves were branded with the same brand as their mothers, thus ensuring that the owner of the cow could claim the calf. When calves were missed, they were called mavericks and could be claimed by whoever caught and branded them. In one instance, Mathew was riding with Joe White when they spotted a big two-and-a-half-year-old maverick. Mathew explained, "Mr. White wanted to get that big one first; it's sort of natural with white men to want the biggest and best thing first. If it had been a little one, he would have let me rope that one first." Normally, a calf would not be branded unless a representative from each of the ranches was part of the group to prevent accusations of cattle theft, but in this case, because it was an older maverick, the men went ahead with the branding. Mathew stopped to build a fire to brand the calf and began heating the short branding iron that they always carried for just such emergencies. Mr. White, meanwhile, chased the maverick over the top of the hill. Mathew suddenly heard Mr. White yelling for him. When Mathew topped the hill, he found that Mr. White had roped the hind legs of the calf, but the calf had escaped the rope, and Mr. White was holding onto the calf by its tail.

"I jumped down, but when I got a hold of him, Mr. White turned loose and started to run. Mr. Joe lit out, and me right after him, and the yearling right after me. . . . when I passed Mr. Joe, I said, 'There he is again!' I heard a jingling, and it was his spurs as his feet went up in the air. A cow can't hook anyone on the ground because its horns are so long. That is one thing a fellow learns if he is willing to lie there and learn his lesson. I ran a while and rested a little bit, and went to catch my horse. I said, 'Do you want me to rope him?' He said, 'What do you think I want?' 'Well, I don't know; if you don't want him, I don't,' I said. He told me that the next time I started running not to start after him."

Cattle were rounded up in the spring and fall, just after calving season, so the young calves could be branded. There were no fences during the early days of cattle ranching in the Panhandle. All the cattle from the different ranches roamed together on the ranges and had to be rounded up and divided with everyone sharing in the effort. For a roundup, the largest ranch would furnish the chuck wagon, and the other ranches would send their cowboys. In this way, no one rancher had to pay for a larger work force than he absolutely needed, but there were sufficient men to find the cattle on a range that might extend hundreds of miles. All the cattle in a fifteen-mile area were collected in one day, and the herd was moved along to the next fifteen-mile section for the next day's roundup. Mathew recalled that cattle liked hiding in the canyons and draws, and ranchers built a drift line near present-day Lubbock to keep the cattle out of the canyons. When the cowboys had amassed a sizable herd, the calves were cut out and branded. Once the entire range was cleared of cattle, which might take as much as four months, the cattle that were to be sold were separated and bunched together for the drive north.

Trail drives, which usually began in May from either Tascosa or Mobeetie, would reach Kiowa, Kansas, in September, and the cowboys would be back home by Christmas. Hooks made many trail drives from the Pecos country with such outfits as the TJ and the Hashknife. The smaller ranchers would put their sale herds in with the large herds going to market and trust the large rancher to pay them for the cattle upon their return. For the most part, Hooks recalls, as long as the ranchers knew each other, "the little fellows got along fine with the big fellows." The huge and sometimes arrogant syndicate ranchers, however, were considered fair game by some of the small ranchers.

Some time later, while Mathew was working for the XIT Syndicate, a young local rancher asked for his help to get one of the prized purebred bull calves from the syndicate's immense, but carefully fenced, pastures. As an employee, Mathew Hooks could come and go through the gates easily, and it took no time to find and separate a good calf and herd him across the country. Part way across the pastures, however, Hooks found a better calf and let the first one go. He herded the second little bull to his waiting friend, who tied the calf up to keep it from returning to its mother and weaned the calf in four days. Many years later, after having earned a reputation for honesty and integrity, Hooks was called into court to testify before a grand jury investigating cattle thefts. He found that the judge was none other than the young rancher whom he had helped. The judge asked Hooks, "Do you know of anyone stealing cattle," then paused, and pointedly added, "now?" Hooks was able to answer truthfully, "No, boss, not now."[33]

Much of the law and order of the country, during the early years, was controlled by vigilantes. These men were usually cowmen determined to stop the cattle and horse theft that had become rampant by the 1880s. According to the cattlemen's associations, as many as forty percent of the cattle that arrived in Dodge City were listed as stolen. In spite of Mathew's early run-in with the vigilantes, his honesty earned him a place as one of their group. They bound themselves together by a password, a casual word that could be passed along in a general conversation unnoticed by others. Though Mathew Hooks refused to divulge this password during his lifetime, he said he would leave it somewhere in his files at the Panhandle-Plains Museum. When word went out among the vigilantes that there was to be a "gathering" or a "trial," the group would come together at a predesignated place, usually with a handy tree. Mathew Hooks held the horses while the committee members conducted their trial under the tree. When the trial was concluded, the accused was usually hung. One young man, after receiving his sentence, asked two favors. The first was to take his boots off, because he had promised his mother that he would not die with his boots on, and the second was to be hung by a man who had never rustled cattle or horses himself. The rope passed from hand to hand around the circle of vigilantes, who soon withdrew for a council. The decision was to let the young man go "if he made a solemn promise he would leave the country right quick and never come back." He left. According to Hooks, there were only twelve to fifteen hangings during the time he was in the Panhandle.[34]

Although many of the ranchers did not realize it at the time, the terrible winter of 1885 and the subsequent drought in 1886, combined with the dreaded tick fever, ruined the free-range cattle industry not only in the Panhandle but throughout Texas. The freeze in January and February of 1886 was so severe that it killed cattle all the way to South Texas. Hooks, who was in Henrietta for the winter, saw so many dead cattle that "you could have put the dead cows three feet apart and had enough to reach to Colorado."[35] Dozens of ranchers went out of business that year, losing all their cattle to either the freeze or the drought that followed. The only operations that would survive into the twentieth century turned to fenced pastures, cattle dipping, and upgraded programs of cattle breeding.[36]

During 1886, Mathew Hooks found there was little need for his services in the Panhandle. Hooks, who had gathered a small herd of horses and cattle as his pay for working roundups, sold his B brand and his herd and moved back to northeast Texas to be with his family. Briefly, he invested his money in a grocery store in the town of Wamba in Bowie County, near Texarkana. After about eighteen months, he arrived one day to find a sign on his door that read, "We give you thirty-six hours to get out," signed by the "White Caps of Sand Gall Gizzard." He closed up the store and "gave 'em thirty-three hours of that back."[37]

Like the other pioneers who had learned to love the arid plains of the Panhandle, Mathew chose to return to Clarendon and the Pecos. After visits to family and friends in Denton, Dallas, and Henrietta, he was back in the Pecos country breaking broncs for T. J. McElroy, Autman, and others by the end of 1887.[38] The cattle business had declined somewhat, as absentee investors and English speculators were weeded out by the freeze and drought of '86, but the completion of the Fort Worth and Denver City Railway just south of Clarendon by 1887 provided new impetus for the remaining ranchers.[39] Mathew's skills were again in demand as horses were needed to trail the cattle from the Pecos River, starting in early March, to reach the railheads along the Fort Worth and Denver Railway in the northern part of the Panhandle in time for the summer shipping.

Although the Fort Worth and Denver shipped cattle year-round, the majority of cattle were shipped after the spring roundup and again after the fall roundup. Because shipping by rail was still in its infancy, most railroads did not supply enough cattle cars to carry the larger number of cattle during the spring and fall. Fourteen cattle cars were provided in each outbound train, so only a few cattle could be taken from each man's herd. The rest of the herd had to be fed at the owner's expense while waiting in the lots along the railroad line, something that might take as long as a month or more. Mathew was responsible for feeding the horses of the remuda until he and the cowboys could take them back to the ranches on the Pecos. Often, he and some of the cowboys were detailed to take the horses back early, leaving only a few to work the cattle in the pens until they were all sold. Many of the ranchers, still used to the trail drives and not interested in paying the high cost of feed at the railhead, would often trail the cattle on to Dodge even with the railroad already in the area. The last of the trail drives to Dodge that Mathew rode with as a wrangler came over the trail in 1896. By then, the railroads had sufficient cattle cars to handle the volume of cattle coming out of the Panhandle, but the cattlemen and cowboys were never fond of the men who checked the cars and decided which cattle to ship. The cowboys called them "bald faced," not necessarily a derogatory term but one that came from the white collars the men wore that made them look like the newly introduced "bald-face" or white-faced Hereford cattle.[40]

During his years in the Panhandle, Mathew Hooks became friends with Tom Clayton when the two men worked for Charles Goodnight on the JA Ranch. "Tommy was one of those boys who liked the open country and horses and cattle." Clayton and Hooks pooled their resources and became partners in the horse business. Each had something the other lacked. "Tom tried hard to be a great rider but he didn't have the physical make-up. On the other hand, I didn't have any business sense and Tom had a pretty good head." The Clayton family was from the Pecos region, so, sometime in the late 1880s or early 1890s, the two men left the JA Ranch at Palo Duro Canyon and returned to the Pecos country in the south. Working from Tom Clayton's small ranch, the two men—Hooks now in his early twenties—began breaking and training horses and selling them throughout the Panhandle. "We made a fine team and I was closer to him than I ever was to any other white man."[41]

During 1894, the two men, with some of the ranch cowboys, were working horses near the Davis Mountains in the Pecos country. Tommy's horse fell, crushing him. Several of the cowboys laid Tommy in a wagon and took him to town, leaving Mathew with the remuda. Deeply concerned for his friend, Mathew "went out and picked a bouquet of the white flowers that Tommy liked so well and I asked the boy to take them to my friend to cheer him up and remind him of the happy days we rode together."[42] The cowboy asked what he should do with the flowers if Tommy were dead. "Just put them on his grave," Mathew answered. When the flowers arrived, Tommy had died, but, as Mathew had requested, his mother laid the small bouquet of white flowers on Tommy's coffin. From this beginning, in honor of his departed friend, and out of respect for the courage and stamina of the early settlers of the Panhandle, Mathew Hooks sent white flowers to the funerals of all the early pioneers. He also began to send flowers to others who showed the same kind of courage and compassion. "I like to give them to distinguished people because of the meaning the flower has for me and because of my respect for the white people," he said.[43]

By the 1890s, times were changing. After the death of Tommy Clayton, Mathew Hooks reassessed his situation. Although Hooks continued to break and train horses, the country was settling up as farmers and merchants came on the railroads. The early ranchers who had made it through the freeze of '86 profited from the limited number of competitors for the cattle market. With their newly acquired wealth, they had built elegant new homes for which they needed servants. Prior to 1880, many towns in the Panhandle had forbidden Negroes to live or even stop over in their towns. The 1880 census indicates that there were a total of fifty-one Negroes in the Panhandle, including a hand-ful of black cowboys and the small community of thirty-one black families at Mobeetie. Among the black cowboys, Mathew counted Dan Sowell of the Figure 4 Ranch, Henry Mangum of the TJM, Bill Freeman at the Quarter Circle Heart, Charles Fowler and Edward Jones at the LFDS, and Brook Lee of the Diamond Tail.[44] The blacks were often harassed, and, although there might be from eight to ten who lived and worked in the area for a short time, they were often run off by the townspeople. "Sometimes there would be only one or two left, and sometimes there would not be any."[45] Eventually, blacks from other parts of Texas and the South arrived to work as domestic help in the fine homes of the newly rich ranchers. The community of Clarendon evidently accepted the new arrivals, perhaps based in part on their friendship with Mathew Hooks. In 1894, the town fathers agreed to let Mathew Hooks have land for a Negro church. With a very limited number of blacks in the area, Mathew brought both a preacher from Fort Worth as well as the beginnings of a small congregation, most of whom were able to find employment in the homes of Clarendon's cit-izens. It was Mathew's first success at building a black community but not his last.[46]

In the waning years of the nineteenth century, the Panhandle was no longer the frontier Mathew had known when he arrived ten years earlier. Newspapers were becoming more readily available, and Mathew, like the ranch owners, kept up with the national news, in particular the struggles of the Populist movement. In 1896 the farmers and ranchers were determined to put the Great Populist, William Jennings Bryan, in the White House. Mathew was working on the Cowan spread at the time, and he and the rest of the hands rode into town to vote. "There were only eight other people besides myself who were going to vote from that section of the country. They said they would throw me in the creek, if I did not vote for Bryan." Mathew, ever his own man, voted for McKinley. Hooks bet Mr. Ross, the Cowan foreman, his horse against fifty dollars that McKinley would win. When they finally saw a copy of the *El Paso Herald*, "it was giving three to one on McKinley's being elected." When McKinley won, much to the dismay of the nation's Populists, Mathew collected. An occasional friendly wager was not against Mathew Hooks's principles.[47]

As civilization, with its roads and towns, spread across the plains, the demand for horse breakers declined. Mathew married Anna Crenshaw, and the couple settled down at his home in Clarendon. "My wife," Mathew said, "was a good woman, a good cook and a wonderful housekeeper," but, as he said, it was hard for her to adjust to his brand of humor. "It took some time," he said, "but she got better at telling jokes." Mathew found out that she also had a powerful sense of intuition. "I found out when she said not to do a thing, I'd better listen." Anna suggested a move to Amarillo so that Mathew, now thirty-three years old, could leave the dangerous job of breaking horses.[48]

By 1900, Amarillo was well established, having been founded in 1887 by a group of Colorado City merchants along the right-of-way of the Fort Worth and Denver City rail line. The newly opened Elmhurst Hotel, in need of workers, hired Anna and Mathew Hooks, who moved from Clarendon to Amarillo, although Mathew continued to claim Clarendon as his home. Anna was employed washing and ironing the hotel linens, and Mathew went to work as a porter for the hotel. For nine years, the couple worked hard, made a decent living, and Mathew continued his friendships with the early ranchers and settlers who had remained in the area.

Although there was still considerable prejudice against the black families, Mathew became a staunch supporter of the new civic organizations that were being formed. Mathew served on jury duty, the first black in Potter County to do so. He was also vitally interested in any organizations that related to the old days. He joined the Old XITs, men who had worked, at one time or another, for the XIT Ranch, which had gone into receivership by the early 1900s. He was also a charter member of the Western Cowpunchers Association of Amarillo and the Western Cowboys Association in Montana. Without fail, he attended the annual meetings of the Old Settlers Reunion at Pampa and the Old Settlers Reunion at the Tri-State Fair. According to Judge James D. Hamlin, "During the last twenty-five years there has not been an important meeting of any kind, conventions, or old settler get-together meetings that Bones is not present, bringing a carnation wrapped in tissue paper which he asks the presiding officer to present with his compliments to the most important guest in attendance."[49]

It was at one of the reunions of the Amarillo Cowboys that his old friends called on Mathew to produce some of his well-known range chili. When he at last pronounced the huge pot of chili done, everyone anxiously lined up for a serving, but Hooks would not allow anyone to eat until he had said grace. He got on his knees and bowed his head, while his old friends, most of them "too stove up to get on their knees," also bowed their heads. His chili prayer was captured for posterity by one of the members in attendance:

> Lord God, You know us ole cowhands is forgetful. . . . We just know daylight and dark, summer, fall, winter and spring. But I sure hope we don't never forget to thank You before we is about to eat a mess of good Chilli. We don't know why in Your wisdom, You been so doggone good to us. The Heathen Chinese don't have no Chilli ever, the Frenchmen is left out. The Rooshins don't know no more about Chilli than a hog does about a side saddle. Even the Meskins don't get a good wiff of it unless they stay around here. Chilli eaters is some of your chosen people. We don't know why You is so doggone good to us. But Lord God, don't never think we ain't grateful for this Chilli we is about to eat. Amen.[50]

In 1909, Mathew Hooks was offered a job as a porter on the Santa Fe Railroad, and he joined what many perceived as a prestigious group. The black porters, who had serviced the elegant Pullman Company sleeping cars for the railroad lines since 1867, were considered the elite of the black labor force. Although they were still underpaid and dependent on tips to make a living wage, they had not only steady jobs but also the opportunity to travel around the country. One wonders whether the cheerful and garrulous Hooks talked as freely and openly with his passengers as he had with his fellow cowboys. Hooks toured the United States, visiting cities as far away as Chicago and San Francisco. He also learned of the efforts by A. Philip Randolph to form a union among the porters. Because blacks made up the vast majority of the workforce on the railroads, Randolph formed the Brotherhood of Sleeping Car Porters in 1925. Mathew Hooks, as an independent cowboy and the only black among the white ranchers of the Panhandle, preferred to place his faith in the paternalism of the white supervisors of the Pullman Company. "One thing about the white folks," he said. "If you do something worthwhile, they will give you credit for it."[51] During the formation of the union in 1925, the company ferreted out the labor leaders and fired any union organizers. In retaliation, Randolph planned a strike in 1928, but without extensive support from the membership the effort failed, leaving the union members angry and defensive and Mathew Hooks thankful that he had not joined the union. The Brotherhood slowly declined and was not revived until 1933 with the support of Franklin Delano Roosevelt and the New Deal. By that time, Mathew Hooks was in his sixties and had retired from the railroad on a disability pension.[52]

Mathew Hooks had never given up his love of horses and the excitement of bronc riding. During 1910, only a year after he had gone to work for the Santa Fe Railroad, he overheard a group of ranchers discussing horses on their train ride back to the Panhandle. "Because I don't like to miss any horse talk," he "sort of hung around dusting the seats." The men were discussing a horse belonging to Mart Davidson of Pampa whom no one had been able to ride. Hooks, even at forty-three, was certain he could ride the horse and, finally, when he could stand it no longer, he broke into the conversation. "I can ride that horse," he stated, quietly confident. The men smiled and assured him that no one could. Ever the gambler, Mathew bet the men $25, an enormous amount of his salary, that he could. The group accepted his bet and determined to have Davidson bring the horse to the train station at Pampa when the train passed through on its return run. Two days later, when the train pulled into Pampa, Mathew got out, removed his coat and porter's cap, and climbed aboard the horse. The horse had been justly described as "a thousand pounds of dynamite," and sitting astride the pitching animal was certainly worse than being on a "hurricane deck," but Mathew rode the horse to a standstill. As the train's passengers cheered, enjoying the one-man rodeo, Mathew climbed off, calmly collected his money, donned his porter's uniform, and reboarded the train. It was a feat that made Mathew Hooks famous up and down the railroad line for the remainder of his twenty years with the Pullman Company.[53]

In 1930, Hooks, then sixty-three years old, had worked on the railroad for over twenty years. His wife Anna had died ten years earlier, in 1920, and he had buried her at the Llano Cemetery in Amarillo. He had married again, briefly, but the marriage ended in divorce, and he did not remarry. He had seen the Panhandle change and grow, and although he had not supported A. Philip Randolph he had been influenced by the growing feeling of black pride that was being espoused by not only Randolph but Marcus Garvey, W. E. B. DuBois, and other black leaders. He knew that there was a need for more black communities such as the one he had started thirty-five years earlier at Clarendon. "When I was a boy," he said, "everywhere I went, folks would say, 'We're not goin' to let any Negroes live here.' I said to myself, 'When I get grown I'm goin' to build a town right beside yours, and not let any white folks live there.'"[54]

When he retired from the railroad, he used his savings and his pension to build a town for his people that would be a credit to the black community. "I wanted our people to have an exclusive town and show the white man we could live as decent and law-abiding citizens so that when one black man committed a crime, the white man couldn't say all darkies were like that."[55]

Mathew Hooks joined sixty other members of the black community in Amarillo to make their dream come true. A parcel of land northwest of Amarillo had been platted for the construction of West Texas State University, but when the Amarillo city fathers failed to encourage its establishment the board of regents moved the location of the university to Canyon. Hooks and the black leaders asked to purchase the land as a community exclusively for blacks. In September 1930, the Amarillo City Commission approved the sale of a twenty-eight-square-block parcel, "bounded on the south by Miller Heights, on the north by Thompson Park, on the east by North Madison Street and on the west by North Hayden Street." North Heights grew rapidly into a successful residential and business community for the blacks of Amarillo. One hundred and thirty-five families built comfortable and attractive homes, in addition to a community center, an auditorium, Methodist, Baptist, and Holiness churches, and the Fred Douglas Elementary School and Patten High School, in which the principal's wife ran the cafeteria.[56] There were also garages, gas stations, and a drug store/general store, owned by Mathew Hooks, at First and Harrison with a second floor where Mathew lived most of the remainder of his life.

In 1932, Hooks and the sixty charter members of the community dedicated a park with lights and a water fountain between Northeast Twenty-First and Twenty-Second Streets and between Davidson and Washington. They planted trees, each one named after a child of the community, so that the children could watch their trees grow as they grew. The black community appreciated the efforts of the aging cowboy, and, within the year, the town fathers decided to rename the park in honor of Mathew Hooks. A statue was later erected for him in the park, and to this day, on June nineteenth, emancipation day, celebrations are still held in Mathew Hooks Memorial Park, with baseball games, barbecues, and speeches.[57]

In 1932, Mathew Hooks, concerned over the underprivileged boys in the community, formed the Dogie Club. Hooks called himself the Head Wrangler and spent his time teaching and educating any of the black boys of the community who were poor or fatherless. The club, which met frequently, helped the young boys learn pride and good citizenship. The boys benefited from the lessons, and many went on to become successful members of the community. At the beginning of World War II, Hooks helped in a recruiting drive for the Selective Service among the young black men of the area. A number of his "Dogies" joined the military and fought with valor in World War II, returning with pride to their West Texas community. Hooks received a certificate of acclamation from the U.S. government for his assistance that he saved in his growing number of scrapbooks.[58]

Mathew Hooks was also active in founding historical groups. In 1933, he founded the Colored Panhandle Pioneer Club. The only requirement was that members had to have lived in the Panhandle for more than twenty-five years. At the first meeting, on June 9 at the North Heights Community Center, there were over sixty black pioneers. As Hooks said, "Folks, it was some roundup. Those mavericks told their experiences in this country when there weren't nothing much but rattlesnakes and dust storms." He was also interested in preserving the history of the area that he saw rapidly slipping away at every funeral he attended. He joined other like-minded old-timers in setting up the Panhandle-Plains Museum and Library and eventually left his extensive scrapbook collection to the museum. His scrapbooks showed his eclectic range of interests, with clippings on world affairs, juvenile problems, crime prevention, politics, and welfare. In 1936, Hooks's scrapbooks were chosen because of their broad coverage and extensive details to represent the history of Negroes in the Panhandle at the Texas Centennial in Dallas. Three years later, in 1939, Mathew Hooks was invited, as the Texas representative, to display the scrapbooks again at a national exhibit in Detroit for the "Seventy-Five Years of Negro Progress."[59]

By the 1940s, Hooks had become "the most famous cowhand still living."[60] Part of his fame came from his white flowers that appeared, for over fifty years, at the funeral of every pioneer from the early Panhandle days. His "Guerdons of Honor" also spread to anyone who had benefited mankind. The Amarillo floral company kept a list of his gifts, and with each one went the same note explaining his desire to honor the pioneer men and women who had built the Panhandle, in particular his friend Tom Clayton. Among those to whom he gave flowers, the Old Soldiers organization received the largest number, eighty-two, while the next largest number, sixty white flowers, went to the Confederate Reunion

Plainsmen, also known as the Sky Busters. During World War II, Hooks sent fifty-seven flowers to a WAVES unit known as the Blue Bonnets, and forty-seven to the Rangerettes, a Women's Army Air Corps unit. Five flowers went to the Scouts of England, and President and Mrs. Franklin Roosevelt each received a flower. The notes of acknowledgment from the presidential couple, as well as from the many other recipients, are carefully preserved in his scrapbooks. When the United Nations Conference met in San Francisco, Hooks sent forty-eight flowers, one to each of the national representatives, some of whom he had met when he was a porter on the trains. During the years from 1930 to 1951, whenever a new building was opened or a church was dedicated in Amarillo, one of Mathew Hooks's white flowers appeared. By the end of his life, Hooks had sent over five hundred white flowers to people from all walks of life and had become famous for his thoughtfulness.[61]

By 1949, at eighty-one years of age, Mathew Hooks had begun to suffer a debilitating illness. Without children or a wife to care for him, he was admitted to Wyatt Memorial Hospital in Amarillo. Unfortunately, the income from his store as well as his life savings had been spent on his young Dogies and to help anyone who had asked for money. His stay in the hospital used up what little was left of his resources. When he was finally released, neither was he able to care for himself nor did he have any money left to hire help. Hearing of his problems, the *Amarillo Globe* ran a story detailing his plight. Friends and funds appeared from everywhere. With the money that was collected, his friends hired a housekeeper, Mrs. Leecie Silas, who left her work at the Amarillo Hotel to devote her attention to caring for Hooks.[62]

Mathew Hooks passed away on February 2, 1951, in Amarillo at eighty-three years of age. One brother, Clem Hooks of Hubbard City, Texas, and a sister, Mrs. Eva Lipscomb of San Diego, survived him. The funeral, held at the Mt. Zion Baptist Church, was attended by dozens of Amarillo citizens. One old white pioneer friend, John Trolinger, had made a vow with Mathew—"Whoever was living when the other died, should offer a white flower as a symbol of friendship between the races." Trolinger carried out the promise and placed a lone white flower on his coffin. Mathew Hooks was buried beside his wife Anna in Llano Cemetery.[63]

Mathew Hooks had come to the Panhandle with the earliest settlers. As he said, "Folks talk about Judge Bean and the Law West of the Pecos, but there wasn't no law out here then." He watched the improvements and comforts of life slowly develop in the area, and he played an active part in the many changes that had taken place. Mathew Hooks helped improve the lot of the early black settlers, first at Clarendon and later at Amarillo. "I've lived through two ages, the horse age and the automobile age. I liked horses and about the time I got to where I liked autos, they started flying." Although he did go flying when his wife had insisted on it, he decided he would not be able to go with the airplanes as he had with the horse and the auto. He had lived a good life and considered himself fortunate. "One time I owned some oil land and could see myself a millionaire. Then I went broke. I got hurt on the railroad and was retired on a pension and I couldn't live like I had before. So I reached up and pulled down my desires to fit my income and now I am a millionaire." He shared his philosophy of life with a class of college students in 1933. "One of the finest things in the world is the friendships you establish when you are young. . . . You can keep friendship always. You may lose everything, but you can't lose that." He believed that if a man loved his country and had faith in that country, it would bring him comfort, life, and friends. For Mathew Hooks, the Panhandle country brought him everything he had hoped for, and his beloved country was enriched by his presence.[64]

Notes

1. The extensive collection of Hooks scrapbooks, interviews, and memorabilia is gathered at the Panhandle-Plains Museum and Library at West Texas A&M University in Canyon. Further sources are in the McCarty Papers at Amarillo Public Library, Amarillo, Texas.

2. Hooks in a July 15, 1939, interview, states that he was born in Orangeville, Robertson County, Texas. Ron Tyler, ed., *The New Handbook of Texas*, Vol. 4 (Austin: Texas State Historical Society, 1996), 1164, cites the only town listed with such a name as located in Fannin County, near the Red River, not in Robertson. Likewise, a history of Robertson County reveals no Orangeville, at any time, in that county.

3. The 1860 Fannin County Census Records list a Cullen or Collin Hooks who owned sixty-five slaves. The name Warren Hooks appears in an undated newspaper clipping from the *Amarillo Globe* in the Hooks scrapbooks.

4. "Bones Hooks," *Amarillo Globe*, n.d., Mathew Hooks file, Amarillo Public Library.

5. "Bones' Bits," Farm and Ranch, *Amarillo Press*, n.d., Mathew Hooks file, Amarillo Public Library.

6. "Old Bones," interview with History 413, April 16, 1933, typescript, Panhandle-Plains Museum Library.

7. Barbara C. Spray, "Mathew Bones Hooks," in Amarillo Genealogical Society, *Texas Panhandle Forefathers*, Vol. 1 (Dallas: National ShareGraphics, 1983), 77.

8. "Recollections of Early Day Texas: Mathew (Bones) Hooks," interview by A. B. Hays, Amarillo, Texas, July 15, 1939, manuscript interview file, Panhandle-Plains Museum Library.

9. Guy Saunders, "The Empty Saddle," Clara T. Hammond, comp., *Amarillo* (Amarillo, Tex.: George Autry, 1971), l39.

10. J. Frank Dobie, *The Mustangs* (Boston: Little, Brown, 1934), 304.

11. Ibid.

12. Jean Ehly, "'Bones' Hooks of the Panhandle," *Frontier Times* 37, no. 4 (June/July 1963): 21; "Old Bones," interview with History 413, 5.

13. "Recollections of Early Day Texas."

14. Interview with History 413.

15. Saunders, "Empty Saddle," 140.

16. This and the following review of Mathew as a young wrangler from Interview with History 413.

17. "Recollections of Early Day Texas."

18. Ibid.; interview with History 413; Amarillo Genealogical Society, *Texas Panhandle Forefathers*, Vol. 1, 76.

19. Saunders, "Empty Saddle," 231.

20. Frederick W. Rathjen, *The Texas Panhandle Frontier* (Austin: University of Texas Press, 1973), 230–31; "Mobeetie," Tyler, ed., *New Handbook of Texas*, s.v., 784–85.

21. Rathjen, *Texas Panhandle Frontier*, 230–31; "Tascosa," Tyler, ed., *New Handbook of Texas*, s.v., 209–10.

22. "Clarendon," Tyler, ed., *New Handbook of Texas*, s.v., 129–30; George Turner, "Black Cowboy 'Bones' Hooks Left His Mark on Frontier West's Lore," *Amarillo Globe Times*, November 4, 1973; Ehly, "Bones Hooks"; Amarillo Genealogical Society, *Texas Panhandle Forefathers*, Vol. 1, 76.

23. Interview with History 413.

24. "Recollections of Early Day Texas."

25. Interview with History 413.

26. Saunders, "Empty Saddle," 139; Interview with History 413.

27. U.S. Works Progress Administration, Federal Writers Project. American Life Histories: Bones Hooks. American Memories Collection, Library of Congress, 1936–40. www.lcwcbJoc.gov.

28. Ibid.

29. Saunders, "Empty Saddle," 232–33.

30. Ibid.

31. Mathew's recollections of this period on the Panhandle from Interview with History 413.

32. The 7D ranch is the same ranch that black cowboys George Adams, Daniel Webster Wallace, and members of the Payne family worked.

33. "How the Vigilantes Worked," folder 166, McCarty Papers, Amarillo Public Library.

34. Ibid. To date the password has not been found in museum records.

35. Interview with History 413.

36. Saunders, "Empty Saddle," 233–24; Ehly, "Bones Hooks," 20; Alwyn Barr, *Black Texans: A History of Negroes in Texas, 1528–1971* (Austin: Jenkins, 1973), 91.

37. "Recollections of Early Day Texas."

38. "Death Takes Bones Hooks," *Amarillo Daily News*, February 3, 1951.

39. Rathjen, *Texas Panhandle Frontier*, 245–46.

40. Interview with History 413.

41. "Recollections of Early Day Texas"; Ehly, "Bones Hooks," 11.

42. "Recollections of Early Day Texas," 5; Saunders, "Empty Saddle," 139.

43. "Recollections of Early Day Texas," 5–6.

44. Rathjen, *Texas Panhandle Frontier*, 237; W. Sherman Savage, *Blacks in the West* (Westport, Conn.: Greenwood Press, 1976), 92.

45. Interview with History 413.

46. Amarillo Genealogical Society, *Texas Panhandle Forefathers*, Vol. 1, 76; Ehly, "Bones Hooks," *Frontier Times*.

47. Interview with History 413.

48. Amarillo Genealogical Society, *Texas Panhandle Forefathers*, Vol. 1, 76.

49. Institute of Texan Cultures, "Mathew Hooks," *The Afro-American Texans* (San Antonio, Tex.: Institute of Texan Cultures, 1987), 17; *Amarillo Press*, July 4, 1996; J. Evetts Haley and William Curry Holden, *The Flamboyant Judge: J. D. Hamlin* (Canyon, Tex.: Palo Duro Press, 1972), 103.

50. "Matthew 'Bones' Hooks Chilli Prayer," African Americans: Matthew "Bones" Hooks Vertical File, Institute of Texan Cultures, San Antonio.

51. Saunders, "Empty Saddle," 140.

52. Paula Pfeffer, *A. Philip Randolph: Pioneer of the Civil Rights Movement* (Baton Rouge: Louisiana State University Press, 1990), 24; Institute of Texan Cultures, "Mathew Hooks," 17; Saunders, "Empty Saddle," 40.

53. Ehly, "Bones Hooks," 22; Savage, *Blacks in the West*, 92.

54. "Bones Bits," Farm and Ranch, *Amarillo Press*, n.d.

55. Saunders, "Empty Saddle," 139.

56. Amarillo Genealogical Society, *Texas Panhandle Forefathers*, 76.

57. Ibid.; Saunders, "Empty Saddle," 139; Turner, "Black Cowboy," *Amarillo Globe Times*, November 14, 1973.

58. Amarillo Genealogical Society, *Texas Panhandle Forefathers*, 77.

59. Ibid.; Turner, "Black Cowboy," *Amarillo Globe Times*, November 14, 1973.

60. Jean M. Burroughs, *On the Trail: Life and Tales of 'Lead Steer' Potter* (Santa Fe: Museum of New Mexico Press, 1980), 136.

61. Ehly, "Bones Hooks," 23.

62. Saunders, "Empty Saddle," 141.

63. Savage, *Blacks in the West*, 92; Ehly, "Bones Hooks," 54.

64. *Amarillo Press*, newspaper clipping, July 4, 1996; Saunders, "Empty Saddle," 40; Interview with History 413.

3

"Havin' a Good Time"

Women Cowhands and Johana July, a Black Seminole Vaquera

CECILIA GUTIERREZ VENABLE

Johana July and Henrietta Williams Foster, or "Aunt Rittie," as she was known, were South Texas black cowhands. Aunt Rittie owned her own home and cattle and thrived in her cattle- and horse-raising environment. Born in Mexico, Johanna July was a member of the Black Seminoles who ultimately resided in Bracketville, Texas. July's mother ran their ranch on the Rio Grande, and as she grew up July learned to work cattle and, in particular, to ride and tame horses. In this chapter, Cecilia Gutierrez Venable tells us much about this interesting female cowhand and, in the process, much about the numerous women in the Old West cattle business.

The terms *vaquero* and cowboy conjure images of a tall, lean, muscled, sun-leath- ered man sporting boots, spurs, chaps, maybe a holster on his hip, a bandana around his neck, and a rope in his gloved hand. His eyes are barely visible beneath his wide-brimmed hat, and the formidable figure exudes rugged mas- culinity. These images are promulgated by media and flaunted in western films. Many of these movies contain themes such as the "pioneering spirit" and the conquest of the frontier. The men are tough and portrayed as conquerors of an adversary or tamers of nature.

Women in these same films are relegated to the borders of the story and placed in a subordinate position, always relying on the strong male, although there are hints that they may also be tough. The females in most westerns are slight, well-coiffed, and radiate a feminine appearance, thus making the male characters seem more masculine. One example is *The Bronze Buckaroo*, a 1939 film in the singing cowboy repertoire, reminiscent of the Gene Autry movies except that it hosts an all-black cast. The female role of Betty Jackson, played by Artie Young, sits on her porch clothed in a crisp flower-patterned dress, her

hands in her lap, her ankles crossed and her head bowed. In deep contempla-
tion, Betty is approached by Bob Blake, played by Herb Jeffries. The tall, dark
stranger towers over Betty as she discusses her missing brother, Joe Jackson.
Bob steps up and lays his hand on her arm and says, "Don't you worry Miss
Betty, we'll find Joe, and we'll find the man who dry-gulched your dad." The
next time Betty appears, she is again in a tailored dress that emphasizes her
curves and dons a white bow at her collar. She tells Bob that the neighbor
offered to buy the ranch, and she would sell if her brother was not alive.[1]

Betty's next appearance finds her astride a horse in her western wear bar-
reling through the desert with Bob. They run into an informative old man,
and Bob decides to go into town. Betty rides toward the ranch alone. Upon
Bob's return, he finds that Betty never came home. He and the ranch hands
are discussing Betty's absence when suddenly her horse runs into the pen. Bob
turns to the cowboys and asks, "Suppose she been throwed off?" A ranch hand
replies, "Oh no, not Miss Betty," and the others nod their agreement. The men
decide to follow the horse in the hope that it will lead them to Betty. In the
meantime, Betty has been kidnapped and reunited with her brother. She struggles to free herself, and four men try to subdue her. Her captors approach her
with a brand, trying to force her to sign over the ranch, but she stands her
ground. In the end, the kidnappers are arrested and Betty reaches for Bob's arm
and clings to him; they mount their horses and ride away with the cowboys
singing in the distance.

This film introduces Betty as a demure woman needing aid to find her
brother. She wears a dress, her hair is neatly in place, and she looks helpless.
Her diminutive stature is emphasized by Bill standing a head taller, so that she
is forced to upraise her doe eyes to speak with him. However, as the film pro-
gresses, the audience learns that Betty actually ran the ranch for months and is
an accomplished rider; she knows the area well and is strong enough to require
four men to hold her. When threatened with a branding iron, she simply braces
herself for the smell of her own burning flesh.

Although this film seemingly perpetuated the stereotype of women as
subordinate actors assuming perceived traditional societal roles for women on
ranches, it also disclosed that women actually worked the ranch and developed
skills similar to their male counterparts. They rode well and performed tasks
when needed, and should the necessity arise they could run the business. In *A
Vaquero of the Brush Country*, J. Frank Dobie described the cowboy as a proud

rider, skilled, observant, alert, resourceful, unyielding, daring, punctilious in a code peculiar to his occupation, and faithful to his trust. His individualism was so marked that he molded in his own image, as it were, all aspirants to his occupation." Dobie considered only men to be cowboys; these traits, however, also applied to women who worked on the ranch. He later defined *vaquero* in his book as a term that in the early days of cattle raising meant "a Spanish or Mexican cowboy." Through time, the term moved away from racial identification to anyone who developed an expertise in working with livestock. In "The Vaquero and Ranching in the Southwest United States 1600–1970," Nora Ramirez described this individual as skilled in "horsemanship, roping ability and knowledge and understanding of cattle." Although several women worked as cowboys and a few may be considered *vaqueras*, their image did not conform with the myth of the brawny male, so their contribution to ranching was dismissed.[2]

Women as cowboys have also been overlooked by scholars. As early twentieth-century scholarship portrayed women's agricultural work in the home, hen house, garden, and field as secondary to that of the male farmer, so too was women's work as a cowboy on the range portrayed as secondary. Their experiences were marginalized because their labor often appeared as part of the family wage, thus largely unpaid. Long-time cowboys Carl Hammond and Mike Hanley noted that they did not know of women who worked as cowboys when they were young, but they did say that women often worked alongside their husbands or other family members. They also posited that women stepped in and became more noticeable on ranches during World War II, when there was a shortage of men to work the livestock. Hammond admitted that his wife "is better help around horses and cattle than any other hand he has hired." Nevertheless, the lack of documentation of women's activities has made it difficult for historians to track their contribution. In *Cowgirls: Women of the American West*, Teresa Jordan posited that women also sought a more diminutive role on the ranch, not because of their inability to handle any task but because they did not want to appear masculine; thus, their direct contribution on the ranch was often hidden. The lack of recorded evidence of women's ranch work coupled with their reluctance to be recognized for their work has posed a conundrum for the study of women as cowboys.[3]

Women's omission as cowboys in the scholarship may also be attributed to their transient positions as ranch hands. When they worked alongside relatives, they had little hope of inheriting the homestead because the ranch usually fell to a male relative, thus forcing women to work in the home, find employment in town, or marry. If a widow inherited the homestead, she had to find a strong ranch foreman or neighbor to aid her in operations, since some men lacked enthusiasm working for a woman. Finally, employers would not actively seek out and hire women as cowboys, forcing them to find a job in the traditional female domain. To circumvent such obstacles, some women altered their appearance to hide their gender. "Little Joe Monahan," a long-time cowboy who worked in Idaho and Oregon in the late nineteenth century, for instance, was discovered to be a woman only upon her death in 1903. Some women were intermittent players on the range, their work essential, yet their contributions went largely unnoticed until the latter half of the twentieth century and the development of women's history as a discipline.[4]

Initial works on women as cowboys were often autobiographies. Hallie Stillwell penned her early escapades in 1991 with *I'll Gather My Geese* and a 2004 addition covering the latter part of her life, *My Goose Is Cooked*. In the same spirit, Sandra Day O'Connor wrote about her experiences in *Lazy B: Growing Up on a Cattle Ranch in the American Southwest*. Other works, such as *I Married a Cowboy* by Connie Reeves, discussed the lives of women living with cowboys, but here the women were not the focus. By the 1980s works such as *Cowgirls* (1982), *Women of the Range* (1993), *Women in Early Texas* (1994), and *Texas Women on the Cattle Trails* (2006) concentrated on women as cowboys. Their focus, however, was on Euro-American women who owned ranches, or on women who pioneered an area with their spouse. These works gave little attention to women of color.[5]

The lack of attention to women of color as cowboys is not surprising. At least one-third of the cowboys were people of Mexican and African descent who worked with Anglo cowboys and were accepted as coworkers, regardless of their race; yet only a few works actually concentrate on the Mexicans, Tejanos, Native Americans, and African-American men who worked livestock. Since men of color went unnoticed as cowboys, women seem nonexistent in this line of work. Armando Alonzo in *Tejano Legacy: Rancheros and Settlers in South Texas 1734–1900* posited that Tejano women worked in the ranching industry as widows of the family operation, and some also had their own livestock and brand independent of their husband's cattle. They often held this as part of their estate and willed separately from their husband's. Although these Tejanas worked the family's cattle and at times their own herd, few studies exist of their activities.[6]

Like Tejanas, African American women also worked as cowboys all over Texas, but few have appeared in scholarly studies.[7] In the 1988 article "Black Women in the West," Glenda Riley noted that histories of black frontier women were also scarce. She attributed some of this omission to the lack of efforts to mine sources to find their stories. For African American women as cowboys this may also ring true, since they are not well represented in the literature. Still, a few women have appeared in vignettes, footnotes, and other works. In the *Black West*, William Katz noted that Mary Fields, a formidable character of Montana, shot well and could protect herself. She hauled freight for the Ursuline nuns at St. Peter's Mission near Cascade but eventually lost that position because the bishop heard of her involvement in a gun battle and considered it inappropriate. In Texas, Aunt Polly Upton, an African American woman who lived on the Melon Creek Ranch, had a small herd of cattle. Louise O'Connor in *Tales from the Antone Bottom* noted that she also rode well. A couple of years later O'Connor wrote a chapter in *Black Cowboys of Texas* on Henrietta Williams Foster, or "Aunt Rittie," a native of Mississippi who came to Texas because her slave owner lived there. Remembered as a tough, resilient woman who could perform whatever task needed, from fieldwork to domestic chores, sewing wounds, and birthing children, Aunt Rittie also worked cattle, rode bareback, and "could ride a horse better than a man."[8]

Though several African American women are remembered for their work as cowboys, their stories are usually gathered from memory and government documents; few have actually recorded their own stories. Johana July (Wilkes Lasley), however, is one who has. As part of Franklin D. Roosevelt's New Deal Programs, the Works Progress Administration (WPA) interviewed Johana. Although the interviewer, Florence Angermiller, added her opinion to the interview, it remains a powerful story of a Black Seminole woman who could and did work as a cowboy and became a skilled *vaquera*.[9]

The WPA report documented Johana as Johanna July, but her family stated that they knew her as JoAnne, which was probably a derivative of the Gullah name Wannah. Gullah, an African language spoken by eighteenth- and nineteenth-century slaves in the New World, fostered the names for many of the Black Seminoles, although the spellings of these names often changed to accommodate regional preferences. Most of Johana's friends and family knew her more fondly by her basket name, Chona. Basket names, or nicknames, were reminiscent of the African Kongolese naming system, which the Black Seminoles have embraced and maintained through the generations. The elders used these basket names when speaking to each other or relating stories or oral traditions about individuals. The usage of basket names was, however, so common that given names fell into obscurity, which prompted one youth to ask the elders to write their real names, so they could pass them on to the children. Since given names may not have been used often, their spellings could change through time both by the individual and the interpreter. This may account for the reason Johana had multiple spellings of her name through the years.[10]

Johana was born in Mexico to Black Seminole parents in 1860. Her father's lineage leads back to important leaders of the Black Seminoles in Florida. The Seminoles emerged from the Creeks; their leader, Chief Cowkeeper, or Mikko Ahaya, brought his people to the Alachua plain near St. Augustine by 1720. Other Creeks congregated in the area, and this group formed a confederacy, which adopted the name "Seminole," derived from the Creek language and meaning "wild or undomesticated." The Seminoles provided a haven for blacks and there numbers increased. Some blacks joined the tribe after escaping slavery, some were purchased by Seminoles, and some free blacks moved to the territory in search of lucrative business opportunities. This population formed several settlements such as Pilaklikaha (Abraham's town), which according to archaeologists served as a hub for trade among the black, Native American, and European communities. This town also supported several prominent individuals, including men with the name July, who acted as interpreters and guides.[11]

The July family also led some skirmishes against U.S. troops. Both Spain and Britain encouraged the Seminoles to contest American incursion. The Black Seminoles, including freedmen and slaves, feared capture and enslavement; consequently, they fought against these trespassers. These battles coupled with the exodus of fugitive slaves who sought sanctuary among the Seminoles further angered American slaveholders. The United States met Seminole resistance, and several wars broke out in Florida and Georgia between 1817 and 1818, collectively named the First Seminole War. These wars highlighted Spain's inability to control its territory. Consequently, Spain ceded its land for $5 million to the United States in 1819.[12]

This newly annexed land encouraged an influx of people to Florida, who coveted slavery and threatened the Seminoles and maroons who lived among them. Because Seminoles along with Cherokees, Choctaws, Creeks, and Chickasaws had brought at least five thousand more blacks with them to Florida by 1830, slaveholders desired land in the area. These conditions escalated tensions with the Seminoles; consequently, when Andrew Jackson assumed the presidency, he scripted the Indian Removal Act of 1830 to free land for the incoming American trespassers. The Treaty of Payne's Landing in 1832 implemented the removal act. This plan involved moving several tribes, including the Seminoles, to Indian Territory (in modern Oklahoma). There the Seminoles would live among the Creeks and become an integral part of that tribe. A year later, in 1833, the Treaty of Fort Gibson provided the Seminoles with land along the Canadian River and the North Fork of the Little River. The Seminole and maroon community farmed and raised livestock, but constant fear of enslavement by Creeks, Cherokees, and other Americans plagued the community. After some had been kidnapped or stolen, the blacks and Seminoles left their land and livestock and fled to Fort Gibson. And though the fort offered some protection, several were still captured and sold as slaves. Living in constant fear, the July family as well as other maroons and Seminoles planned an escape to Mexico.[13]

One of the maroon leaders of the expedition south of the border was John Horse (Cowaya, John Caballo), an interpreter for the U.S. Army as well as a spokesman for the Seminoles in Washington. He spoke on numerous occasions on behalf of blacks and Seminoles to U.S. officials. Wild Cat (Kowakochi Coacoochee), a Seminole leader, had been captured with several other Seminoles and blacks because they resisted relocation. They were subsequently chained and sent to New Orleans, and then on to Indian Territory. Both men sought an existence free of Creek domination and of enslavement, so they secretly met with Mexican officials who wanted settlement along their border. The Mexican government found it difficult to entice people to the area because of continued raids, so they offered citizenship to the Seminoles and blacks if they would move to the region. Since slavery had been abolished in Mexico, blacks could live with little fear of enslavement. John Horse and Wild Cat prepared for their journey, and when opportunity arose they gathered people from Florida and Fort Gibson in 1849 and journeyed to Mexico. The party reached the Rio Grande near Eagle Pass only to find the water high and turbulent. The travelers built rafts and crossed the rapid river for Mexico in 1850.[14]

The group set up camp, and John Horse met with Mexican officials.

Eventually, the government agreed to give the party land and an official designation as "Mascogos." This classification came with strings, however; officials expected the Mascogos to adopt Spanish names and surnames and be baptized as Catholics. Most of the people never gave up their African traditions, but some adopted a few Catholic practices. The Black Seminoles lived near Piedras Negras, a small Mexican town just across the border from Eagle Pass. There, they had to keep extremely vigilant for fear of marauding Americans who crept onto Mexican soil to capture and enslave people. Finally, the Mexican government relented to their complaints and gave the Mascogos land, equipment, and seed in the Hacienda de Nacimiento in exchange for their aid in fighting Apaches and Comanches.[15]

The Mascogos set to work building homes on their land. These houses resembled Mexican *jacals* and were fashioned by shaving and tying tree limbs together and chinking the spaces with stones and mud. The roofs consisted of leaved plants lashed together to prevent rain from pouring into the structure. A fireplace in front of the shelter was used to keep the home warm, one of the remnants from their lives in Indian Territory, which differentiated it from the typical Mexican *jacal*. The group also attached arbors to the house, which held the family's saddles and provided shade from the scorching sun. The coverings offered a cooler place to sleep while protecting the family from the rain.[16]

The men, however, had little time to spend in these homes, because the Mexican government continually needed their help to subdue Indian uprisings. With the absence of the men, the women strengthened communal ties and continued as a matrifocal society, which harkened back to their African roots. The women split chores among themselves, which included farming and caring for livestock. Women made decisions for the group, and when men married they moved to their wife's home.[17]

The Mascogo women proved successful in producing crops and healthy livestock in Nacimiento. They maintained an irrigation system that helped provide much-needed water to sustain life in the area. As a consequence of their success, wealthy Mexicans sought to infringe on their land, so the government decided to move the Mascogos to Parras de la Fuentes in southwest Coahuila in 1859. Johana's family probably made this trip, and she may have been born in Parras. Conditions at Parras, however, proved dangerous for the Mascogos because other tribes invaded their land and captured and killed people in the community. The Mascogos pleaded to return to Nacimiento, but the Mexican government refused them permission. Eventually, the Seminoles fell into the middle of political strife between Santiago Vidaurri, governor of Nuevo Leon y Coahuila, and Benito Juárez, leader of the Mexican reform movement that supported the expansion of the Mascogos' rights in Mexico. Maximilian and the French then invaded Mexico and burned most of the Mascogo homes, before Juárez and General Porfirio Díaz ended their destructive spree. The Mascogos returned to Nacimiento only to find Kickapoos and other blacks on their land. With cries from these groups that they had abandoned the land, the Mascogos had to make several trips to discuss their plight with Juárez. Finally, the government returned their land, but this did not allay the people's fears or bring them peace; Mexico's tumultuous political strife over the next few years combined with drought, a smallpox epidemic, and strife with other Indian tribes tempted many Mascogos to return to the United States and Indian Territory.[18]

Eagerness to return to the United States drove John Horse and John Kibbetts (Si-tee-tas-to-nachy, or Snake Warrior) to negotiate with the U.S. Army as early as 1868. The army offered the Mascogos positions as scouts in a new branch known as the Seminole Negro Indian Scouts. These scouts would assist the army to crush Indian raids in Texas. In return, the scouts and their families could cross the river and live near Fort Duncan. This fort, part of a string of garrisons built by the United States along the Rio Grande to secure the border beginning in 1848, was established by Gen. George M. Brooke. The fort housed infantry, but many of these soldiers were inexperienced in handling Indian raids. With the influx of new settlers, the U.S. government needed additional protection for its citizens—in this case, the Seminoles' expertise. In compensation for their services, the Mascogos would receive land.[19]

Johana's family returned to the United States in 1869, when she was almost ten, perhaps fleeing the smallpox outbreak that hit Nacimiento. In anticipation of a final agreement between the United States and the Seminoles, the family settled near Fort Duncan and farmed as well as raised livestock. Johana's father taught her to hunt, fish, and care for livestock. Work was often shared and gender-specific within the Black Seminole community, with women cooking, gardening, and caring for family, and men caring for livestock and hunting. Johana, however, preferred to labor with her father. He must have recognized her ability with the horses, working goats and cattle, because he allowed her to work with him. Her mother must also have noticed her skill with animals and supported her absence from domestic chores. Though Seminole women often prepared food and farmed, they had also been in the livestock business as early as the 1800s, when Buckra (Bucker) Woman raised and sold cattle for the Spanish.[20]

In the tradition of the Mexican *vaquero*, Johana's father handed down his knowledge and skills with livestock to a member of his family, Johana. She enjoyed working with her father, but unfortunately his life was cut short. With the death of her father, Johana assumed the management of the livestock and horses. In a WPA interview with Johana, interviewer Florence Angermiller remarked that Johana was "practically forced into the job of breaking horses after her father died." Other interpretations of Johana's story also assumed she was forced into this job; however, this may not have been true. Since the Mascogos had lived in Mexico for several years, and the men routinely left their homes to aid Mexican officials with marauding tribes, the women cared for the livestock in the men's absence. Johana's father also scouted, which meant he had to be away from the family at times; consequently, Joanna cared for the animals and at her father's death simply assumed the duties as a matter of course.[21]

Along with raising livestock, another job Johana mastered was breaking horses. The ability to train horses had a long history of being valued in the New World. When the Spanish conquistadores arrived in New Spain, they brought horses and their black slaves to care for them. Because the horses were important for Spanish survival and dominance over the native population, the conquistadores prohibited Indians from caring for and riding their mounts. Consequently, the ability to raise and break horses defined race and class. With the expansion of ranching and the need to increase the horse population for working livestock, the Spanish rescinded colonial law and allowed Indians, blacks, and mestizos to tend the horses. These groups improved their skills and adapted the Spanish tradition of horsemanship (*charreria*) and the *vaquero* culture.[22]

Immersed in the *vaquero* culture working with her father and later with others who lived near the fort, Johana knew how to ride well. She preferred to ride bareback with only a rope tied around the horse's nose to guide it. For breaking horses Johana adopted her own style of gentling her stock. Some *vaqueros* walked their horses in deep sand or mud to tire them out; as noted earlier, Johana used the river. In the WPA interview, she explained her method:

I would pull off my clothes and get in to de clothes I intended to bathe in and I would lead 'em right into de Rio Grande and keep 'em in dere till dey got pretty well worried. When dey was wild, wild, I would lead 'im down to de river and get 'im out in water where he couldn't stan' up and I would swim up and get 'im by de mane an' ease up on 'im. He couldn't pitch and when I did let 'im out of det deep water he didn't want to pitch. Sometimes dey wasn't so wore out an' would take a runin' spree wid me when dey got out in shallow water where dey could get der feet on de ground and dey would run clear up into de corral. But I was young and I was havin' a good time."[23]

Johana's routine allowed the horses to tire swimming in the river, preventing them from bucking and running too far. She also multitasked her work by washing her clothes while she exhausted her horse. Johana enjoyed her work, although at times it could be dangerous outside of the fort or town without protection. She told the story of going out and cutting hay with her horses. Fatigued from her task, she decided to rest but noticed that the horses seemed skittish, with their ears twitching. Johana sensed something amiss and called to her horse. She jumped on his back and turned, only to see two Indians racing toward her. She dug in her heals and rode hard to the fort. Arriving, Johana jumped off her horse and told the soldiers about being chased by a couple of Indians. The men immediately gave chase and followed the Indians into Mexico. After this incident, Johana, unscathed and undeterred, continued riding in search of rich pastures for her horses, despite the dangers lurking around the next hill.

At eighteen, Johana married a U.S. Army scout. Since he was stationed at Fort Clark, she left her mother and family for a small home near Las Moras Creek. Leaving her relatives proved difficult; Johana had grown up surrounded by her mother and extended family. Growing up in Mexico, she witnessed the Seminole women banding together in the absence of the men and supporting each other to build a thriving community. Johana left this network behind when she relocated; she no longer had relatives she could consult, seek aid from, or simply converse with. The lack of a safety net coupled with her inexperience for domestic chores resulted in her tolerating an abusive husband. His anger, fueled by her inadequate training, turned extremely violent. Finally, Johana decided to return home after a rough altercation with her husband. She quietly crept out of the house and ran to the pasture where she found one of the neighbor's horses. She cut a spanish dagger and wove it into a rope and tied it around the horses head. She jumped on the horse and kicked his flanks to fly, but she "couldn't get dat old pony out of a trot."

In fear that he would trail after her, she rode through the night, covering the forty-five miles to her home. "As I got to Fort Duncan I heard de sentry call out, 'Four o'clock an' all is well!' I know I said to myself, 'All may be well, but I don't feel so well after dis ride!" Johana stayed with her mother, but she was always vigilant of her surroundings because she feared the wrath of her spouse. She revealed that "he come down dere [her mother's home] three or four times to get me but I wouldn't go. He shot at me two different times but he missed me, den he tried to rope me, but de Lawd fixed it so my head was too low and de rope went over. I got to de brush an' he never could find me. He would have killed me, en' I knowed it!"

Johana remained with her extended family and continued raising livestock and breaking horses until she married again. Her second marriage of almost two decades, to Ned Wilkes around 1881, produced four children: John, Ned, Lucinda, and Amanda. Unlike her first husband, Ned respected her talents and allowed her to use her skills while also enhancing her domestic talents with caring and cooking for the children. Wilkes had passed away by 1900 and Johana and her family were one of the few families remaining in the area, because many of the Seminoles were ordered to Fort Ringold in 1897. Johana married for the last time to Charles Lasley, by 1910.[24]

With all the children grown, Johana Lasley and her husband worked with livestock, broke horses, hunted, and sold hides. She recalled: "I helped my last husband break hosses an' mules. I 'member one bad mule. He was the meanest one I ever had any dealins wid. He was 'hip-shotten.' I had to tie his good front leg to his good back leg an', don't you know, he'd catch me by de clothes and toss me and shake me if he could get hold of me. I never did break 'im, I got fraid of 'im."

Though Johana worked outdoors in the pastures or corrals, she still had time for her family, noted her niece, Ethel Warrior. After raising her four children, she also cared for her granddaughter, Ora May Roach. By 1940, Johana was a widow once again and living alone on Rufford Street in Brackettville, Texas. Johana July Wilkes Lasley died sometime after World War II, according to nephew William Warrior, and was buried in the Brackettville cemetery.[25]

Johana July's life is illustrative of the lives other *vaqueras* who lived on ranches or found employment opportunities working with livestock. Contrary to what we see in films and other popular media, women were cowboys too; they worked livestock, rode horses, and managed ranches. Though much of the literature on women as cowboys centers on Anglo women, several women of color also participated in this arena. Some worked for part of a family wage or aided a spouse, but they still acquired skills to handle the business and when the need arose could assume the responsibility of running the operation. Johana July Wilkes Lasley's life is a fitting example of woman as cowgirl and *vaquera*. Her Black Seminole roots enhanced her ability to acquire skills to work with livestock. Growing up with the military, she witnessed women accomplishing any task set before them in the absence of men. This allowed her the freedom to master the skills needed to run her business. Her life also matched many other women's transient lives as cowgirls because she grew up raising animals and taming them, but with the demands of family dividing her efforts. When the children vacated the nest, she once again resumed her passion working with animals and "havin' a good time!"

Notes

1. Bell Hooks, *Reel to Real: Race, Sex and Class at the Movies* (New York: Routledge, 1996), 3; Frederick Jackson Turner, "The Significance of the Frontier in American History," in *Bobs-Merrill Reprint Series in History*, reprinted from Annual Report of the American Historical Association the Year 1893, 199–201; Yvonne Tasker, *Working Girls: Gender and Sexuality in Popular Cinema* (New York: Routledge, 1998), 55; E. Ann Kaplan, *Women and Film: Both Sides of the Camera* (New York: Routledge, 1983), 2–3; *The Bronze Buckaroo*, prod. by Dick L'Estrange and dir. by Vin Taylor, Timeless Western Movies, 1939.

2. Lillian Schlissel, Vicki L. Ruiz, and Janice Monk, *Western Women: Their Land, Their Lives* (Albuquerque: University of New Mexico Press, 1988), 172–73; J. Frank Dobie, *A Vaquero of the Brush Country* (Austin: University of Texas Press, 1929), xiv, 3, 6; Nora E. Ramirez, "The Vaquero and Ranching in the Southwest United States 1600–1970" (Ph.D. dissertation, Indiana University, 1979), ii.

3. Katherine Jellison, *Entitled to Power: Farm Women and Technology, 1913–1963* (Chapel Hill: University of North Carolina Press, 1993), x, 1; Judith N. McArthur and Harold L. Smith, *Texas through Women's Eyes: The Twentieth-Century Experience*

(Austin: University of Texas Press, 2010), 62; Lawrence Clayton, Jim Hoy, and Jerald Underwood, *Vaqueros, Cowboys and Buckaroos* (Austin: University of Texas Press, 2001), 206; Teresa Jordan, *Cowgirls: Women of the American West* (Lincoln: University of Nebraska Press, 1982), xiii–xiv; Elizabeth Maret, *Women of the Range: Women's Roles in the Texas Beef Cattle Industry* (College Station: Texas A&M University Press, 1993), 15.

4. Jordan, *Cowgirls*, xiii–xiv; Maret, *Women of the Range*, 15; Richard W. Slatta, *Comparing Cowboys and Frontiers: New Perspectives on the History of the Americas* (Norman: University of Oklahoma Press, 1997), 183; Clayton, Hoy, and Underwood, *Vaqueros, Cowboys*, 206; Sara R. Massey, *Texas Women on the Cattle Trails* (College Station: Texas A&M University, 2006), 4–5.

5. Hallie Crawford Stillwell, *I'll Gather My Geese* (College Station: Texas A&M University Press, 1991); Hallie Stillwell, *My Goose Is Cooked* (Alpine, Tex.: Center for Big Bend Studies, 2004); Sandra Day O'Connor and H. Alan Day, *Lazy B: Growing Up on a Cattle Ranch in the American Southwest* (New York: Random House, 2003); Connie Reeves, *I Married a Cowboy* (New York: Eakin Press, 1995); Jordan, *Cowgirls;* Maret, *Women of the Range;* Evelyn M. Carrington, ed., *Women in Early Texas* (Austin: Texas State Historical Association, 1994); Massey, *Texas Women on the Cattle Trails.*

6. J. Marvin Hunter, comp., *The Trail Drivers of Texas*, Vol. 1 (Austin: University of Texas Press, 1985), 453; Armando C. Alonzo, *Tejano Legacy: Rancheros and Settlers in South Texas 1734–1900* (Albuquerque: University of New Mexico Press, 1998), 189–90, 239–40; Charles A. Siringo, *A Texas Cowboy, or Fifteen Years on the Hurricane Deck of a Spanish Pony* (Simon and Brown, 2013), 56; Jack Bailey, *A Texas Cowboy's Journal: Up the Trail to Kansas in 1868*, ed. David Dary (Norman: University of Oklahoma Press, 2006), 16.

7. Philip Durham and Everett L. Jones, *The Negro Cowboys* (Lincoln: University of Nebraska Press, 1965); Franklin Folsom, *The Black Cowboy: The Life and Legend of George McJunkin* (Niwot, Colo.: Roberts Rinehart, 1992); Gina De Angelis, *The Black Cowboys* (Philadelphia: Chelsea House, 1998); Patrick Minges, *Black Indian Slave Narratives* (Winston-Salem, N.C.: John F. Blair, 2004); Clayton, Hoy, and Underwood, *Vaqueros, Cowboys;* Colonel Bailey C. Hanes, *Bill Pickett, Bulldogger: The Biography of a Black Cowboy* (Norman: University of Oklahoma Press, 1977); Sara R Massey, ed., *Black Cowboys of Texas* (College Station: Texas A&M University Press, 2000). All of these books discuss African Americans as cowboys, but only two books even mention women working as cowboys.

8. Glenda Riley, "American Daughters: Black Women in the West," *Montana* 38 (Spring 1988): 14–17; William Loren Katz, *The Black West* (Seattle: Open Hand, 1987), 155–56; Louise O'Connor, *Tales from the Santone River Bottom* (Victoria, Tex.: Wexford, 1998), 131; Louise S. O'Connor, "Henrietta Williams Foster, 'Aunt Rittie': A Cowgirl of the Texas Coastal Bend," in Massey, *Black Cowboys of Texas*, 7–72. Foster is also mentioned in Alwyn Barr, *The African Texans* (College Station: Texas

A&M University Press, 2004), 37; and Bruce A. Glasrud, ed., *African Americans in South Texas History* (College Station: Texas A&M University Press, 2011), 9.

9. This and following interview excerpts from U.S. Works Progress Administration, Federal Writers Project, American Live Histories: Johanna July. Interview by Florence Angermiller, American Memories Collection, Library of Congress, 1936–1940, www.loc.gov/resouce/wpalh3.32061505/#seq.6 (accessed March 29, 2014).

10. Shirley Boteler Mock, *Dreaming with the Ancestors: Black Seminole Women in Texas and Mexico* (Norman: University of Oklahoma Press, 2010), 91, 210, 219, 226; Alcione M. Amos, "Black Seminoles: The Gullah Connection," *Black Scholar* 41 (Spring 2011): 34; U.S. Bureau of the Census, *Fifteenth Census of the United States, 1930, 1940* (Washington, D.C.: National Archives and Records, 1930), T626; censuses for 1930 and 1940 list Johana as Johanna or Johanne Lasley.

11. U.S. Bureau of the Census, *1910, 1920, 1930, 1940* (Washington, D.C.: National Archives and Records); Amos. "Black Seminoles," 43; Mock, *Dreaming with the Ancestors*, 28, 31; Kevin Mulroy, *The Seminole Freedmen: A History* (Norman: University of Oklahoma Press, 2007), 9, 13, 36, 140.

12. Mulroy, *Seminole Freedmen*, 140, 17, 19.

13. Ibid., 53–57; Mock, *Dreaming with the Ancestors*, 31, 44–45; Susan A. Miller, "Seminoles and Africans under Seminole Law: Sources and Discourses of Tribal Sovereignty and 'Black Indian' Entitlement," *Wicazo Sa Review* 20 (Spring 2005): 26–27; J. Leitch Wright Jr., *Creeks and Seminoles* (Lincoln: University of Nebraska Press, 1986), 313.

14. Mock, *Dreaming with the Ancestors*, 51–57, 69–70; Kenneth Wiggins Porter, "The Seminole Negro-Indian Scouts 1870–1881," *Southwestern Historical Quarterly* 55 (January 1952): 359–60.

15. Mock, *Dreaming with the Ancestors*, 79–75; Kevin Mulroy, *Freedom on the Border: The Seminole Maroons in Florida, the Indian Territory, Coahuila, and Texas* (Lubbock: Texas Tech University Press, 1993), 62–63.

16. Mock, *Dreaming with the Ancestors*, 93–94.

17. Ibid., 77–80.

18. Mulroy, *Freedom on the Border*, 107–109; Mock, *Dreaming with the Ancestors*, 82–86. It is uncertain who actually made the trip because the records were lost in the Mexican Revolution.

19. Mock, *Dreaming with the Ancestors*, 89–91; William H. Leckie with Shirley A. Leckie, *The Buffalo Soldiers: A Narrative of the Black Cavalry in the West* (Norman: University of Oklahoma Press, 2003), 33, 144; Mulroy, *Freedom on the Border*, 110–13; Porter, "Seminole Negro-Indian Scouts," 360–65; Randolph B. Campbell, *Gone to Texas: A History of the Lone Star State* (New York: Oxford University Press, 2003), 196–98.

20. Porter, "Seminole Negro-Indian Scouts," 359–60; Jim Coffey, "Johanna July: A Horse Breaking Woman," in Massey, *Black Cowboys of Texas*, 75; Mock, *Dreaming with the Ancestors*, 30; Mulroy, *Seminole Freedmen*, 13.

21. Works Progress Administration, Johanna July interview; Mock, *Dreaming with the Ancestors*, 30; Mulroy, *Seminole Freedmen*, 91; Coffey, "Johanna July," 76.

22. Clayton, Hoy, and Underwood, *Vaqueros, Cowboys*, 5–8; Slatta, *Comparing Cowboys and Frontiers*,74; Anita González, *Afro-Mexico: Dancing between Myth and Reality* (Austin: University of Texas Press, 2010), 19; Olga Najera-Ramirez, "Engendering Nationalism: Identity, Discourse, and the Mexican Charro," *Anthropological Quarterly* 67 (January 1994), 2.

23. This quotation and the remaining narrative details from Works Progress Administration, Johanna July interview by Florence Angermiller, except where noted.

24. War Department letter dated May 17, 1897, from Clarence R. Edwards 1st Lieut. and Qr. Master 23rd Infantry Commissary to Commanding Officer, Detachment Seminole-Negro Indian Scouts, Fort Ringgold, in vertical file at Archives of the Big Bend Bryan Wildenthal Memorial Library, Sul Ross State University, Alpine, Texas; U.S. Bureau of the Census, *Twelfth Census of the United States, 1900* (Washington, D.C.: National Archives and Records), Administration 1900 T623; in 1900, Johana Wilkes was listed as white, but in 1910, 1920, 1930, and 1940 she was labeled as black.

25. Coffey, "Johanna July," 80; Bureau of the Census, *Fourteenth Census of the United States*, Administration 1900 T625.

4

Black Cowboy

Daniel Webster "80 John" Wallace

DOUGLAS HALES

Another West Texas cowhand to lead an enterprising life was D. W. Wallace. Douglas Hales's biographical chapter portrays a man who not only worked as a cowboy but eventually owned and operated a ranch of significant proportions. Wallace, as Hales comments, "became one of the few successful and enduring African American ranchers in the nineteenth-century West." Born in 1860, Daniel Wallace left home in early 1876 to pursue his dream of becoming a cowboy. He soon hooked up with John Nunn and then with Clay Mann, with whom he worked for eleven years. Mann helped Wallace learn about cattle raising and ranch management. As time moved on, Wallace purchased land of his own in Mitchell County. And he prospered. When he died in 1939, he owned sixteen sections of land.

On a cold March morning in 1876, his thoughts dominated by cattle and cowboys, Daniel Webster Wallace stole away from home. He joined a cattle drive and the event forever changed his life.

Born into slavery on September 15, 1860, Wallace grew up on a small farm near the Texas Gulf Coast in Victoria County. Following the emancipation of slaves at the close of the Civil War in 1865, he moved with his former owners, the O'Daniels, some eighty miles north to a larger farm in Fayette County. The O'Daniels, records suggest, were "good people," and the Wallace family trusted them. In fact, Wallace's mother remained with Macy O'Daniel for the rest of her life, and in turn Mrs. O'Daniel raised Wallace's younger brothers after their mother's death.

Originally published as Douglas Hales, "Black Cowboy: Daniel Webster '80 John' Wallace," in *The Cowboy Way: An Exploration of History and Culture*, edited by Paul H. Carlson (Lubbock: Texas Tech University Press, 2000), 33–43. Reprinted by permission of Texas Tech University Press and the author.

On the Fayette County property, young Wallace, like many other African Americans in the rural South of the post–Civil War era, seemed destined for a life of farm work in the region's cotton and corn fields. But such pursuits held little interest for him. Besides, Wallace knew that black cowboys were working in his part of Texas. No doubt he had seen them for himself as cattle and cowboys passed the O'Daniel place on a regular basis. The brief glimpses of cowboy life that he could observe from the farm must have appealed to his spirit.

So, on that cold March morning in 1876, after completing his predawn chores, fifteen-year-old Daniel Wallace left to pursue his dreams. His life's journey led him to the cowboy way and into the western cattle industry, where he became one of the few successful and enduring African American ranchers in the nineteenth-century West.[1]

His initiation as a cowboy came quickly. When Wallace approached the cattle drovers, the trail boss asked him to show that he could handle a horse. Wallace found the tough little cow pony he was assigned much harder to handle than the old plow horses back on the farm. He climbed into the saddle, but not knowing what to do next he waited for the horse to move. When it moved, it bucked—vigorously. Refusing to be thrown, however, Wallace dug his feet into the stirrups, held on to the saddle horn, and somehow stayed aboard the half-wild mount. Impressed with Wallace's determination and tenacity, the trail boss gave him a job.

The cattle drive went from Victoria County through Wallace's Fayette County to land still controlled by American Indians. It ended near Buffalo Gap at the corner of Runnels and Taylor Counties in west-central Texas near modern Abilene. Now with cattle trailing experience for a reference and $1.50 in his pocket, Wallace went looking for a permanent job as a cowboy.[2]

Traveling southeast to Lampasas County, Wallace found a position with Sam Gholson, a small rancher with a reputation as an excellent "Indian fighter." After Wallace had been in Gholson's employment a short time, John Nunn from South Texas came through Lampasas with a herd of cattle. He was looking for unclaimed grassland on which to start a ranch. As Nunn had found elsewhere, however, local ranchers in the Lampasas area told him to keep his herd moving. In dire need of additional cowhands to continue his quest, Nunn, on Gholson's suggestion, hired Wallace, who immediately left with Nunn and the cattle in search of good grass.

Wallace became one of Nunn's most valuable workers. Nunn, known as a "Christian gentleman" who allowed no profanity in his presence, assigned Wallace the important job of "wrangler" or "hoss stink"—a position that included keeping track of horses, taming wild ones, and being the first to awaken each morning so that he might rouse the camp. For Wallace the work was fine. But Nunn, after again being rejected from occupied grasslands, moved to Sand Rock Springs, twelve miles from the present town of Snyder in Scurry County. Here he settled in and here Wallace worked with him for an additional seventeen months.[3]

Because of the often harsh and dangerous conditions on cattle drives and on the open range, cowhands understood that it was essential to cooperate with each other. Therefore, black cowboys were often exempted from the severe anti-black attitudes exhibited through much of American society in the post–Civil War era. As a black man, however, and often the only African American in the outfit, Wallace was on occasion subjected to racial attacks. When they occurred, he confronted his attacker head on. One such event took place while Wallace worked for Nunn. A large man known as a "bully from a neighboring herd" came to a Nunn cow camp not far from Sand Rock Springs, and in front of Wallace he "bragged of the many things he had done to cowboys of color." Wallace, who stood six feet, three inches tall but was only seventeen years old and a bit thin, immediately challenged the big man to a fight Then, in short order Wallace defeated the unpopular bully and, according to one source, won the respect of both his adversary and his fellow cowboys. In fact, he became something of a legend on the southern plains.[4]

Wallace proved himself in other ways. He was an excellent roper, for example, and several times he accepted friendly challenges to rope a buffalo while riding his horse. One time when he tried the dangerous trick, he came close to losing his life. Most of the time he completed the daring act with success.[5]

In 1878, Wallace received a letter from Mary O'Daniel notifying him that his mother was seriously ill and wanted to see him. Accordingly, he left Nunn's employ to make the long journey back to Fayette County. Unfortunately, the letter, which was several months old, had arrived late, and his mother had passed away before he could make it back. After taking care of his mother's affairs, Wallace took a position with Clay Mann, a well-known rancher in the Colorado City area. Seventeen years old and already a seasoned cowboy, Wallace traveled some four hundred miles to begin work at the new job.

Over the next eleven years Mann and Wallace developed a close personal and working relationship. As his reputation grew, Wallace came to be called "80 John," a name taken from Mann's popular "80" cattle brand. He began work on Mann's ranch near the present-day town of Colorado City. The Silver Creek operation was a ranch in the making. At first no housing was available, and ranch hands had to make do with abandoned dugouts left by buffalo hunters, or "more often," according to Wallace, "we used our wagons and the ground with our blankets for a bed and a saddle for a pillow. . . . It was common to find a snake rolled up in your bedding or to be awakened early in the morning by the howl of the wolf or the holler of the panther." Indian raids were still quite common in this part of Texas, and Wallace always slept with a gun under his head. He remembered Indians stealing "all of our horses in '78 and most of them in '79, but we stayed there all the year of '80." Perhaps about the same time, but probably a few years earlier, Comanche warriors stole one of his favorite horses. He tracked the band for several days before giving up the chase.[6]

One of his most dangerous encounters with Native Americans took place in Mexico. In the early summer of 1883, Mann acquired a ranch in the Mexican state of Chihuahua. He sent his brother John Mann, Wallace, and several other cowboys with four thousand head of cattle to establish his presence on the property. Unfortunately, Indians controlled the same area and took a dim view of intruders, and Mexican citizens along the way warned the Americans of the danger. According to Wallace, "We knew not what to do but go on where Mann told us to go." After crossing the Chihuahuan desert the Americans arrived at the ranch site in late August, built a small headquarters, and kept a close vigil for Indian people. They saw no Indians until October 18, when a number of warriors appeared and "raided our camp, burned our wagons and pens, killed our milk cows, took all the horses we weren't riding and waylaid us in the hills." In an attempt to break out, John Mann and another man were killed, while, according to Wallace, "the rest of us ran as fast as we could to the open prairie, away from the mountains." After the Indians had left, Wallace managed to return to bury the scalped and mutilated bodies of his fallen comrades. Mann's cowboys rounded up what cattle they could find and moved to a neighboring ranch before heading back to Texas a year later. In 1886, Mann sold the ranch to Randolph Hearst.[7]

Wallace and his favorite horse "Peck," who "was no bigger than a half a bushel," rode range lines all across Mann's holdings, land from eastern Mitchell County to the Double Mountain Fork of the Brazos River in Kent County.

Eventually Wallace became Mann's right-hand man and his companion on cattle drives and expeditions for more land. Mann trusted Wallace, whose straightforward response to assignments was, "I will do my best." Mann also entrusted Wallace with the protection of his family. In addition, he trusted Wallace with the buying and selling of cattle. Wallace recalled numerous times he was sent alone with large sums of Mann's money. To buy new stock, once he went to Midland, Texas, with $30,000 in cash in his pocket. When Mann died in 1889, his wife thought so highly of Wallace that she asked him to take over the training of her two young sons.[8]

Wallace credited Mann with teaching him the fundamentals of cattle raising and good ranch management. In fact, Wallace began his own cattle herd through a "gentleman's agreement" with Mann. For a two-year period he earned $720 but drew only $120, applying the remainder to purchase cattle. Mann allowed Wallace's stock with the "Wallase" brand to be run along with his own cattle. As the herd grew, Mann encouraged his young cowhand to purchase land, and in 1885 Wallace bought two sections of railroad land southwest of present-day Loraine in Mitchell County. Later he homesteaded the property.[9]

In the winter months during this time Wallace attended a school for blacks in Navarro County. There he met and fell in love with Laura Dee Owen, a recent graduate of the school. On April 8, 1888, the couple married. Not long afterward Mann died, and Wallace and Laura took steps to become full-time ranchers on their own spread. Now in business for himself, "80 John" Wallace changed his brand from "Wallase" to a "D-triangle." He cut native wood, probably mesquite, for posts to fence his land, and he worked part-time for wages at cattle pens and for other ranchers, including the Slaughter and Spade ranches. And, when a local bank loaned him money to buy Durham and Hereford heifers, he moved to improve his herd.

Daniel Webster "80 John" Wallace became a connected and well-respected resident of Mitchell County. In 1905 he purchased two additional sections of land on Buck and Silver Creeks, tributaries of the Colorado River, and this property became the Wallace Silver Creek Ranch. The increased acreage and stored feed helped Wallace through some tough droughts.[10]

Wallace also joined the Texas and Southwestern Cattle Raiser's Association. For the next thirty years he attended meetings of the organization and earned the respect of its mainly white members. Indeed, an event that occurred while he was on a train en route to one such meeting illustrated the respect. Railroad cars in Texas at the time were segregated, with separate cars for blacks and whites. But several white ranchers came into the black car where Wallace was riding and greeted the black cattleman. When told they would have to return to the whites-only car, one man refused, stating, "I have known 80 John for thirty years. We ate and slept on the ground together. I see no reason that makes it impossible for me to set here now."[11]

Like other cattlemen, Wallace had his share of troubles. The most difficult time came with a drought in 1894. He first moved his cattle to better pasturage in Oklahoma, but the grass there did not last, and he had to sell his herd. Because of depressed prices, he sold at a loss and faced possible ruin. As in other critical times in his life, once again he received help from some friends. Winfield Scott, an old acquaintance and retired rancher living in Fort Worth, furnished him with a $10,000 line of credit to restock his ranch, and soon Wallace prospered again. To deal with future droughts, Wallace allocated twelve hundred acres of prime land for feed crops. Another drought in 1917 posed no real setback for Wallace, even when, for better grazing, he had to send a portion of his herd to New Mexico.

Wallace prospered. He hired cowboys, both black and white, bought more land, and brought in tenants to farm some of the more productive bottomlands. In 1915 he resurveyed some of his land, particularly the original railroad land. Upon completing the new survey, he found that one hundred acres of the original purchase had not been paid for. Fearing it might be taken from him at a later date, he notified the state and purchased the land. It was a wise move, for in 1953, several years after his death, wildcatters found oil on those same one hundred acres. His descendants benefited from his prescience.[12]

Meanwhile, as the droughts illustrate, a successful ranching operation needs good water. Always in short supply in West Texas, water was a precious commodity. Wallace, however, had a knack for finding it. He developed a reputation in the use of a "divining rod," and he was often being sought by other ranchers who wanted him to find water for them. He also used his "skill" to locate sites for windmills on his own property.[13]

The Great Depression of the 1930s brought hard times to the American cattle industry. In his seventies during the Depression, Wallace was nonetheless determined to ride out the troubles. Fortunately, through frugal and efficient management he ended the period debt free.

After Franklin D. Roosevelt's election to the presidency in 1932, the federal government moved to help cattlemen through the New Deal programs.
Wallace refused most aid, but he did accept help through the Emergency
Buying Program of 1934, a law that allowed the president to establish the
Surplus Relief Corporation. Through this program, the government hoped to
raise cattle prices by buying surplus cattle. In turn, Wallace saw no reason not
to sell to the government at thirteen dollars per head some seventy-six of his
older and in some cases sick cattle.

Through such aid, Wallace, unlike many (if not most) cattlemen during the
period, remained profitable. In fact, during the Depression, he bought and paid
for two additional sections of land that adjoined his property near Loraine in
Mitchell County. As a result, with the coming of World War II, the Wallace
ranching operation was in a position to benefit from the high demand for beef
during the booming wartime economy.[14]

Daniel Webster "80 John" Wallace died on March 28, 1939. At the time he
owned sixteen sections of land, including farmland operated by ten different
tenant families. Today the ranch is operated by his descendants.

Wallace learned his ranching lessons well. He came to understand the
importance of making improvements for both the protection of his livestock
and the comfort of his family. For example, he was a good carpenter, and
through the years he built a large ranch house, numerous barns, and cattle pens
and made other improvements on his property.

His life was an amazing and successful one. At the time of his death,
Wallace had four children and four grandchildren. Even though he himself
had very little formal education, he sent each of his children through school,
including college, and he assisted several other young people with their education. In Colorado City, Wallace donated the land on which an African
American school was built. In Loraine, he financed the building of the First
Baptist Church, which also served as a school for black children.[15] He was a
young black cowboy who became a highly respected cattleman.

The information available on African American ranchers like "80 John"
Wallace is limited. Compared to white cattlemen, black ranchers never existed
in large numbers. For Wallace there was little time to worry about his historical significance—being one of the few black cowboys who built a large
cattle ranching operation. Moreover, few historians before the 1960s studied
or wrote about African American contributions to the West. During Wallace's

lifetime little was mentioned about black ranchers or cowboys, at least in Texas, except for the contribution of the *Cattleman,* a magazine for ranchers. In 1936, John M. Hendrix wrote a bland but fair article entitled "Tribute Paid to Negro Cowmen." It is a brief account of Wallace's life, but the short piece also treats such legendary black cowboys as Bill Pickett, William Coleman, and Tige Avery.

Beginning in the 1950s, interest in black cowmen began to increase. The *West Texas Historical Association Year Book* in 1952 published a sketch on Wallace, one he dictated to a friend shortly before his own death in 1939. Hertha Webb's M.A thesis, a largely forgotten piece on Wallace from Prairie View A&M University, was completed in 1957. Mainly, it represents interviews with Wallace's daughter Mary Wallace Fowler, but the brief work adds some information to Wallace's life story. Hettye Wallace Branch, another Wallace daughter, published a small book about her father in 1960; it is a romanticized view of cowboy life and adds little new information. William S. Savage published "The Negro Cowboy on the Texas Plains" in the *Negro History Bulletin* in 1961, but he relied mainly on previously published material.

Each of these works is to be commended for bringing a black cowboy turned cattleman to the attention of scholars and the public at large. At the same time, the shortage of information on black cowboys shows the price society pays when an important segment of the country's population is excluded from serious study.

Daniel Webster "80 John" Wallace, an African American, moved from slave to farm laborer and then from cowboy to cattleman. In some ways his story was typical of American cowboys: he started young and on a trail drive before working for others; he collected his own small herd while employed as a cowboy; and he eventually acquired his own cattle operation, one he built into a successful ranching enterprise. In other ways his story is atypical: here was a black cowboy who became a respected cattleman and a major contributor to his community and to African American schools. He was one of the few western ranchers who survived the shakeout of the mid-1880s and the drought and national financial depression of the 1890s. His ranch some 110 years later remains in his family's possession. Clearly, "80 John" Wallace was one of the most remarkable black cowboys of the American West, and his story deserves retelling.

Notes

1. R. C. Crane, ed., "D. W. Wallace ('80 John'): A Negro Cattleman on the Texas Frontier," *West Texas Historical Association Year Book* 28 (October 1952): 113–14; Hettye Wallace Branch, *The Story of "80 John"* (New York: Greenwich Book, 1960), 13–14; Alwyn Barr, *Black Texans: A History of African Americans in Texas*, 1528–1995, 2nd ed. (Norman: University of Oklahoma Press, 1996), 91, 149. The Crane article is actually a reprint of a sketch dictated by Wallace shortly before his death. In this article Wallace identifies his former owner as Mary Cross, though most sources identify her as Mary O'Daniel.

2. Branch, *Story of "80 John,"* 13–14; John M. Hendrix, "Tribute Paid to Negro Cowmen," *Cattleman* 22 (February 1936): 25.

3. William S. Savage, "The Negro Cowboy on the Texas Plains," *Negro History Bulletin* 24 (April 1961): 157; Crane, "D. W. Wallace," 114–15; Branch, *Story of "80 John,"* 15. Gholson's reputation as an Indian fighter seemed to be based purely on word of mouth.

4. Branch, *Story of "80 John,"* 15–18.

5. Ibid.

6. Ibid., 18–22; Crane, "D. W. Wallace," 116–18; Ira B. Jones and Rupert Richardson, "Colorado City, the Cattleman's Capital," *West Texas Historical Association Year Book* 19 (October 1943): 38.

7. Crane, "D. W. Wallace," 117–18; Branch, *Story of "80 John,"* 22, 29–30. The accounts of Wallace and Branch differ in their descriptions of the Mexico episode. Where differences occur I use the first-hand account of Wallace.

8. Branch, *Story of "80 John,"* 28, 36; Hertha Auburn Webb, "D. W. '80 John' Wallace— Black Cattleman, 1875–1939" (M.A. thesis, Prairie View A&M University, 1957), 22–25.

9. Branch, *Story of "80 John,"* 30, 36; Webb, "D. W. '80 John' Wallace," 22. Wallace purposely spelled his brand using an "s" instead of "c."

10. Webb, "D. W. '80 John' Wallace," 22, 30–32; Branch, *Story of "80 John,"* 30, 36–39.

11. Branch, *Story of "80 John,"* 37–38.

12. Webb, "D. W. '80 John' Wallace," 36–37.

13. Ibid.; Branch, *Story of "80 John,"* 30–32, 41.

14. Webb, "D. W. '80 John' Wallace," 33–36.

15. Ibid., 32–33, 38–39; Branch, *Story of "80 John,"* 489.

5

Nat Love, a.k.a. Deadwood Dick

A Wild Ride

MICHAEL N. SEARLES

Michael N. "Cowboy Mike" Searles concludes this section with his study of Nat Love. Love self-published an autobiography in 1907, *The Life and Adventures of Nat Love, Better Known in the Cattle Country as "Deadwood Dick,"* printed with a cover photo of himself decked out in fine cowboy attire. By this time, though, he had not only lived the life of a black cowboy but spent years as a hotel and railroad porter. His autobiography and cover photo portray a man who is the ultimate in accomplishments and abilities as a cowboy. Race was not an important aspect of his book. He was a black man who worked in a white-dominated field, but it was not exclusively white. African Americans could also be active in the cowboy community. Love's autobiography emphasizes the fact that blacks were part of the West as cowboys and workers and porters, and sometimes in separate roles, but certainly present.

Nat Love, the iconic image of an Old West black cowboy, authored *The Life and Adventures of Nat Love, A True History of Slavery Days, Life on the Great Cattle Ranches and on the Plains of the "Wild and Woolly" West, Based on Facts, and Personal Experiences of the Author*. Love's name, photo, or likeness appears on books, a graphic novel, magazines, a play, children materials, and a clothing company.[1] Yet his fame is clouded with controversy. Were the experiences in his autobiography real, or literary excesses found in the cowboy fiction of the day? Whether he called himself Nat or Nate still interests devotees and scholars. But the greatest challenge in riding Love's trail is that few sources corroborate his story.

Even Love's choice of the "Deadwood Dick" sobriquet was fraught with controversy. Love stated in his autobiography that he was given the name Deadwood Dick by citizens of Deadwood, South Dakota, on July 4, 1876, because of his marksmanship and cowboy skills. Yet the name Deadwood Dick was claimed by no less than six individuals. "Banjo Dick" Brown, a mining camp entertainer and actor, assumed the name around the time of Love's arrival. A year earlier, the mercurial Morgan Levy, a.k.a. Dick Ackermann, allegedly was bequeathed the same title for taming and civilizing the town. Later, Richard "Little Dick" Cole, a stagecoach driver, was said to use the name to scare off would-be robbers. A fifth Deadwood Dick, Cornishman Richard Bullock, gained renown as a professional bullion guard on Deadwood stagecoaches and railroads.[2] To further complicate matters, Edward L. Wheeler, a writer of "dime novels," created the fictional character Deadwood Dick in a series of stories published from 1877 to 1897.[3]

Nat Love revealed in his *Life and Adventures* that he was born in an old log cabin on his master's plantation in Davidson County, Tennessee, in June 1854. Love's childhood remembrances included many pleasantries. He mentioned finding a demijohn of wine hidden by his mother in the garden that he and his brother and sister drank until they were "dead drunk." He later told a story about neighborhood boys chasing rabbits and being confronted by a big red fox. The fox so startled Love that he ran as fast as he could, fearing the fox was nipping at his shirttail. The stories were universal in nature and could have been told about children of any race, social class, or state of bondage.

In 1860, the state of Tennessee recorded a population of 275,719 slaves, a little less than 25 percent of the total population. Though only 20 percent of Tennessee's white population owned slaves, those who did had a median of 15.1 slaves each.[4] Love spoke of his master as kindly, but he condemned the meanest slave owners and the cruelty of the institution. He referred to other slave masters as task masters and perfect devils in human form who delighted in torturing black human beings. Love attributed no special virtue to the slave-owning class, acknowledging that they achieved their sovereignty by chance and the accident of birth. Though many things in life were evil and horrendous, Love found nothing worse than slavery.

When Lincoln's election and the subsequent firing on Fort Sumter propelled southern states out of the Union, Tennessee was the last to secede. The lack of enthusiasm for leaving the Union was reflected in the referendum June 8, 1861, in which Davidson County voted 5,635 in favor and 5,572 against secession. A mere sixty-three votes separated those who wanted national separation from those who did not.[5]

Slavery in Nashville reflected an urban pattern like that in other southern cities. Perhaps prominent Tennessee historian Bobby L. Lovett put it best:

During the era of slavery . . . Nashvillians usually lived in an integrated society without any laws to segregate the races though the free Negroes lived in a quasi-free status with an existence that was defined by state and local laws as well as the unwritten rules of white benevolence and paternalism. The rural whites generally had no need for segregation laws when slaves lived under the tight control of their masters, and as long as persons of African descent were slaves they usually were not viewed as economic competition with the whites.[6]

Middle Tennessee, with its majority white population, did not reflect some of the harsh tendencies of the Deep South; however, the absence of Reconstruction gave the Redemption movement a head start in the state. Seventy-five miles south of Nashville, the Ku Klux Klan was organized in Pulaski, Tennessee, in December 1865. Violence against blacks marred the lives of Tennesseans as they sought to assert their newly acquired status. Even with this mixed pattern, Nell Painter in *Exodusters* stated that Tennessee blacks' sense of continuity made them reluctant to forsake the generational home of their birth.[7]

Robert E. Love of Davidson County owned considerable property in the Nashville area; his "property" included Nat and twenty other slaves.[8] Nat spoke of the end of slavery with his father, mother, brother, and sister while working twenty acres of rented land planting corn, tobacco, and vegetables. After harvesting their first crop and soon after planting a second crop, Nat's father, his sister Sally, and Sally's husband died. In a passing reference, Nat mentioned that his late master and his brother left the old place and went north. However, Robert E. Love's name appears in the 1870 and 1880 federal censuses as a resident of the same county and district as he lived in during 1860. Nat Love never expected to have his autobiography examined by scholars and, possibly for literary effect, kept his past obscure.

Love provided the names of his brother and sister, Jordan and Sally, but failed to name his father or his mother. In the 1870 census, the black family of Sampson Love was recorded as living in Davidson County, Tennessee. In that census, the following individuals and their ages were listed as members of the Sampson Love household: Sampson Love (fifty-two), Melissa Love (sixty-two), Jordan Love (twenty-four), Anias Love (twenty), Ellen Love (nineteen), and Martha Goodwin (sixteen). Jordan Love at twenty-four corresponds to the name and approximate age that Nat Love gave for his older brother in his autobiography. Several sources state that Sampson Love was Nat's father, though Nat never confirmed this.[9] Sources generally indicate that his mother's name is not known; however, in the 1870 census Sampson was living with a female housekeeper named Melissa Love. Melissa Love would have been around forty-six when Nat Love was born, but no evidence has surfaced to indicate that she was his mother.

There is little indication as to the relationship among the six individuals living with Sampson Love except their ages, gender, place of birth, and race. Interestingly, in the census Martha Goodwin is listed as a white domestic servant born in Indiana. There is no census indication of a relationship between Jordan and Ellen Love, but a Jordan Love married an Ellen Read or Reed in Floyd, Indiana, on December 13, 1868, and Jordan and Ellen Love appeared in the household of Sampson Love in 1870.[10] By 1880, Jordan and Ellen were absent from Sampson Love's household, but their names appeared in the 1880 census as residents of New Albany, Indiana, with two children: Ida (nine) born in Tennessee about 1871, and Albert Love (two) born in Indiana about 1878.[11]

Nat Love spoke of the difficult times faced by his mother and his two nieces, children of his deceased sister, Sally. He found work with a Mr. Brooks, giving Love the opportunity to purchase food and badly needed clothing. With items acquired from neighbors and other sources, the wolf was kept from the family's door. Love worked for Mr. Brooks for the next few months until falling out with him over wages. The need to find other employment provided an unexpected opportunity when he stumbled upon a horse ranch owned by a Mr. Williams. His acquaintance with Mr. Williams's adolescent sons and an arrangement to break unruly young colts for ten cents each provided an introduction to his later career. Love did not state how the arrangement was made, but it had a quasi-clandestine feel to it. When Mr. Williams and presumably his wife went to church on Sunday, he left his two sons at home. This was the time when Love came over and broke the colts.[12]

Love detailed how he mounted and rode the frisky mounts until they were saddle-broke. The final episode of the story is a bargain made with the two boys to ride a horse called Black Highwayman. Love refused to ride this horse for the customary dime and, after some bargaining, agreed on twenty-five cents. As might be predicted, Black Highwayman gave Love the ride of his life, running past the Williams's ranch, jumping fences into neighboring pastures, until it succumbed in complete exhaustion. A final note in this adventure was the loss of the twenty-five cents paid in advance by the Williams boys, a quarter the boys would not replace.[13]

The experience Love had breaking horses in Tennessee served him well as a cowboy. Middle Tennessee was horse country, and horse ranches were common. Even before the famed Tennessee walking horse, the state was established as the center of horse breeding and racing. Black men during times of slavery had demonstrated their ability to train and breed horses. On the Belle Meade plantation, the most famous stud farm in Nashville, head groom, trainer, and breeder "Uncle" Bob Greene was credited with breeding some of ranch's first great stallions. Bob Greene spent his life caring for the plantation's horses and had the opportunity to greet and shake hands with President Grover Cleveland when he and his wife visited. Today, "Uncle" Bob's photo and portrait are part of the Belle Meade collection.[14]

Several events allowed Love to leave home with confidence. A man named Johnson announced a fifty-cent raffle for a "fine beautiful horse." As luck would have it, Love won the raffle and sold the horse back to Mr. Johnson for $50. Mr. Johnson then held a second raffle, which Love won for a second time. He then resold the horse back to Mr. Johnson for another $50. Though a second chance drawing of Love's ticket would have likely raised a few eyebrows or pistols, he made no reference to ill will by the unlucky raffle ticket holders. With nearly $100 in his possession, Love gave half of the money to his mother and left her in the care of an uncle and his brother Jordan.[15]

Love set out on his westward trek to Kansas on February 10, 1869, eight years before the famed Black Exodus. Though he gave scant details about his travels to the Sunflower State, blacks had been making the migration since the 1854 formation of Kansas Territory and Nebraska Territory. According to the 1860 census, 625 free and two enslaved African Americans were residents of the territory prior to the free state of Kansas entering the Union in 1861. After the Civil War, Kansas was seen by blacks as a promised land, for the 1859 Kansas Constitution welcomed all settlers regardless of their ethnic or racial background. The 1862 Homestead Act, which allowed blacks an opportunity to claim homestead lands, added to Kansas's attraction. The significant rise of African Americans from 627 to 17,108 in 1870 was representative of the growing popularity of Kansas among blacks.[16]

Black cowboys began driving cattle up the trail to Kansas soon after the Civil War ended. Love arrived in Dodge City as the demand for beef was growing. The abundance of cattle in South Texas with the increased call for beef signaled the beginning of the great cattle drives of the 1870s and 1880s. The presence of black cowboys had a long history in Texas.[17] Black cowboys were cited in *Trail Drivers of Texas*, the most authoritative source on old-time trail drives. Though the black cowboys were usually called by a single name, their presence was acknowledged. Their activities were the same or similar to those of their white counterparts. Love spoke of having breakfast with a Texas outfit that had several "colored" cowboys. Many men from various parts of the world experienced cowboy life, but only a few made it their lifetime occupation. When a greenhorn wanted to join an outfit, it was not unusual to test his mettle. Black cowboys often were given unbroken or "green broke" horses to ride.

Nat's first assignment as a cowboy was to ride old "Good Eye." Knowing the danger associated with riding outlaw horses, a fellow black cowboy, Bronco Jim, offered a few clues about the horse Nat was about to ride. He warned that Good Eye pitched quite a bit, but Nat, in traditional Nat Love fashion, expressed confidence that he could master the task. Love seldom admitted any circumstance that got the better of him, but he came close to acknowledging his vulnerability when he wrote, "I thought I had rode pitching horses before, but from the time I mounted old Good Eye I knew I had not learned what pitching was. This proved the worst horse to ride I had ever mounted in my life, but I stayed with him and the cow boys were the most surprised outfit you ever saw, as they had taken me for a tenderfoot, pure and simple."[18]

Just as Love was called Red River Dick by the trail boss of the Texas outfit, many black cowboys were known by a nickname or their first name with the obligatory appellation "Black" or "Nigger." Some terms that are highly offensive today may not have drawn the same consternation during the time. Sometimes calling a cowboy black or some other color was a way of distinguishing him from a white cowboy with the same or similar name. Addison Jones, a West Texas black cowboy who gained considerable fame as an all-around cowboy, was rarely called Add but was known throughout cattle country as Nigger Add. It is likely that few cowboys ever knew Add's surname. This use of nicknames and given names was not, however, limited to black cowboys; some white cowboys also went through life with just one name.[19]

Love wrote about adventures that likely enthralled the early twentieth-cen-

tury public as the first western movie, *The Great Train Robbery*, must have done
in 1903. Readers who "cut their teeth" on the pulp fiction westerns expected
nothing less. Love's feats as a rider, marksman, Indian fighter, and all-around
cowboy rivaled those of Pawnee Bill, Buckskin Sam, or even Ed Wheeler's legendary Deadwood Dick. A good horseback rider could ride up to forty miles
in a day; Love sometimes rode eighty or even one hundred miles in a day. He
experienced dangerous night rides after stampeding cattle, fought large con-
tingents of Indians, hunted wild buffalo, faced outlaws, and had the "pleasure"
of harassing Mexicans. On one adventure his horse was slightly wounded, but
Love generally escaped these episodes without a scratch.[20]

With so much hyperbole, one must wonder if Love ever told the entire
truth about anything. On July 4, 1875, he passed through Laramie, Wyoming,
just in time to hear about the jailbreak of notorious desperado Jack Watson.
Unlike the many references that cannot be verified, Jack Watson was a real
character that fits Love's description. Watson had a terrible reputation for
getting into trouble with the law. He was a very good shot with a handgun,
and few law officers sought to challenge him. Trouble seemed to be Watson's
middle name, as a previous member of the Hat Creek gang and later as the
leader of his own gang. On May 24, 1875, Watson and a young cohort came into
Laramie to get a court document for a horse and were confronted by Sheriff
J. R. Brophy and Deputy Larry Fee, who attempted to serve an outstanding
warrant for Watson's arrest. Watson and his partner drew their pistols and fired,
leaving Sheriff Brophy and Deputy Fee wounded, then made their escape.[21]
Nat Love's description of Watson as the most desperate criminal ever placed
behind prison bars and his account of the shooting were consistent with the
record. In terms of timing, the incident took place a couple of months before
Love arrived in Laramie, and whereas Love stated that Watson broke out of
jail, actually he made a daring getaway before he could be arrested. However,
his fellow gang member, Richard Rogers, alias Sam Jackson, was apprehended
and jailed.

A year later nearly to the day of his arrival in Laramie, Love and his fellow cowboys delivered three thousand head of cattle to a buyer outside of
Deadwood. July 4, 1876, was a big day in Deadwood Gulch and in the nation.
The centennial celebration of the nation's birth brought a goodly amount of
excitement to the freshly minted mining town. Between January and July 1876,
the *Black Hills Pioneer* newspaper began printing; the first stagecoach arrived;

Charlie Utter led a wagon train that conveyed an ample supply of gamblers and prostitutes; and the Grand Central Hotel opened with Lucretia "Aunt Lou" Marchbanks, a cook and former slave, preparing biscuits, flapjacks, bacon, and beans to rave reviews.[22]

In 1875, John B. Pearson discovered gold in Deadwood Creek, and miners rushed to the area. Even though Deadwood was on Sioux land, gold fever overrode federal treaties and laws. It was into this raw environment that Nat Love rode in July 1876. He wrote of the festivities that met him upon his arrival, and according to the *Pioneer* newspaper the first real gala social event occurred on that day. The paper also described miners firing one hundred guns between midnight on July 3 and daylight, raising the American flag, and singing patriotic songs and hearing speeches.[23] No reference to the rodeo and marksmanship contest that Love mentioned was recorded.

Love met many of the famous and infamous men of the Old West during his years in the saddle. In most cases he not only met them, he became friends with them. Bat Masterson, Buffalo Bill, and Billy the Kid would sit down and have a drink with the famous Deadwood Dick no matter what was happening in their lives. Love also had the benefit of being at the right place at the right time. He was present at some of the most significant events in western history. As he and his fellow cowboys were driving cattle to Deadwood, they were just two days behind the soldiers who would be defeated at the Little Big Horn. Love and the boys had no idea that defeat and death awaited Custer, for if they had known they would have ridden to his defense. Violent encounters with the Sioux in Montana and the Dakotas were an ongoing concern since the discovery of gold in the Black Hills and, though the news of the Custer battle probably did not reach the citizens of Deadwood until nearly a month later, Love barely missed being a participant.[24]

Love did not indicate where the famous photo of himself in his fighting clothes was taken. One source suggests that it was taken around 1880 in Dodge City, Kansas; the Denver Public Library's Digital Photo Division dates the photo at 1894–99. Though no current source identifies the place or date of the photo, the popularity of cowboys and other westerners taking photos cannot be questioned. Only two photographers are listed in the 1878 *Deadwood Business Directory*, but seven others plied their trade there in 1876. When the dates are slightly expanded, the list grows to nineteen.[25] Photography was experiencing rapid growth during the second half of the century along with

America's fascination with the West. Many aspiring and working cowboys patronized photographic studios to have a permanent image of their time in the West, and, like Nat Love, they prominently displayed the tools of their trade in those photos.

Cowboy life was suited to boys as young as twelve who took their places among men in tending and moving cattle. As cowboys aged, they became chuck wagon cooks or trail bosses, or they found other lines of work. Several factors influenced cowboys' desire to leave the life: the physical toll on the cowboy's body, marriage, and the decline in cattle drives. The same railroads that had opened new markets for cattle now were bringing settlers who were opposed to cattle trampling their crops. Open range ranching had been practiced extensively in the West after the Civil War and provided vast amounts of cattle that could be driven up the trail to Kansas, Wyoming, and points north. The cattle drives that had been a profitable mainstay for cowboy ranchers now had to compete with barbed wire, heavy snow storms, and cattle town fears of Texas fever.

Although Love did not specifically admit it, his marriage to Alice in Denver on August 22, 1889, signaled the end of the cowboy life for him. If there was any doubt about Nat's remembrances, it was in his recollection of his marriage date. On the Index of Colorado Marriages, 1858–1939, Nat Love married Alice Owens on August 2, 1888, in Denver County. Since there is no conceivable reason for Love to fabricate the date of his marriage, this statement by Ramon Adams seems particularly apt: "Although this Negro author is supposed to be writing of his own experiences, he either has a bad memory or a good imagination."[26] I propose that Nat Love had both a bad memory and a good imagination.

Love experienced the cowboy life for twenty years before hanging up his saddle and, like black cowboy Mathew "Bones" Hooks, transitioned from riding trails to riding the trains that were changing so much in the West. Though the freedom on the range was something Love missed, he initially made a seamless transition from cowboy to Pullman porter, a position assigned exclusively to black men by the Pullman Palace Car Company. The taste for travel that had prompted him to leave Tennessee was a factor in his decision to try railroading. He applied for a porter's position in Denver and was interviewed by Pullman superintendent John S. Runnells. Runnells served as general counsel, vice-president, and future president of the Pullman Company.[27] Love never seemed to have any trouble gaining access to and the confidence of those in top positions. Although his interview with Mr. Runnells was successful, an unpleasant incident on his first trip proved disturbing. Even after encouraging words from Runnells, Love decided to resign. After a short stint selling vegetables from a horse-drawn wagon and conversing with fellow porters, Love decided to give the Pullman service another try.

In Love's interview with Pullman superintendent J. M. Smith he was asked why he initially quit. Love responded that the tips did not meet his expectations. Smith then told Love something he never forgot: the whole secret of success was in pleasing "all" of your passengers. Apparently, Love accepted the advice and his earnings increased. Superintendent Smith's interest in the Pullman Service included having special agents ride the trains and report to him about the conduct of its employees. It was the Pullman Company's paternalistic policy to keep a tight rein on everything that George Pullman owned and oversaw. Love did not complain about the extra eyes on him. In fact, he bragged that his exemplary behavior got him assigned more profitable routes and a higher salary.[28]

Love was not inclined to voice grievances, whether riding the trails or the rails; however, he did reveal an occasion when his friendly demeanor was not reciprocated. He often received generous tips from the passengers he served, but not always. Some passengers described as not so financially "well blessed" gave smaller sums; he did not complain when those who had little gave little. The other side of the coin was when a man who was financially "well blessed" gave him a two-cent tip. The man also gave Love a piece of his mind when he said that some of the porters needed calling down and others needed a knocking down. This was a time when black men were supposed to know their place and stay in it. Yet, even before the formation of the Brotherhood of Sleeping Car Porters, Pullman porters exhibited a confidence not generally observed in black men of other professions.[29]

Nat and Alice Love did not live in Denver long, and by 1891 they resided in the Salt Lake City area.[30] Love transferred from Denver to the Ogden division and later to the San Pedro, Los Angeles, and Salt Lake Railroad. In 1898 he attracted the attention of the *Salt Lake Tribune* in the Railroad News section: "Nat Love of this city, one of the most obliging Pullman porters on the Overland Limited, is back from two long trips. He went to Tampa with a soldier train and then went to Mexico with B. L. Winchell. He met with a serious accident recently in Denver falling from the train and breaking his arm. He has been in Salt Lake for three years."[31]

In June 1900, Nat and Alice Love were listed as residing in the First Precinct, Salt Lake City. In responding to federal census questions, Alice stated that she was the mother of four children, with two living. Nat made no reference to having a child, which suggests that Alice had the children before they married. In 1905, Nat once again graced the pages of the *Salt Lake Tribune*. This time the article was in larger and bolder in print: "Colored Porter as Author— Nat Love, or 'Deadwood Dick' will Tell His Experiences."

> "Nat Love, or Deadwood Dick" is the title of a book that an old railroader is preparing for the press. Nat Love is the author's name, and he is a colored porter who has been in the employ of the Pullman company for nearly twenty years. But Nat is more than a porter, for he claims to be the original "Deadwood Dick," for he won the sobriquet, as he says, because he was the "best roper, and rider and long distance shot." This was down in the Panhandle country some thirty years ago, and now "Dick" is going to feast the public with his experiences, both on the range and on the railroad. And the book should be a triller [*sic*], for "Dick" has been wounded fourteen different places and, as is perfectly correct according to fiction, lives to tell the tale.[32]

By 1910, Nat Love and his family had moved to Los Angeles, California, ending his career as a Pullman porter. Nat would later find employment with the General Securities Company, and in May he was self-employed repairing window sashes and blinds. In the 1910 federal census, Nat and Alice Love were listed as renting a residence in the Malibu Township in Los Angeles. Alice reported there that she had given birth to five children, with none living. Since Alice had reported four children born to her in the 1900 census, possibly she and Nat had a child that died. By 1914 the Loves resided in Santa Monica in a house that they owned when Nat Love died on February 11, 1921.[33]

Love's passing was noted in the *Santa Monica Evening Outlook*. On the day of his death, the newspaper printed the following obituary: "Love, Nathan, age 77, died Friday morning, corner Michigan Avenue and Twenty-second Street. Survived by wife Alice Love. Worked for city department of Santa Monica. Funeral Services Monday, February 14, at 3 p.m. Interment Woodlawn."[34]

Nat Love's final indignity or affirmation of a partly manufactured life was the tombstone that marked his grave. The stone shows the name Love and Nathan (1854–1921) and Alice (1845–1946) with "Famous Black Cowboy— Loving Wife" engraved under their names. On top of the tombstone it reads "Bradford Dick—101 years old." Love's physical longevity fell short of the listed centenarian status by twenty-four years, and it is ironic that a man who spent his life trying to convince everyone that he was the real Deadwood Dick should have that honor omitted from his headstone. No one knows why "Bradford Dick" replaced "Deadwood Dick." Possibly someone seeking to honor Love listed a long forgotten black cowboy or conflated Deadwood Dick with Brick Bradford, a popular daily science fiction comic strip in the 1930s. Brick, who was white with blond hair, had little resemblance to Love, but Brick was a time traveler, and in a way so was Nat Love. He was born at a time when people traveled by horse-drawn vehicles, participated in the great years of railway travel, lived to see the Ford Model T dominate the roadways, and died on the eve of airline passenger service. Nat Love rode a cowboy's life to immortality, and what a ride it was.

Notes

1. Blake Allmendinger, "Deadwood Dick: The Black Cowboy as Cultural Timber," *Journal of American Culture* 16, no. 4 (Winter 1993): 79–89; Kenneth Speirs, "Writing Self (Effacingly): E-Race-D Presences in *The Life and Adventures of Nat Love*," *Western American Literature* 40, no. 3 (Fall 2005): 301–20; Susan Scheckel, "Home on the Train: Race and Mobility in the *Life and Adventures of Nat Love*," *American Literature* 74, no. 2 (June 2002): 219–50; Brackette F. Williams, "Nat Love Rides into the Sunset of Slavery and Racism," in *Nat Love, The Adventures of Nat Love, Better Known in the Cattle Country as "Deadwood Dick,"* by Nat Love, ed. Brackette F. Williams (Lincoln: University of Nebraska Press, 1995), vii–xviii; Tricia Martineau Wagner, *Black Cowboys of the Old West: True, Sensational, and Little Known Stories from History* (Guilford, Conn.: TwoDot, 2011); Patricia McKissack and Frederick L. McKissack Jr., *Best Shot in the West: The Adventures of Nat Love* (San Francisco: Chronicle Books, 2012); Charlotte R. Clark, *Black Cowboy: The Story of Nat Love* (Eau Claire, Wisc.: E. M. Hale, 1970).

2. Richard W. Slatta, "Deadwood Dick," in *The Mythical West: An Encyclopedia of Legend, Lore, and Popular Culture* (Santa Barbara, Calif.: ABC-CLIO, 2001): 119–20.

3. Edward L. Wheeler, *The Deadwood Library* (New York: Arthur Westbrook, 1899).

4. Wagner, *Black Cowboys*, 48–62; Scheckel, "Home on the Train."

5. Bobby L. Lovett, *The African-American History of Nashville, Tennessee, 1780–1930* (Fayetteville: University of Arkansas Press, 1999), 45.

6. Ibid., 76.

7. Nell Irvin Painter, *Exodusters: Black Migration to Kansas after Reconstruction* (New York: W. W. Norton, 1992), 113.

8. 1860 U.S. Federal Census—Slave Schedules, http//interactive.ancestryinstitution. com/Print/7668/TNM653 1281–0445/4144129?landscape (accessed September 9, 2014).

9. Monroe Lee Billington and Roger D. Hardaway, eds., *African Americans on the Western Frontier* (Niwot: University Press of Colorado, 1998); Harry Thomas, "Summary of Life of Nat Love," *Documenting the American South*, University Library, University of North Carolina at Chapel Hill, 2000, http://docsouth.unc. edu/neh/natlove/summary.html; Caroline Smith, "Nat Love 1854–1921," www.ency-clopedia.com/topic/Nat_Love.aspx; Harold W. Felton, *Nat Love, Negro Cowboy* (New York: Dodd, Mead, 1969).

10. Lovett, *African-American History*, 72.

11. "Indiana Marriages, 1780–1992," index, Familysearch, https//familysearch.org/pal (accessed August 2, 2014).

12. Nat Love, *Life and Adventures*, 28–32; Wagner, *Black Cowboys*, 48–62.

13. Love, *Life and Adventures*, 28–32.

14. Ridley Wills II, *The History of Belle Meade: Mansion, Plantation and Stud* (Nashville, Tenn.: Vanderbilt University Press, 1991).

15. Love, *Life and Adventures*, 33–39.

16. "African Americans in Kansas," Kansaspedia, Kansas Historical Society, www.kshs. org/kansapedia/african-americans-in-kansas/15123 (accessed August 12, 2014).

17. Richard W. Slatta, *Cowboys of the Americas* (New Haven: Yale University Press, 1990); Terry G. Jordan, *Trails to Texas: Southern Roots of Western Cattle Ranching* (Lincoln: University of Nebraska Press, 1981).

18. Love, *Life and Adventures*, 41.

19. Michael N. Searles, "Addison Jones: The Most Noted Negro Cowboy That Ever 'Topped Off' a Horse," in *Black Cowboys of Texas*, ed. Sara A. Massey, 193–205 (College Station: Texas A&M University Press, 2000).

20. Scheckel, "Home on the Train"; Love, *Life and Adventures*; Charity Fox, "Cowboys, Porters, and the Mythic West: Satire and Frontier Masculinity in *The Life and Adventures of Nat Love*," in *Fathers, Preachers, Rebels, Men*, ed. Peter Castor, 184–202 (Columbus: Ohio State University Press, 2011).

21. Robert K. DeArment, *Assault on the Deadwood Stage: Road Agents and Shotgun Messengers* (Norman: University of Oklahoma Press, 2011), 40.

22. Deadwood South Dakota Timeline, www.legendsofamerica.com/sd-deadwood-timeline.html (accessed August 26, 2014).

23. Nancy Niethammer Kovats, "Black Hills Pioneer: First Newspaper of Deadwood, Dakota Territory, 1876–1877," South Dakota Historical Society, 1978, 218–19.

24. Ibid., 204.

25. Robert Kolbe and Brian Bade, *They Captured the Moment: Dakotas Photographers, 1853–1920* (Sioux Falls, S.Dak.: Pine Hill Press, 2006).

26. Ramon F. Adams, *Burs under the Saddle: A Second Look at Books and Histories of the West* (Norman: University of Oklahoma Press, 1964), 352.

27. Albert Nelson Marquis, *The Book of Chicagoans: A Biographical Dictionary of Leading Living Men of the City of Chicago* (Chicago: A. N. Marquis, 1911), 586.

28. Beth Tompkins Bates, *Pullman Porters and the Rise of the Protest Politics in Black America, 1925–1945* (Chapel Hill: University of North Carolina Press, 2001), 42.

29. Love, *Life and Adventures*, 131–44.

30. Alton Hornsby Jr., ed., *Black America: A State by State Historical Encyclopedia* (Santa Barbara, Calif.: Greenwood, 2011), 843.

31. *Salt Lake Tribune*, June 21, 1898.

32. *Salt Lake Tribune*, November 29, 1905.

33. *Santa Monica, Ocean Park, Venice, Sawtelle and Westgate Directory 1913 and 1919–20.* Compiled by Los Angeles Directory Company, 1913 and 1919.

34. *Santa Monica Evening Outlook*, February 11, 1921.

PART II

❊

Performing Cowboys

6

Shadow Riders of the Subterranean Circuit

A Descriptive Account of Black Rodeo in the Texas Gulf Coast Region

DEMETRIUS W. PEARSON

Black cowboys utilized the skills they developed as cowhands to act as performers as well, especially by participating in rodeos. Demetrius W. Pearson portrays life as rodeo performers in what he refers to as the "Subterranean Circuit" in Texas. As Pearson defines it, this circuit (referred to by Wendy Watriss as the "Soul Circuit") "is rarely reported in the media, few are aware of its history and existence, arenas are in obscure locales, and attendance comprises the devotees." This circuit, and others around the country, emerged initially because blacks were excluded from participating in regular, whites-only rodeos (Bill Pickett, for example, referred to himself as Mexican in order to perform at a few). Lately the obstacle to black attendance at nationally sponsored rodeo events is that few have jobs that allow them to be absent from work often enough. The Texas circuit, the largest in the nation, has existed since the late 1940s.

African Americans have experienced unparalleled racial intolerance and discrimination in every conceivable form since their arrival in America over four hundred years ago. This form of disenfranchisement has operated in all aspects of society, including work and play. North American rodeo, whose origins can be traced to festival pastimes in Mexico and its cattle industry, evolved into a quasi-sport form in the United States during the late nineteenth century. This work-related sport form incorporated the social and cultural controls endemic to American society. As a result, even though blacks were inextricably involved in the cattle industry, rodeo, and "the West," American history has frequently

Originally published as Demetrius W. Pearson, "Shadow Riders of the Subterranean Circuit: A Descriptive Account of Black Rodeo in the Texas Gulf Coast Region," *Journal of American Culture* 27, no. 2 (June 2004): 190–98. Reprinted with permission of the *Journal of American Culture* and the author.

misrepresented, marginalized, or omitted their contributions. However, some researchers have argued that the term "cowboy" may have first been used to denote a black slave's role in the cattle industry.[1]

Rodeo, like baseball and other American sports, was participated in and influenced by African American athletes whose legacy within the sport has also been frequently overlooked. Interestingly, unbeknownst to many, a rodeo circuit exists in Texas comprising primarily African American rodeo cowboys. The participants, past and present, have received minimal media exposure, as have the venues housing their sport, yet they continue to compete and maintain the cultural trappings of the past.

This serendipitous rodeo circuit offers a unique opportunity to analyze the nuances of ethnic rodeo in an environment novel to most scholars. Staged in small rural environs, this branch of rodeo reflects sanctioned mainstream rodeo yet departs from it in several respects. Veteran cowboys and observers have dubbed it the "Soul Circuit."

I have referred to it as the "Subterranean Circuit" because of several unique features: it is rarely reported in the media, few are aware of its history and existence, arenas are in obscure locales, and attendance comprises the devotees. In addition, the rodeo cowboys have been referred to as "Shadow Riders" because they have historically participated in rodeo competitions in the shadows of their white counterparts. The Subterranean Circuit is a loosely structured network of ethnic rodeos that have operated in the Gulf Coast region of Texas since the 1940s. This area is unique in that it has the largest number of African American rodeo cowboys in the world, as does the state of Texas with respect to rodeo cowboys in general.[2]

Rodeo and Americana: A Brief Historical Review

American rodeo has recently experienced a resurgence in popularity since its dramatic decline in the late 1950s. Akin to the Hollywood-produced western, rodeo may have fallen victim to a more radical social and political climate in the 1960s. Today, an estimated 23 million fans attend Professional Rodeo Cowboys Association (PRCA)–sanctioned rodeos annually.[3] This figure does not include the countless unsanctioned professional rodeos held in small rural towns around the country. Evidence of rodeo's resurgence has also been demonstrated by network viewership. The Nashville Network televises Professional Bull Riders (PBR) and PRCA competitions to approximately 1.5 million households weekly. PRCA officials noted that more than fifteen million viewers watched professional rodeo on television in 1998.[4] Considering the data, it is difficult to dismiss rodeo as a viable sport and entertainment option.

Critics and sport purists alike have questioned rodeo's athletic pedigree and sport skill requirements and have characterized it as spectacle. However, contemporary rodeo incorporates the requisite elements detailed by Jay Coakley for any sport form. In addition, rodeo rests upon rich cultural tradition and history, ritualistic lore, and fanatical bravado conceivably unparalleled in modern sports.[5] Perhaps no other sport in the United States except baseball is seen as epitomizing American values, traditions, and lifestyles as does rodeo. These may have been factors contributing to the popularity and patriotic fervor exhibited by rodeo during World War II.

Historically, rodeo parallels American culture because it was participated in and influenced by minority athletes whose legacy has been marginalized and overlooked. An example of this omission is Bill Pickett, an African American from Taylor, Texas, who is credited for having invented "bulldogging," a popular rodeo event commonly known as steer wrestling. Until he became a celebrity for his trademark bulldogging technique, Pickett was forced to dress as a Mexican toreador because rodeos did not admit black contestants. Early accounts of the ranching industry in and around Texas, Oklahoma, and the Mexican border address various cultural and festival pastimes. Rodeos were a common fixture within this region and engaged in by Anglos, Hispanics, African Americans, and Native Americans.[6] Although rarely depicted in film, historical evidence suggests that at least one in three cowboys was "of color."[7] As a result, an estimated nine thousand African Americans participated in the cattle industry in the late 1800s. As Elizabeth A. Lawrence noted, "It was a society of white Anglo-Saxon domination, in which Mexican and black cowboys were often discriminated against, and were not generally promoted to foremen."[8] Often they were hired to do the hardest and most dangerous jobs.

Unable to compete in rodeos of the day because of unwritten policies excluding them, African Americans began to organize their own competitions and associations. Ernest Jackson Jr. conveyed this point: "Although the Professional Rodeo Cowboys Association (PRCA) never had a written policy that excluded minority competitors, it is interesting to read comments from

older cowboys . . . reference to 'the days of segregated rodeo.' Until around
the 1950s, the lack of black professional cowboys and some underlying racism
kept most blacks from competing with whites. To combat this situation, black
cowboys of the 1940s formed the Southwestern Colored Cowboys Association
(SCCA)."[9]

Although such policies based on race no longer exist, professional rodeos
comprising primarily African American cowboys still operate throughout the
country. These little-known subterranean circuits continue to offer a viable
sport opportunity and entertainment option. Even though more has been written in the past decade about the sport and lifestyle of the rodeo cowboy,[10] little
seems to have been documented regarding African American involvement in
rodeo. In many respects, these rodeo cowboys remain relatively invisible.

The Soul Circuit Setting

The Soul Circuit or Subterranean Circuit is located in and around the Texas
Gulf Coast region. Many of the individuals interviewed and discussed in this
chapter are descendents of former slaves brought to Texas to labor on sugar
and cotton plantations and cattle ranches in Fort Bend, Brazoria, Liberty, and
Jefferson Counties. Others are descendents of former slaves who had migrated
to the lush grasslands of the Texas Gulf Coast from Arkansas and Louisiana
after the Civil War. Many were attracted to the coastal counties because of the
labor demands and quest for land. Mid- to late-nineteenth-century African
Americans residing in these rural environs were often employed as migrant
farmers, domestics, livestock caretakers, and cowboys. As a result, black settlements (e.g., Kendleton) and towns densely populated by African Americans
(e.g., Prairie View, Richmond, Egypt) emerged. As with other indigenous
groups within Texas, festive pastimes that included ranch livestock became
prevalent. Ro-day-os (or the Anglicized term "rod-ee-os") were staged to test
various skills of the ranch hands. Because Jim Crow laws relegated African
Americans to second-class citizenry, few blacks were permitted to participate in
white-promoted rodeos. As a result, African Americans staged their own competitions. Population patterns, much like today, dictated where the early rodeos
were staged. Many of the early sites make up the contemporary Soul Circuit.
The term Soul Circuit, fondly used by veteran performers and spectators,

denotes the loosely structured schedule of minority rodeos held in and around the Texas Gulf Coast region. This area includes Houston and much smaller cities to the east (e.g., Beaumont, Raywood, and Liberty); Dallas and surrounding cities to the north (e.g., Fort Worth, Madisonville, and Fairfield); San Antonio and quaint prairie towns to the west (e.g., Navasota and Hempstead); and small rural communities like Egypt, McBeth, and Kendleton. Some of these areas are historically significant because of their ties to the cattle, agriculture, and slave industries.

Shadow Riders

The rodeo cowboys who make up the Soul Circuit are part-time rodeo performers for the most part. Many hold full-time jobs while rodeoing. This factor has a major impact on African Americans' access to the nationally sanctioned PRCA rodeos. Because of their full-time employment, limited disposable income, and lack of sponsorship, few African American cowboys, contrary to their white counterparts, find it possible to leave their jobs mid-week to travel to distant rodeo sites. These circumstances are akin to the plight of African American athletes in auto racing. As a result, most African American rodeo cowboys are attracted to the small, unsanctioned, open rodeos frequently scheduled on the weekends. These rodeos are usually within a 200- to 250-mile radius of the rodeo cowboy's hometown.

Although many of those I interviewed indicated that they had participated in rodeos at an early age, most had little formal training in the sport. Unlike their white counterparts who may have engaged in structured programs like 4-H Clubs, Little Britches Rodeos, and scholastic rodeo programs, few of the minority cowboys expressed such involvement, nor had many participated in weekend rodeo schools or college rodeo programs. Of those interviewed, few had actually honed their skills on a working ranch. This fact was articulated by a veteran Soul Circuit cowboy and once-aspiring Negro League ballplayer who grew up on a ranch and herded cattle during the Jim Crow era. L.R. lamented, "Ninety-nine percent of the rodeo cowboys competing in this rodeo don't know what to do on a ranch. I came up through the ranks. We used to break horses for $10.00 a head and could only practice at stock contractor breakouts. They're not as talented as we were partly due to the opportunities to do other things."

Many contemporary Soul Circuit cowboys admitted that they learned their rodeo skills from watching television, "shadowing" veteran cowboys over the years, and trial and error in the arena. C.M., a PRCA card holder and Soul Circuit competitor, stated, "I actually got started by watching rodeo competitions on TV. I was about twelve [years old] when a cousin and his friends got me in it." He indicated that his rodeo involvement tends to be a bit different from that of his Soul Circuit counterparts: "Since I'm employed as a rancher I have a flexible schedule. It also helps to have a boss that's a calf roper. He competes too. My schedule is not too hectic so I can travel out of state about once a month. I don't have a major preference toward sanctioned or unsanctioned competitions. Where the show is and the cost determine if I am riding."

C.M.'s experiences are somewhat different from those of his counterparts because he has calf-roped at the collegiate level, is a PRCA member, and plans part of his rodeo schedule based on PRCA information and the *Cowboy Sports News*. Few who ride the Soul Circuit have the aforementioned benefits. Yet, with limited formal training and ranching experience to draw upon, Soul Circuit rodeo cowboys continue to seek fame and fortune via the less heralded small-circuit, weekend rodeos, in rural Texas environs.

Rodeo Venues

Facilities reminiscent of the years of segregated baseball appear to be prevalent at Soul Circuit rodeo venues. Although the viability of some of the sites might be questioned, event promoters frequently make do with the dimly lighted, cramped, and dilapidated facilities. Worn and rusted pens, splinter-infested wooden bleachers, unfinished press boxes with barely audible sound systems, and makeshift concession and pay booths are part of the legacy and reality of the circuit. Space dimensions of the rodeo arenas vary considerably depending upon ownership. Whereas fairgrounds I observed tended to be spacious, with ample competition area and seating, private ranches and local rodeo arenas often lacked extensive seating. The competition areas, albeit quaint, were large enough for the requisite events. The event most apt to be compromised was barrel racing because of its space requirements for the start-up and deceleration phases.

Parking at many Soul Circuit rodeos was not of major concern, particularly in comparison to densely populated urban sites. The rural environment in which many of these venues were located afforded certain amenities. At some venues, it was common practice for spectators to back their pickup trucks to the arena fence and view the rodeo from the truck's bed. The more contemporary rodeo arenas or fairgrounds often had standard parking lots. Regardless of the venue, parking fees were modest, ranging from one dollar to three dollars. Several venues either had no parking fee or the cost was included in the ticket price. A major shortcoming at some of the smaller venues was the portable restrooms, which were spartan at best. These facilities were less than ideal, particularly at rodeos scheduled in the evening.

Spectator amenities varied depending upon the respective venue. Generally, rodeos held at fairgrounds offered a more comfortable environment. Frequently county owned and operated, these facilities were often covered and equipped with indoor restrooms. Lighting, parking, and signage were standard, and concession windows and stands were easily accessible. Because the rentals of such facilities were more costly than smaller local sites, promoters frequently made concerted efforts to solicit sponsors to defray operating costs. Thus, advertising banners and placards were frequently draped across and affixed to arena rails and fencing.

Concession stands and food windows are major revenue sources at all sport and entertainment venues, and Soul Circuit rodeos were no exception. Assorted items were available to be purchased, including western attire, riding gear, jewelry, beverages, and food. Akin to mainstream rodeos that highlight barbecue-flavored meats, Soul Circuit "cuisine" also featured fried fish and boudain (Cajun sausage). Both foods are culturally significant and indigenous to the devotees, as well as fan favorites and dietary staples.

Marketing and Promotional Strategies

The marketing and promotional strategies employed in the Soul Circuit were provincial and lacking contemporary technological advances. Unlike many mainstream rodeo circuits that used audio-visual, print, and electronic media to market and promote events, the Soul Circuit primarily depended on handbills, posters, public address announcements (at rodeos), and word of mouth. The absence of the more sophisticated forms of advertising appeared to be due in part to limited revenue streams, lack of corporate sponsors, nominal promotional budgets, and spectator resources (e.g., computers). Thus, the promotional activities primarily attracted local cowboys and rodeo fans from around the general area.

The Cowboys of Color rodeos, which consisted of a series of individual rodeo competitions cosponsored by Ford and held in five Texas cities (San Antonio, Austin, Houston, Fort Worth, and Mesquite) in 2001, were the only minority-oriented rodeos that used contemporary technological advances to advertise. The promoter (C.H.) of this invitational rodeo series was adamant about the importance of implementing new promotional strategies with conventional techniques. Billboards, websites, radio and television spots, handbills, calendars, souvenir programs, and apparel were employed for promotional purposes. C.H. contends that ethnic rodeos can be successful endeavors if they attract corporate sponsors that can help sell their product. According to C.H., "Anything that Blacks are candidates to buy can help underwrite cost and promote the rodeo. Tobacco, beer, banking, food, electronics, news services, utility companies and small businesses (e.g., legal and tax services, funeral homes, and feed stores) are potential sponsors. The important thing is, you have to sell them on a quality rodeo. No one wants to be associated with a bad product."

The Cowboys of Color invitational rodeos have been very successful in attracting corporate sponsorship, which in turn has enhanced the image of the rodeo and provided multiple advertising outlets, more participants, and increased winning payouts. This rodeo series was most like mainstream rodeos with respect to marketing and promotion yet maintained the trappings of ethnic rodeos (e.g., food, music, specialty events, and postrodeo entertainment).

Among the more noteworthy marketing and promotional ploys implemented by Soul Circuit promoters were the postrodeo dances and specialty events. The rodeo dance is a staple and major component within black rodeo. With live entertainment, frequently featuring zydeco music (a combination of Cajun, rhythm and blues, and country and western), the rodeo dance provides additional value to the cost of admission. In many of the small rural locales in Texas, the rodeo and dance compete favorably with high school football for the entertainment dollar. However, because of the need to maximize the potential spectator base, many rodeos were scheduled for Saturday evenings and Sunday afternoons so as not to conflict with football during the fall months.

To further attract a paying audience, ethnic rodeo promoters have often included specialty events. These events frequently include rough-stock and timed roping competitions for young children ("pee wees" and "juniors") and older adults ("old timers"). The specialty events served multiple purposes: rodeo socialization for the youth, a feeder system program for the rodeo circuit, inclusion for young and old rodeo contestants, revenue generation via entrant fees, and an increased spectator base. As promoter H.D. mentioned, "Youth and Old Timer events is cash money. They bring out other family members who pay to get in and eat and drink."

Rodeo Competitions

Soul Circuit rodeos, much like mainstream rodeos, began with a grand entry. This standard ritual consisted of rodeo contestants lined up in single file on horseback circling the arena in a parade-like manner. During the grand entry, both American and Texas flags were presented to the audience. A "riderless horse," which symbolizes a death in the rodeo family during the year, was also a part of the procession. H.C., a former rodeo cowboy and now rodeo promoter, discussed the practice: "The riderless horse symbolizes death: rider, promoter, or any individual closely tied to the rodeo. It could be one person or several individuals." Various dignitaries and the rodeo promoter and stock contractor participated in this ritual.

The vast majority of Soul Circuit rodeos observed were advertised as "open competitions." This basically meant that contestants did not have to be PRCA members or affiliated with a sanctioned rodeo organization. In essence, people could compete if they paid the requisite event registration fee. Many of the rodeos were lengthy and loosely structured. On average, competitions varied in length from three to eight hours. The lengthiness of the rodeos was primarily due to two major factors: "walk-up" registration and basic organizational structure. In an effort to increase the payout and generate additional revenue, promoters often waived advanced registration. This administrative decision enabled rodeo cowboys to register for an event immediately before it began. Unfortunately, this option compromised any time schedule that was to be maintained, slowed down the rodeo, and invariably led to long breaks between events. F.W., a celebrated PRCA member and former Soul Circuit rider, commented on the aforementioned shortcomings: "I roped at all of 'em

over the years: McBeth, Navasota, Madisonville, you name it. One of the problems is they're too long. I can make more money in one PRCA event than I
can in a whole rodeo out here. [In addition], registration should be in advance.
A cowboy shouldn't be allowed to pay right before the event begins. This makes
the rodeo drag." Other cowboys expressed similar sentiments regarding the
organizational structure, but they were less likely to be overly critical because
of their limited options.

Conclusion

African American cowboys were less likely to be employed in work settings
in which they could leave their jobs midweek to travel to distant rodeos. As a
result, they primarily participated in unsanctioned weekend competitions close
to home. None of the rodeos on the Soul Circuit was sanctioned by the PRCA,
the largest national and international governing body of professional rodeo.
Although these rodeos are viable professional competitions, the payouts are
nominal and exposure is minimal; therefore, they rarely enhance the market-
ability of the rodeo athlete.

Because of financial constraints and job stability concerns, African American
cowboys were more apt to participate in the smaller, closer, unsanctioned ethnic
rodeos. In these competitions, points and yearly financial earnings were never
tallied, thereby making rankings impossible. The lack of meticulous record
keeping and a standardized ranking system adversely affected these cowboys
because they invariably lacked the requisite documentation to qualify for the
more celebrated competitions nationally.

Participation on the Soul Circuit was a viable means for honing skills
and earning a living, but limited event sponsorship minimized the athletes'
earning potential. Because few events were underwritten or received money
from corporate sponsors, rodeo promoters relied primarily on entrance fees to
cover expenses and pay event winners. Therefore, open registration was usually
practiced to accommodate late registrants to assure a larger pool of money.
This promotional strategy frequently increased the number of competitors but
slowed down the rodeo. One highly successful PRCA rodeo cowboy and former Soul Circuit participant stated that he could make $7,000 to $8,000 riding
in one or two PRCA competitions in the same amount of time that he could

make $700 in a Soul Circuit competition. According to him, at this stage of his career, it was not a good investment of his time. Other rodeo cowboys had similar views because it is common practice for them to compete in several rodeos concurrently.

Previous segregation policies that prohibited or discouraged African American participation have had a lingering effect on many of the veteran competitors. On several occasions, African American cowboys recalled incidents in which they were not welcomed at some of the mainstream rodeos. Several recounted incidents in which they were required to ride before the fans had entered the arena, while others competed after they had left. Incidents of unfair judging and the refusal to pay individuals for winning or placing were also mentioned. These and other incidents were among the reasons given for the formation of ethnic rodeos, riding clubs, and associations. Younger rodeo cowboys were less likely to experience such overt discrimination and rarely expressed such sentiments. Several veteran rodeo cowboys who participated on the Soul Circuit implied that the caliber of contestants and crowd support are far less than they used to be. They equated the present-day Soul Circuit with the latter years of the Negro Leagues.

Shrewd marketing and promotional strategies have made the Soul Circuit a viable sport and entertainment option. The use of conventional modes of advertising and the staging of competitions in small rural environs have kept promotional costs down. Additionally, the scheduling of nontraditional rodeo events like junior roping, old-timers roping, and open break-away has increased the pool of paying competitors and has built a potential "feeder system" into the circuit. From a sociological perspective, this approach may be viewed as a form of "prole sport" (working class) socialization, whereby three generations of rodeo cowboys could be competing at the same venue.

Another marketing ploy and salient feature of the Soul Circuit was the rodeo dance. This commonly scheduled activity, which is covered in the rodeo admission fee, afforded both competitors and spectators an opportunity to fraternize. It also served as an additional revenue generator for the event promoter. Akin to the much larger Houston Livestock Show and Rodeo (HLSR), which featured a top entertainer each of the twenty-three nights of the rodeo, the Soul Circuit rodeo dance attracted fans and nonfans alike. Zydeco was frequently the music of choice because of its ethnic lyrics and historical significance. Juneteenth (June 19), not July fourth, is "Cowboy Christmas" in black rodeo circles. This historically significant date has traditionally been considered emancipation day for African Americans in Texas. Like Independence Day for mainstream rodeo, more ethnic rodeos are held on Juneteenth than any other single day of the year.

Although few rodeo cowboys competing on this circuit of marginally promoted rodeos in secluded rural hamlets devoid of media exposure will ever earn PRCA credentials and notoriety, they continue to perform. Consistent with the past and reminiscently akin to the Negro Leagues after integration, this subterranean circuit has managed to maintain the vestiges of its cultural tradition.

Notes

1. Andy Newman, "Deep in the Heart of Brooklyn, Cowboys and Kosher Food," *New York Times*, September 1, 1997, late ed., B1.

2. Ernest Jackson Jr., *Celebrating Black Cowboys in 2000* (Houston: Clear Channel Communications, 2000), 12; Wendy Watriss, "The Soul Circuit," *Geo* 2 (December 1980), 143.

3. Skip Hollandsworth, "Sweetheart of the Rodeo," *Texas Monthly*, May 1999, 154.

4. Professional Rodeo Cowboys Association, *Media Guide* (Colorado Springs, Colo.: Professional Rodeo Cowboys Association, 1999), 20.

5. Jay. J. Coakley, *Sport in Society: Issues and Controversies*, 7th ed. (Boston: McGraw-Hill, 2001), 20; Demetrius W. Pearson and C. Allen Haney, "The Rodeo Cowboy: Cultural Icon, Athlete, or Entrepreneur?" *Journal of Sport and Social Issues* 23, no. 3 (1999), 308.

6. Kendall Blanchard, *The Anthropology of Sport: An Introduction*, rev. ed. (Westport, Conn.: Bergin and Garvey, 1995), 157; Elizabeth A. Lawrence, *Rodeo: An Anthropologist Looks at the Wild and the Tame* (Chicago: University of Chicago Press, 1982), 67; Sara R. Massey, ed., *Black Cowboys of Texas* (College Station: Texas A&M University Press, 2000), 14.

7. Ernie Collins and Jim McIngvale, "'Y'all and 'Us' Are Pardners in Texas," *Houston Chronicle*, February 16, 1997, C1; William L. Katz, *The Black West* (New York: Simon and Schuster, 1996), 146; Kenneth W. Porter, *The Negro on the American Frontier* (New York: Arno, 1970), 495.

8. Lawrence, *Rodeo*, 67.

9. Jackson, *Celebrating*, 12.

10. Angeline Bushy, "Understanding Health Practices and Health Care Needs of Western U.S. Rodeo Participants: An Ethnographic Approach," *Family Community Health* 3, no. 1 (1990), 47; Michael C. Meyers, Arnold LeUnes, and Anthony E. Bourgeois, "Psychological Skills Assessment and Athletic Performance in Collegiate Rodeo Athletes," *Journal of Sport Behavior* 19, no. 2 (1996), 134; Demetrius W. Pearson and C. Allen Haney, "The Rodeo Cowboy as an American Icon: The Perceived Social and Cultural Significance," *Journal of American Culture* 22, no. 4 (1999), 17.

7

Oklahoma's African American Rodeo Performers

ROGER D. HARDAWAY

Texas was not the only state in which black cowboys joined and performed at rodeos, as Roger D. Hardaway notes in this information-filled chapter. Hardaway explores the emergence of black rodeo performers from the earliest beginnings of the sport in the late nineteenth and early twentieth centuries to later with Bill Pickett and George Hooker, a champion "trick rider," all the way to the end of the twentieth century. He points out the top performers of each era and does not exclude women performers, with a mention of Oklahoma City rider and nurse Carolyn Carter, who began performing in 1985. Most of the Oklahoma rodeo performers, Hardaway reports, as in Texas, travel the lesser-known circuits, since they too cannot leave jobs for long. Hardaway also remarks that some Oklahoma performers live out-of-state while others are members of a family of rodeo riders. Overall, he states, the contribution of Oklahoma's black rodeo performers "is likely to continue indefinitely into the future."

In the late nineteenth century, the cattle industry boomed in the American West. Hundreds of thousands of wild bovines were rounded up and branded to form the nucleus of one of the most important economic enterprises in the United States at that time. The cattle industry was centered in Texas, a former slave state with many black residents. Consequently, several thousand of the cowboys who worked on western ranches and ranges were former slaves or their descendants.[1] Likewise, when the sport of rodeo evolved out of the cattle industry before the end of the century, many of the cowboys who honed their cattle- and horse-handling skills into entertaining performances for appreciative audiences were African Americans.[2]

Originally published as Roger D. Hardaway, "Oklahoma's African American Rodeo Performers," *Chronicles of Oklahoma* 89, no. 2 (Summer 2011): 152–75. Reprinted with permission of the author.

Not surprisingly, cattle raising became big business in Indian and Oklahoma Territories. The U.S. government's Americanization program urged Native Americans to become farmers and ranchers. And when the late nineteenth-century land runs brought thousands of non-Indians to the future Sooner State, they, too, raised crops and cattle. As a result, many Oklahomans became cowboys; and because of the legacy of black slavery that had existed in Indian Territory prior to the Civil War, many Oklahoma cowboys were African Americans. Some of these black cowboys—like their counterparts in Texas and other western states—eventually made the transition from ranch hand to rodeo performer.[3]

The first African American rodeo participant whose exploits are significant to a study of the sport's history was Bill Pickett. Born in Texas on December 5, 1870, Pickett moved to Oklahoma in 1908 when he was thirty-seven years old. Once north of the Red River, Pickett went to work for the Miller family's 101 Ranch and performed roping and riding feats all over the world with the 101's "Wild West" show. In addition to being a great example of a transition figure taking cowboy skills from ranches to rodeo arenas, Pickett is also the only person of any race to be credited with creating a rodeo event.[4]

Pickett's handling of cattle without the use of a rope has become legendary in rodeo history. As a young man in Texas, he had seen bulldogs immobilize cows by biting their lips. The bovines, in pain and frightened, would stand still or lie down to minimize the damage the dogs' teeth could do to their flesh. Pickett perfected the art of grabbing cattle by their horns and then biting them on their upper lips until they lay calmly on the ground. This activity evolved into the rodeo sport of steer wrestling—often still referred to by rodeo performers and fans as "bulldogging." When not performing ranch work or entertaining audiences at wild west shows, Pickett participated in rodeos in order to supplement his income. In addition to wrestling steers, Pickett occasionally rode broncs and worked as a "pickup man" helping other bronc riders dismount after their rides. In 1971, Pickett became the first African American cowboy to be inducted into the Hall of Fame of the National Cowboy and Western Heritage Museum located in Oklahoma City.[5]

Another African American cowboy who excelled in the 101's wild west shows was George Hooker, who was born in 1860 and came to Oklahoma from his native Arizona. For several years, Hooker rode broncs in Miller Brothers productions and—like Pickett—in rodeos. His chief talent, however, was in displaying horse-riding skills that became known eventually as "trick riding." Today, trick riders are considered "specialty acts" who perform at rodeos for pay and to entertain the audience—much like clowns. In the early twentieth century, however, when Hooker was one of the best trick riders in the country, he often defeated other competitors in rodeos; in those instances, his remuneration was based upon the quality of his performance rather than a contracted price—as was the case when he worked for the Miller brothers.[6]

Just as Pickett and Hooker were able to participate in the new sport of rodeo, both also had the opportunity to earn some money by exhibiting their skills in another new medium—the motion picture industry. These cowboys are credited with having been featured in two movies each, although it is likely that "stock" footage of their performances (especially Hooker's) were used in other cinematic productions. Before Hooker came to Oklahoma, he landed roles in two westerns starring Tom Mix. Both were shot in Prescott, Arizona, where Mix—also a veteran of the 101 Ranch wild west shows—lived for several years performing in movies filmed by the Selig Polyscope Company. The two in which Hooker acted—*A Romance of the Rio Grande* and *Why the Sheriff Is a Bachelor*— were each approximately ten to fifteen minutes in length and released in 1911. Interestingly, Hooker, who was part Hispanic, played a Mexican American rather than an African American in each film. He was a contract actor for Selig for several years and undoubtedly performed in uncredited roles in other Mix films. Pickett's movie career was a little more impressive than Hooker's. In 1921, Pickett's rodeo skills were central to the documentary *The Bull-Dogger*. The following year, he was in a film about an outlaw gang entitled *The Crimson Skull*. All four of these movies featuring Oklahoma's African American rodeo performers were made, of course, during filmdom's "silent era."[7]

Eventually, wild west shows began to lose favor with audiences, and by the early 1930s they were basically a thing of the past. As these productions became less popular, however, rodeos became more so. And as wild west shows had featured a few performers displaying skills that were common years later in rodeos, so, too, did rodeos feature some aspects of their wild west predecessors. Consequently, during the early days of rodeo, the sport was not well organized. In fact, it was hardly a sport at all, but rather entertainment designed to make audiences laugh rather than to be awed by participants' athletic prowess. Promoters kept few records; moreover, rules were not standardized and varied from one venue to the next. Furthermore, early twentieth-century rodeos did not always emphasize contests between competitors seeking to perform the same act but in a quicker time or more accomplished manner than their fellow cowboys.[8]

Another feature of early rodeos was that promoters of particular events often exaggerated their significance in the sport. Thus, many rodeos touted their winning cowboys as "world champions" when they were, in fact, only the champion of a single competition. In time, rodeo organizers and performers devised ranking systems that allowed cowboys to accumulate points during an entire annual season and be crowned champions (or world champions) for a particular year. Even then, various organizations would crown champions so that several cowboys could lay claim to the title just as performers in the early twentieth century did for winning one contest.[9]

At least two African American rodeo performers from Oklahoma called themselves "world champions" when that title meant only that they had won one event. In 1904 Knox Simmons won the calf-roping title at the St. Louis world's fair. Simmons was light-skinned, and organizers apparently thought he was Caucasian or Native American. When his true racial makeup became known, he was retroactively disqualified from the competition. Simmons was born in Tennessee around 1864 but moved as a young adult to Ardmore, Oklahoma, with his parents and siblings. Prominent African American attorney Buck Franklin recalled in his autobiography that his first case as a lawyer in Ardmore was to represent Simmons's mother in an action to recover a stallion her son had sold (without her permission) to pay off some alleged gambling debts. According to Franklin, Knox Simmons "never worked. He lived entirely off his mother and had reduced her almost to poverty." Eventually, Simmons served time in the Oklahoma state penitentiary for stealing cattle in a case that did not involve his mother's livestock. In 1915, Simmons (who was about fifty years old at the time) was murdered on a street in Ardmore in a case that has never been solved. Nevertheless, Simmons was inducted in 2006 into the National Cowboys of Color Museum and Hall of Fame located in Fort Worth, Texas.[10]

Oklahoma's other African American "world champion" in the early twentieth century was Bennie Miller. Born in South Carolina in 1912, Miller moved to Texas as a child and came north to work on the 101 Ranch when he was about fifteen years old. He was working for the Miller brothers when he won a bull riding event held at Marland, Oklahoma, in 1929. Since Marland was in the heart of the 101, it is likely that the contest Miller won was staged by his bosses. After a few years in the Sooner State, Miller travelled around the country for eighteen years with a rodeo company based in Texas. He eventually settled in New York City and became a venerated member of a local group known as the Federation of Black Cowboys. When he died in November 2009, Miller's obituary notices touted him as a world champion cowboy because of the bull riding contest he had won eighty years earlier.[11]

In the decades following Miller's great achievement, other black Oklahomans made their livings (and their marks) following the rodeo circuit. Bill Pickett's nephew, Joe Pickett—perhaps to escape the shadow of his famous uncle—rodeoed under the pseudonym of "Lucky Boy Williams." Like Miller, Williams travelled around the country for several years as a member of a rodeo troupe. At a rodeo in Pittsburgh, Pennsylvania, in 1936, Williams won the bull riding event and placed second in steer wrestling; he also regularly competed in and won saddle bronc competitions.[12] That groups of cowboys were hiring on and touring with rodeo companies, performing at all the stops the companies made, underscores the fact that during the 1930s and 1940s rodeo was still undergoing a transition from the entertainment spectacle of its predecessor, the wild west show.

Another African American involved in rodeos in Oklahoma for several decades beginning in the 1920s was Jesse (or Jess) Howard. He was born in Kansas in 1885 and moved to Oklahoma when he was a small child. In 1922, Howard—who was a rancher by this time—and a Caucasian partner, Hosea English, founded a rodeo in Cleo Springs that was successful for around twenty years. Howard also competed in rodeos—including his own—in calf roping. After the Cleo Springs rodeo ended, Howard continued in the rodeo business as a stock contractor—one who provides the broncs, bulls, calves, and steers that cowboys ride, rope, and wrestle during the rodeo.[13]

In the 1940s the two most prominent African American rodeo performers from Oklahoma were Marvel Rogers and Floyd "Buck" Wyatt. The two often travelled to rodeo events together. Rogers was the more flamboyant of the two. He was born in Arkansas in 1924 but moved to Oklahoma when he was a youngster. Eventually, he went to work for Lynn Beutler's rodeo organization and learned to wrestle steers and ride roughstock. He often rode bulls and saddle broncs while puffing on a cigar. One of his most impressive victories was winning the 1947 bull riding championship at Ellensburg, Washington.[14]

Buck Wyatt also rode bulls but his specialty was bareback broncs. He won bull riding titles at Chicago in 1936, Ellensburg in 1941, Lewiston, Idaho, in 1946, and Missoula, Montana, in 1948. At the latter event, he was also crowned best "all-around cowboy," an award given to the performer who makes the most money participating in two or more categories. As impressive as his bull riding feats were, the most significant item on Wyatt's rodeo resume is that he finished fourth in the bareback riding world standings at the end of the season in 1942.[15]

The sanctioning body for rankings that year was the Rodeo Association of America (RAA), one of the organizations that eventually merged to become the Rodeo Cowboys Association (RCA)—now known as the PRCA (the "P" standing for "Professional"). The PRCA today recognizes the RAA standings of 1942 (and other years) as the organization's official rankings. Had the National Finals Rodeo (which was created in 1959 to provide a spectacular finish to each annual rodeo season) been in existence in 1942, Wyatt would have become the first African American to qualify to participate in that most important of all rodeo events.[16]

The next generation of African American rodeo performers—after Rogers and Wyatt— included Gerald Vaughn and Luther Johnson, who were active in the 1960s (and later years). Vaughn was a steer wrestler, and Johnson rode bulls and broncs. Both had long and relatively successful careers. Johnson became a rodeo organizer and stock contractor after his competing days were over.[17]

Two others attended Oklahoma State University on rodeo scholarships. Both were born in the late 1930s and both also became involved in producing rodeos that gave other African Americans an opportunity to hone their skills while entertaining audiences and becoming role models for African American youngsters who might think that there are not—and never have been—any black cowboys. Bud Bramwell was born in Connecticut but he always wanted to live in the West and participate in rodeos. He became proficient in two events—steer wrestling and calf roping. After college, he moved back to the East Coast. In the early 1970s he was president of the American Black Cowboy Association and produced rodeos in—among other places—New York City. He was also a featured performer in the 1972 documentary film *Black Rodeo*. Moreover, he regularly participated in weekly events at Cowtown Rodeo in New Jersey as well as at other eastern venues. He had his greatest success as a professional rodeo performer in the late 1970s when he was the year-end all-around champion of the First Frontier Circuit of the PRCA in 1975, 1977, and 1978. He won the circuit's steer wrestling title four times—in 1975, 1976, 1977, and 1984. The First Frontier is one of twelve geographical regions the PRCA created in 1975 to allow competitors who do not wish to compete nationwide to win local championships. The First Frontier Circuit includes thirteen states in the northeastern section of the United States.[18]

Cleo Hearn was born in Seminole, Oklahoma, in 1939. In addition to rodeoing at Oklahoma State University, he was a member of the football team for a while. He was drafted into the U.S. Army prior to graduation and finished his bachelor's degree at Langston University after he was discharged from the service. He participated as a calf roper in the Cheyenne Frontier Days Rodeo for thirty-seven straight years, and he won the calf roping event at the Denver rodeo in 1970. Later, he founded the Cowboys of Color rodeo, which features African American, Native American, Asian American, and Hispanic cowboys and cowgirls. Eventually, he relocated to Texas, where he worked for the Ford Motor Company and continued to rodeo part-time along with his four calf-roping sons.[19]

Several African American rodeo performers from the Sooner State have excelled in the various minor league professional rodeo organizations that exist below the PRCA and that provide additional opportunities for cowboys and cowgirls to earn money while entertaining audiences. The best of these circuits is the International Professional Rodeo Association (IPRA), headquartered in Oklahoma City. While it stages rodeos all over the United States and parts of Canada, it is especially active in Oklahoma. Two others operating from home offices in Oklahoma are the American Cowboys Rodeo Association (ACRA) of Tahlequah and the Cowboys Regional Rodeo Association (CRRA) of Stilwell. Most of the participants in these minor league circuits are part-time performers who hold down full-time jobs because they do not earn enough money rodeoing to survive. Moreover, following the lead of the PRCA, these organizations have created season-ending finals competitions that culminate in the crowning of their annual champions.[20]

Four African Americans from Oklahoma have been crowned year-end champions of the IPRA. The first of these was Clarence LeBlanc, who won the steer wrestling title in 1983 and again in 1990. LeBlanc, of Okmulgee, is from a prominent rodeo family. His father, Roy, produced rodeos for years. Another of Roy's sons, Kenneth, was also a successful steer wrestler who qualified for the

IPRA's year-end celebration, the International Finals Rodeo (IFR), which—like the NFR—is limited to the circuit's top fifteen money-winners during the regular season. Kenneth's ex-wife, Marilyn, a barrel racer, is one of only two African American women to qualify for the IFR.[21] Arthur Stoner of Midwest City won three IPRA bareback riding championships—in 1991, 1992, and 1994. His promising career was cut short in 1995 when he died suddenly at the age of twenty-five from bacterial spinal meningitis.[22]

Two other African Americans to win IPRA titles are among a group of five Oklahomans who have qualified for the NFR. Danell Tipton of Spencer won the IPRA bull riding title in 1995. He qualified for the NFR in 1998, finishing eighth in the world standings, and in 2000, when he ended up in twelfth place. He was one of four bull riders featured in the 2007 documentary film *Shut Up and Ride*.[23] Steer wrestler Ronnie Fields of Oklahoma City won IPRA championships in 2000, 2001, and 2002. He also was the champion of the PRCA's Prairie Circuit in 2003 and of the American Cowboys Rodeo Association (ACRA) in 2000, 2002, and 2003. He qualified for the NFR in 2004 (finishing in third place in the world standings), distinguishing himself by winning the overall competition of the ten-round event; that is, he wrestled his ten steers in a faster aggregate time than that of the other fourteen cowboys participating in the rodeo. Fields also finished third in the world in 2005 and twelfth in 2006 (when a leg injury forced him to miss the last five rounds of the NFR).[24]

Three other African Americans from Oklahoma—Ervin Williams, Chris Littlejohn, and Lee Akin—qualified for the NFR in bull riding during their careers. Williams, of Tulsa, qualified for the NFR three times, finishing third in the world standings in 1989, fifth in 1990, and ninth in 1991. Like Tipton and others, Williams competed in IPRA rodeos before moving on to the PRCA circuit.[25] Littlejohn, a friend of Williams from Tulsa, went to the NFR four straight years—1994 through 1997—finishing in fourteenth, eleventh, eleventh, and fifteenth places in the world. He was also the champion of the PRCA's Great Lakes Circuit in 1997. A spinal injury he suffered at a rodeo in Missouri in 2009 ended his rodeo career.[26]

Akin grew up in a rodeo family in California and came to the Sooner State to rodeo at Southwestern Oklahoma State University in Weatherford. He went to the NFR in 1997, 2000, and 2001. He finished ninth in the world in 1997 and third in each of the latter two years. In 2002, Akin switched his allegiance to the Professional Bull Riders (PBR) association, a second major league rodeo circuit that is—unlike the PRCA—limited to the most popular rodeo event. He qualified for the PBR World Finals year-end event for the circuit's top forty-five riders for four consecutive years, 2002 through 2005. In March 2007, Akin's career came to a sudden end when he suffered a fractured skull when a bull stepped on him at a rodeo in Alabama. He suffered extensive brain damage and has had a long and slow period of rehabilitation since his accident.[27] His tragic story, like that of Littlejohn, underscores the fact that while rodeoing is fun and exciting it is also tremendously dangerous.

An NFR qualifier who did not live in Oklahoma during much of his career but does now is steer wrestler Tommy Cook. Cook grew up in Texas but lived in Utah when he qualified for the National Finals Rodeo in 1998 and 1999; he finished in tenth place in the world standings in the former year and eighth in the latter. Other honors Cook has received include being the champion of the Cowboys Professional Rodeo Association, a minor league organization, in 1992; and winning the Cheyenne Frontier Days Rodeo and being the champion of the PRCA's Wilderness Circuit—both in 1999. Another interesting aspect of Cook's rodeo career is that he makes extra money shoeing the horses of his fellow cowboys at almost every rodeo he attends. In 2007 Cook moved to McAlester, Oklahoma.[28]

Another Oklahoman who has excelled in rodeo arenas is barrel racer Carolyn Carter of Oklahoma City. A nurse by trade, Carter has competed part-time in rodeos since 1985, primarily on the Bill Pickett Invitational Rodeo (BPIR) circuit. The BPIR mostly consists of African American contestants who do not rodeo for a living. While the competition is less talented than at most other rodeos, the BPIR nevertheless gives those who are interested in rodeo a chance to participate, to earn a little money, and to improve their performances through competition. Carter has passed her love of rodeo down to her daughter, Tiphani, who also competes in BPIR events.[29]

In more recent times, several other African Americans from the Sooner State have competed successfully in rodeos at all levels. In 2003, Stephen Reagor of Tulsa won the National Intercollegiate Rodeo Association calf roping crown while competing for Bacone College, the first time an African American had won any college rodeo championship. Reagor currently competes in PRCA and other professional rodeo venues; he qualified for the finals of the PRCA's Prairie Circuit in 2009. Steve Starks of Rentiesville has qualified for the IFR in steer wrestling. Glenn Jackson has won several calf roping titles in the BPIR and finished second in the standings of the IPRA in 2009. Eric Bennett of Tulsa was the CRRA steer wrestling champion in 2002. Denard Butler and Chase Crane are competing in steer wrestling in PRCA and other rodeos after careers at Bacone College and Connors State College, respectively. Derek Goff, a calf roper from Eufala, has qualified several times for the finals of the ACRA and the CRRA. Alexza Fullbright of Wainwright is an up-and-coming barrel racer.[30]

Quite a number of Oklahoma's African American rodeo performers are, like the LeBlancs, members of families that include other rodeo competitors. Marvel Rogers Jr. is a successful steer wrestler who has qualified for the IFR several times and was runner-up in the standings of the ACRA in 2010. Luther Johnson Jr. was—like his father—a bull rider. Gerald Vaughn Jr. followed in his father's footsteps and became a steer wrestler; he qualified for the IFR twice. Danell Tipton's brother, Demeko, also qualified for the IFR several times as a bull rider. Ronnie Fields's brother, Cornell, has likewise qualified many times for the IFR as a steer wrestler; he has also worked as a "hazer," the cowboy who rides alongside a steer and directs it toward the steer wrestler. Hazers typically receive a percentage of the money earned by their steer-wrestling partners. Randy Jackson, who won the CRRA's calf roping title in 2005, was also the organization's all-around cowboy that year—participating also in steer wrestling; his father, Nelson Jackson, was a professional calf roper for several years.[31]

A few other Oklahomans contribute to the sport of rodeo in a variety of ways. Elmer and Charlene Anderson, along with their son Doyle, of Guthrie, have for years operated a successful stock contracting business. Jesse Guillory, who lived in Oklahoma for several years but now resides in Texas, won several BPIR titles in bareback bronc riding and steer wrestling; he also qualified for the IFR as a steer wrestler and currently works as a "field representative" for the IPRA after serving for several years as the general manager of the BPIR. Ron Hunter of Holdenville is a rodeo clown when he is not pursuing his day-time job of high school principal in Weleetka; he has participated in the IFR, the CRRA finals, and PRCA events. Brian White of Oklahoma City is a former bull rider who is currently a bullfighter—one of those who protect bull riders after they have been bucked off in the arena. Sam Gress, originally from Kansas, came to Northwestern Oklahoma State University to rodeo and is currently a successful bullfighter who has worked events sanctioned by the PRCA, PBR, and other associations. Jeff Rector, another Kansan who attended

Northwestern Oklahoma State University on a rodeo scholarship, is currently
the only African American pickup man in the PRCA; as previously noted, the
job of a pickup man is to help bareback and saddle bronc riders dismount from
their horses after their rides are completed.[32]

Just as African Americans played a significant role in the western cattle
industry during the late nineteenth century, they have excelled in the rodeo arenas of the twentieth and twenty-first centuries. And because Oklahoma has a
long tradition in rodeo and a sizeable black population, it is not surprising that
several of the more accomplished African American rodeo performers have
been from the Sooner State. Unfortunately, the number of African American
rodeo stars at the highest levels of competition is quite small. No single annual
edition of the NFR has had more than four African American qualifiers out
of 120 total participants. Still, each year finds new contestants participating in
professional rodeos on either a part-time or full-time basis. Consequently, it
appears that the contribution Oklahoma's African American rodeo performers
will make to the sport is likely to continue indefinitely into the future.

Notes

1. The literature on the cattle industry is vast. Among the more established sources
   are Lewis Atherton, *The Cattle Kings* (Bloomington: Indiana University Press, 1961);
   Gene M. Gressley, *Bankers and Cattlemen* (New York: Alfred A. Knopf, 1966); and
   Edward Everett Dale, *The Range Cattle Industry: Ranching on the Great Plains from
   1865 to 1925*, new ed. (Norman: University of Oklahoma Press, 1960). General works
   on cowboys include Richard W. Slatta, *Cowboys of the Americas* (New Haven: Yale
   University Press, 1990); and Joe B. Frantz and Julian E. Choate Jr., *The American
   Cowboy: The Myth and the Reality* (Norman: University of Oklahoma Press, 1955).
   Black working cowboys are the subject of Philip Durham and Everett L. Jones, *The
   Negro Cowboys* (New York: Dodd, Mead, 1965); Kenneth W. Porter, "Negro Labor in
   the Western Cattle Industry, 1866–1900," *Labor History* 10 (Summer 1969): 346–74;
   and Roger D. Hardaway, "African American Cowboys on the Western Frontier,"
   Negro History Bulletin 64, nos. 1–4 (January/December 2001): 27–32.

2. The history of the sport of rodeo is covered in Clifford P. Westermeier, *Man, Beast,
   Dust: The Story of Rodeo* (Lincoln: University of Nebraska Press, 1947); Kristine
   Fredriksson, *American Rodeo: From Buffalo Bill to Big Business* (College Station:
   Texas A&M University Press, 1985); and Wayne S. Wooden and Gavin Ehringer,
   Rodeo in America: Wranglers, Roughstock, and Paydirt (Lawrence: University Press of
   Kansas, 1996).

3. The best (but outdated) survey of African American rodeo performers is Clifford P. Westermeier, "Black Rodeo Cowboys," *Red River Valley Historical Review* 3 (Summer 1978): 4–27. Two articles that focus exclusively on Texas are Wendy Watriss, "The Soul Circuit," *Geo* 2 (December 1980): 134–50; and Demetrius W. Pearson, "Shadow Riders of the Subterranean Circuit: A Descriptive Account of Black Rodeo in the Texas Gulf Coast Region," *Journal of American Culture* 27, no. 2 (June 2004): 190–98.

4. Jerrold J. Mundis, "He Took the Bull by the Horns," *American Heritage* 19, no. 1 (December 1967): 50–55; and Jim Hoy, "Bill Pickett in the Flint Hills," in *Flint Hills Cowboys: Tales from the Tallgrass Prairie* (Lawrence: University Press of Kansas, 2006).

5. The definitive biography of Bill Pickett is Bailey C. Hanes, *Bill Pickett, Bulldogger: The Biography of a Black Cowboy* (Norman: University of Oklahoma Press, 1977). For the history of the 101 Ranch, see Ellsworth Collings, *The 101 Ranch* (Norman: University of Oklahoma Press, 1937). The 101 Ranch's wild west show is the subject of Michael Wallis, *The Real Wild West: The 101 Ranch and the Creation of the American West* (New York: St. Martin's Press, 1999).

6. *Prescott Journal-Miner*, July 5, November 11, and November 25, 1913.

7. Information on Hooker's and Pickett's movie careers is available at the Internet Movie Database website, www.imdb.com. Hooker's career as a contract player with the Selig Polyscope Company is mentioned in *Prescott Journal-Miner*, July 5, 1913, 5; and January 9, 1914, 7. Hanes, *Bill Pickett, Bulldogger*, 134, describes Hooker as being "of Negro and Mexican extraction."

8. Michael Allen, *Rodeo Cowboys in the North American Imagination* (Reno: University of Nevada Press, 1998), especially chapter 1, "Real Cowboys: A Brief History of Rodeo"; see also Wooden and Ehringer, *Rodeo in America*, especially chapter 1, "Introduction and Brief History of Rodeo."

9. Wooden and Ehringer, *Rodeo in America*, 15–16.

10. "Knox Simmons," biography posted on the website of the National Cowboys of Color Museum and Hall of Fame, www.cowboysofcolor.org; Buck Colbert Franklin, *My Life and an Era: The Autobiography of Buck Colbert Franklin*, ed. John Hope Franklin and John Whittington Franklin (Baton Rouge: Louisiana State University Press, 1997), 136; *Simmons v. State* (Oklahoma Court of Criminal Appeals), 114 P. 752 (1910).

11. Lenwood Fletcher and Alice Hyman, "Bennie Miller Passes On," *New York Amsterdam News*, December 3–9, 2009; Cyril Josh Barker, "Bennie Miller: Harlem Says Goodbye to Black Cowboy," *New York Amsterdam News*, December 10–16, 2009.

12. Westermeier, *Man, Beast, Dust*, 235; *Pittsburgh Post-Gazette*, April 18, 1936, 5; Earl Morris, "Day and Night," *Theatre World* 62, no. 46 (February 26, 1942), 3B.

13. "Official Program, English and Howard's 16th Annual Rodeo and Round-Up, July 23–24–25, 1937, Cleo Springs, Okla."; Michael McNutt, "Couple Envisions Music

Hall, Arena near Cleo Springs," *Daily Oklahoman*, December 4, 1994, 7; *Kiowa (Kansas) News*, August 20, 1947, 1; "Cleo Springs Rancher, Rodeo Promoter Dies," *Fairview Republican*, October 10, 1968. I gratefully acknowledge the assistance of Jana Brown, a native of Cleo Springs and a graduate of Northwestern Oklahoma State University, who provided much information on the life of Jesse Howard.

14. Willard H. Porter, "He Was a Marvel, and They Want to Do a Movie," *Daily Oklahoman*, September 30, 1984; *Ellensburg (Washington) Daily Record*, September 2, 1950, 26; Wooden and Ehringer, *Rodeo in America*, 208.

15. "Roberts Is RAA Champion," *Billboard* 55, no. 7 (February 13, 1943), 37, 43; *Ellensburg (Washington) Daily Record*, September 2, 1950, 26; website of the Lewiston, Idaho, rodeo, www.lewistonroundup.org; website of the Reno rodeo, www.renorodeo.com; Morris, "Day and Night," 3B; author interview with Jimmy Wyatt, January 19, 2011.

16. Wooden and Ehringer, *Rodeo in America*, 15–16; website of the PRCA, www.prca.com; Leisl Carr Childers, "The National Finals Rodeo: The Evolution of an Urban Entertainment Phenomenon," *Nevada Historical Society Quarterly* 51 (Winter 2008): 267–91; Kendra Santos, ed., *The Finals: A Complete History of the First 50 Years of the Wrangler National Finals Rodeo* (Colorado Springs, Colo.: Professional Rodeo Cowboys Association, 2009).

17. Roy Reed, "Black Rodeos Gaining Nationwide Popularity," *New York Times*, September 1, 1975, 8; Bill Pennington, "Rodeo's the Thing for Giants' New Runner; LeShon Johnson Learned Tricks of the Trade on His Father's Ranch in Oklahoma," *New York Times*, May 15, 1998; Rhonda Stewart, "Bull Riding Bash at Tullahassee Was Stocked with Solid Action," *Muskogee Phoenix*, October 4, 2007; Rhonda Stewart, "Rodeos Get Peachy This Weekend," *Muskogee Phoenix*, July 15, 2009; Rhonda Stewart, "Green Country Has Rich Heritage of African American Rodeo Competitors," *Muskogee Phoenix*, February 25, 2009.

18. "Black Rodeos," *Black Enterprise* 2, no. 9 (April 1972), 39–40, 42–44; "Black Rodeo Reminds of Heritage," *Daily Oklahoman*, September 6, 1971, 16; Angela Carella, "City Men Live Life in the Saddle," *Stamford (Connecticut) Advocate*, June 12, 2010; "First Frontier Champions," http://sports.espn.go.com/prorodeo; "The Circuit System," http://www.prorodeo.com.

19. Chris Perkins, "This Family Loves Rodeo Calf Roping," *St. Louis Post-Dispatch*, May 14, 1995, 12F; Art Chapman, "Pride in Their Ride," *Fort Worth Star-Telegram*, September 2, 1999; "Cleo Hearn Summary Cowboys of Color Rodeo," *Educated Horsemen*, www.theeducatedhorsemen.org.

20. Information on these organizations is available on their respective websites: IPRA, www.iprarodeo.com; ACRA, http://acrarodeo.com; and CRRA, www.crrarodeo.com.

21. Whit Canning, "Success Runs in Family for LeBlancs in Rodeo," *Fort Worth Star-Telegram*, March 30, 1992; Glenn Hibdon, "LeBlanc: Steer Wrestling's Running Man," *Tulsa World*, April 18, 1991; Ira Berkow, "The Rocky Trail of a Rodeo Cowboy,"

New York Times, September 25, 1981, D17–18; Tim Stanley, "Rodeo Pioneer Taught Tough Lessons," *Tulsa World*, November 26, 2009; Matt Gleason, "The Roy LeBlanc Okmulgee Invitational Rodeo Has Been Renamed for a Legend," *Tulsa World*, August 12, 2010; Glenn Hibdon, "Busy Rodeo Circuit Fills in Life's Blanks for LeBlancs," *Tulsa World*, January 18, 1996; Nora K. Froeschle, "Barrel Racer Keeps Riding to Success," *Tulsa World*, June 2, 1999.

22. Steve Habel, "Rodeo Brings Milestone for Rookie Competitor," *Austin American-Statesman*, March 28, 1992; Jason Z. Cohen, "Rodeo Champ Arthur Stoner Is Dead at 25," *(Fort Wayne) Journal-Gazette*, March 18, 1995; Eric Bradshaw, "Rodeo Honors Life of Deceased Local Cowboy," *(Midwest City) Sun*, June 22, 2006.

23. Bryan Painter, "Tipton Following List to Success," *Daily Oklahoman*, October 11, 1998; Bryan Painter, "Despite Some Untimely Ribbing, Tipton on Top," *Daily Oklahoman*, September 23, 2000; Bryan Painter, "Tipton's Mind Is in the Middle: Pro Bull-Rider Not Easily Shaken," *Daily Oklahoman*, December 10, 2000; http://sports.espn.go.com (PRCA results for 1998 and 2000); Eric Bradshaw, "Bull Rider Honored, Hosts Rodeo Saturday," *(Midwest City) Sun*, August 22, 2007; Peter Vonder Haar, "Shut Up and Ride [review]," www.filmthreat.com.

24. Bryan Painter, "Rodeo Star Knows Value of Education," *Daily Oklahoman*, January 10, 1999; Bryan Painter, "Fields Wins Dream Title: Millwood Grad Takes Steer Wrestling Crown," *Daily Oklahoman*, January 21, 2001; Kim Watkins, "IPRA World Champion Ronnie Fields Knows Secret to Life," *IPRA News*, www.iprarodeo.com; Ted Harbin, "Fields' Spirituality Helps Him Cope with Family Loss," *Daily Oklahoman*, January 11, 2002; Jerry Shottenkirk, "Fields Gets His Payday in the Dirt," *Daily Oklahoman*, November 15, 2003; Ed Guthrie, "Fields Is a Star in the Making," *Daily Oklahoman*, November 5, 2005; http://sports.espn.go.com (PRCA results for 2003, 2004, 2005, and 2006); www.acrarodeo.com (ACRA results for 2000, 2002, 2003).

25. Jerry McConnell, "Perseverance Pays Off for Bullriders," *Daily Oklahoman*, February 4, 1990; Bryan Painter, "Williams Watched, Learned at NFR," *Daily Oklahoman*, December 20, 1992; http://sports.espn.go.com (PRCA results for 1989, 1990, and 1991).

26. Glenn Hibdon, "Tulsa's Littlejohn Finds Niche in Pursuit of NFR Crown," *Tulsa World*, December 3, 1996; Frank Carroll, "Rodeo Exciting but Not Colorful: Although African-Americans Have Starred on Horseback, Only a Handful Ride the Circuit," *Orlando Sentinel*, February 23, 1997; Ted Harbin, "Bull Rider Chris Littlejohn Bucking the Odds after Spine Injury," *World of Rodeo*, July 13, 2009, www.worldofrodeo.com; http://sports.espn.go.com (PRCA results for 1994, 1995, 1996, and 1997).

27. Barbara Wilcox, "He's Akin to Join the Best Bull Riders at Grand National," *(Walnut Creek, California) Contra Costa Times*, October 24, 1996; Carroll, "Rodeo Exciting but Not Colorful"; Bryan Painter, "Akin Back in Business on Bulls," *Daily*

Oklahoman, November 18, 2000; Jeff Wolf, "National Finals Rodeo: Cowboys Follow Different Paths to Painful Profession," *Las Vegas Review-Journal*, December 12, 2001; Jason Schneider, "Bull-Riding Akin Seeks to Inspire Others: Lone African-American Has Run into Racism during Days on the PBR Tour," *Florida Times-Union*, December 27, 2003; Candace K. Clarke, "Lee Akin: A Rider Breaking Boundaries and Making a Difference," *(St. Petersburg, Florida) Weekly Challenger*, February 23, 2005; Tim Gayle, "Akin Still in Coma after Suffering Skull Fracture," *Daily Oklahoman*, March 10, 2007; Ed Godfrey, "Akin Has Second Surgery, Still in Critical Condition," *Daily Oklahoman*, March 13, 2007; Ed Godfrey, "How One Bull Rider Bucked the Odds," *Daily Oklahoman*, February 15, 2008; Tim Ghianni, "Long Road Home," *Pro Bull Rider*, May 2009; Keith Ryan Cartwright, "Akin Undergoes Successful Surgery," PBR press release, July 27, 2009, www.pbrnow.com; http://sports.espn.go.com (PRCA results for 1997, 2000, and 2001); www.pbrnow. com (PBR results for 2002, 2003, 2004, and 2005).

28. Ed Knocke, "Texas Steer Wrestler Nears Legendary Feat," *Dallas Morning News*, September 7, 1995; Paula Parrish, "Tough Work, If You Can Do It," *(Colorado Springs) Gazette*, August 16, 1999; www.cpra.net (CPRA past champions); http:// sports.espn.go.com (PRCA results for 1998 and 1999).

29. Shanida Smith, "Cowboys, Cowgirls Display Their Skills," *Richmond Times-Dispatch*, September 30, 1999; Jennifer Brown, "Cowboys of Color: Rodeo with a New Look," *Joplin (Missouri) Globe*, August 1, 2002; www.billpickettrodeo.com (biographies of Carolyn and Tiphani Carter); Kyle Partain, "Carolyn Carter-Emmett," *Western Horseman*, May 2010, 50.

30. Cory Young, "Local Cowboy Ropes, Rides to National Title," *Tulsa World*, July 23, 2003; Rhonda Stewart, "Green Country Has Rich History of African American Rodeo Competitors," *Muskogee Phoenix*, February 25, 2009; Joey Bunch, "Green Only Color That Matters," *Denver Post*, January 20, 2009; www.crrarodeo.com (CRRA results for 2002); Brad Hallier, "Picking Up the Slack," *Hutchinson (Kansas) News*, July 15, 2009; Doug Russell, "Rodeo Finals Begin Here Thursday," *McAlester (Oklahoma) News Capital and Democrat*, November 11, 2004; Rhonda Stewart, "Wainwright Girl Ropes High in Mile-High City," *Muskogee Phoenix*, January 19, 2011.

31. Bob Colon, "Marvel-ous Transformation: Former Carl Albert Runner Now Wrestles Steers," *Daily Oklahoman*, January 18, 1997; Rhonda Stewart, "Bull Riding Bash at Tullahassee Was Stocked with Solid Action," *Muskogee Phoenix*, October 4, 2007; Todd Newville, "On the Road . . . with Demeko Tipton," *IPRA Online*, July, 2003, www.iprarodeo.com; Lynda Hillman-Rapley, "Local Guy Wins Second World Steer Wrestling Championship," *(Grand Bend, Ontario) Lakeshore Advance*, January 25, 2010; Glenn Hibdon, "Jackson's Only Tie to Real Job Is Calf Roping," *Tulsa World*, January 16, 1997; Ron Lubke, "Rodeo Gives Minority Cowpunchers the Chance to Rope in Their Dream," *Austin American-Statesman*, May 5, 1991; Todd Newville to the author, January 12, 2003.

32. Sue Blakely, "Meet the Rodeo Man," *(Auburn, New York) Citizen*, September 10, 1978; Chris Brawley, "30-Year-Old Rodeo Hand Who's Going on 11 Is Giving Life a Ride," *Daily Oklahoman*, June 27, 1983; Tammie Hiatt, "Jesse Guillory Joins IPRA Staff," *Rodeo News*, June 1, 2009, 147; www.iprarodeo.com (Ron Hunter Profile); author interview with Ron Hunter, August 31, 2011; Charlyn Fargo, "Bull-Headed: Rodeo Bullfighter Knows the 'Science' of His Work," *(Springfield, Illinois) State Journal-Register*, July 20, 2000; Kelly Hill, "Man vs. Beast: Bullfighters Highlight Klein Rodeo," *Grand Rapids Press*, September 2, 2004; Steve Carpenter, "Hutchinson High Graduate Finding Niche As Bullfighter," *Hutchinson (Kansas) News*, July 18, 2002; Roger McKenzie, "Former Ranger Gets the Best of Bulls," *Alva Review-Courier*, July 15, 2007; Kyle Partain, "Pick-Up Game: Jeff Rector Wants to Make Wrangler NFR History," *ProRodeo Sports News* 59, no. 12 (June 24, 2011): 18–19.

8

The Bronze Buckaroo Rides Again

Herb Jeffries Is Still Keepin' On

MARY A. DEMPSEY

Black cowboys held about one-fifth to one-fourth of the positions occupied by cowboys in the latter nineteenth and into the twentieth century. Nevertheless, if one views films produced in Hollywood beginning in the 1930s that feature cowboys, blacks were seldom included. As Mary A. Dempsey shows us, one black performer, Herb Jeffries, decided that films featuring blacks ought to be produced. In the late 1930s, on film, Herb Jeffries became a cowboy, Bob Blake, whose nickname was "The Bronze Buckaroo." Jeffries acted, edited, and wrote songs for the films. A few of his songs are found on a CD titled *The Bronze Buckaroo Rides Again*. As Dempsey put it, Jeffries did the unthinkable: "He convinced Hollywood to make all-black cowboy movies." Herb Jeffries passed away in 2014, after publication of Dempsey's article and before publication of this book. In our hearts he "is still keepin' on."

During the 1930s, when the film exploits of singing cowboys Gene Autry and Roy Rogers packed audiences into dime movie houses, jazz singer Herbert Jeffries (then known as Herbert Jeffrey) did the unthinkable: He convinced Hollywood to make all-black cowboy movies—and then he starred in the films, singing his own western compositions.[1]

Six decades have passed since he first played cowboy Bob Blake, better known as the Bronze Buckaroo, meting out Old West justice along with bunkhouse admonitions against liquor and cigarettes and against shooting—except in self-defense. But the still elegant Jeffries remembers with clarity the films, the filmmaking, and the urgency that drove him forward.

His foray into the entertainment world began in the late 1920s, when he

Originally published as Mary A. Dempsey, "The Bronze Buckaroo Rides Again: Herb Jeffries Is Still Keepin' On," *American Visions* 12 (August/September 1997): 22–26. Reprinted with permission of the publisher and author.

serenaded dancing couples at the Graystone Ballroom in his native Detroit. Then it was on to Chicago to sing with Earl "Fatha" Hines at the Grand Terrace Nightclub. A national tour with Hines took Jeffries to the South for the first time, opening his eyes to Jim Crow in its rawest forms. "When we went down South that's where I first saw discriminatory theaters, including at the U.S. capital, where blacks sat in segregated balconies," Jeffries recalls of the 1933–35 tour. He remembers watching African Americans queue outside segregated southern theaters to watch Sunday matinee "horse operas" with all-white casts. "I said: 'Wait a minute. Blacks helped pioneer the West.'"

A stop during a northern road trip further exposed an already raw nerve. "There was a bunch of children running down the street. A little black boy was with them, crying," Jeffries recalls. "He said they wouldn't let him play cowboy. But in the real West, one of every four cowboys was black."

Jeffries decided that America's movie audiences needed a history lesson, so in 1936 he took off for California, determined to make the first all-black cowboy movie. "I wanted to be in cowboy pictures," he explains. "I didn't care whether I was a star; I just wanted to be part of the technology of making them happen."

He spent nearly a year looking for backers, futilely courting the millionaires who ruled the urban numbers rackets. Then he turned up at the office of producer Jed Buell, who two years later would release the western musical *The Terror of Tiny Town*, a novelty flick featuring a cast of little people. Buell was skeptical that audiences would pay to see westerns boasting all-black casts, but after bouncing the idea off a Dallas film distributor he decided to proceed with the venture.

A search began for African Americans who could ride, sing, and act. "We tested ten or twelve, and none could do all three," recalls Jeffries. So the singer—who as a youngster had learned to ride horses at his grandfather's farm in Michigan—found himself cast as Bob Blake. Jeffries then convinced Spence Williams, who later portrayed Andy in television's *Amos 'n' Andy*, to write a script and sign on as the film's costar. Comedian Mantan Moreland became the Bronze Buckaroo's sidekick. The rest of the cast was drawn from the pool of African American actors working on Tarzan pictures.

A three-month stint at a dude ranch added lasso tricks, branding, and fancy equestrian footwork to Jeffries's familiarity with horses—but it didn't prepare him for the rigors of low-budget black filmmaking. "Sometimes, we worked fourteen hour a day," he recalls with a chuckle. Horses stepped on my foot. I fell off the horse. Sometimes I was so tired and sore that I couldn't get my leg over the horse, so I'd jump up from an apple box."

Working with a budget of less than $80,000 (and earning only $5,000 for himself from each film), the energetic Jeffries not only starred in the movie and performed his own stunts; he also wrote and sang the music and edited the film. And he has no illusions about the quality of the movies; today he affectionately refers to them as "the first bunch of C-minus westerns," while noting that he worked with a budget that was just a fraction of those assigned to the B westerns of Autry and Rogers.

Before the end of 1936, *Harlem on the Prairie* made its debut at New York's Rialto theater on Broadway. In Jeffries's next two sequels, *Two-Gun Man from Harlem* and *Harlem Rides the Range*, the blues-style music of *Prairie* evolved into a more western sound, with songs like "Git Along Mule," "The Cowpoke's Life Is the Only Life for Me," and "Almost Time for Roundup."

Although the West portrayed in Jeffries's films was no more realistic than that depicted in the Hollywood offerings of the major studios, some music historians have noted that Bob Blake's harmonies were more authentic than those featured in mainstream cowboy films, because Jeffries borrowed from gospel and Appalachian traditions, as did the songs of those who really rode the range in the heyday of the cattle drives from Texas to Kansas. A fourth movie, *The Bronze Buckaroo*, was released in 1939. The series ended with *Ten Notches to Tombstone*, which was never completed.

While black westerns added cachet to the professional resume of the debonair Jeffries, they didn't bring him wealth; so in 1939 he returned to music. Two years later, he recorded "Flamingo" with Duke Ellington's orchestra on the RCA label. (In the process, RCA had the singer change his surname from Jeffrey to Jeffries.) The song sold nearly a million copies and propelled Jeffries to fame, encouraging him to embark on a career as a solo act.

This endeavor never really took off and, after the Japanese attack on Pearl Harbor, Jeffries enlisted in the armed forces. By the war's end, there were fewer segregated theaters, the audience for westerns had waned, and some of the hottest jazz nightclubs were in Europe. So in 1951 Jeffries headed to France, where he found renewed success and opened up a club on the Côte d'Azur, which he named the Flamingo after his 1941 smash hit. "I had good French musicians mixed with American musicians, and I ran the club, performed, and was chief bottle washer, janitor, and host," he says with a laugh. His effort was rewarded: he moved from his first Flamingo club to a venue three times larger and then added a Riviera branch in Cap d'Antibes, between Nice and Cannes.

A September 1953 *Life* magazine profile sparked renewed stateside interest in Jeffries, and he began receiving invitations to play at clubs such as the Macambo in New York City. For the next six years, he shuttled across the Atlantic, singing in clubs in both Europe and the United States, until he decided to settle in Los Angeles.

Back home in the United States, Jeffries continued to sing in clubs, in theaters, on cruise ships. The years were interwoven with marriages—five of them and as many children, including a son born while Jeffries was in his seventies, married to a woman fifty years his junior. He acted on television occasionally (showing up in episodes of *The Virginian, The Name of the Game,* and *Hawaii Five-O*) and had a role in the 1977 movie *Portrait of a Hitman* (starring Jack Palance), but his western movies were nearly forgotten.

Then the long-lost Bob Blake flicks resurfaced in a cache of old film cans discovered not long ago in a collapsed cellar in Tyler, Texas. *Harlem Rides Again* was released on videotape, and fragments of the Bob Blake films appeared in Mario Van Peebles's 1993 movie *Posse*, spawning an interest in Jeffries's historic role in breaking Hollywood's race barriers and leading to his participation in the Public Broadcasting Service's show *California Gold* and the Turner Broadcasting Service's documentary on the legacy of black cowboys on the American frontier, *The Untold West.*

"To say I was the first black singing cowboy on the face of this earth is a great satisfaction," Jeffries acknowledges. If these words seem a summation of a man whose day has passed, think again, for the still active eighty-six-year-old performer quickly adds: "But that's history. Today I'm the new kid in western music."

He may be the new kid, but he's once again a smashing success, singing western music (which, he emphasizes, is different from country music) against a symphonic backdrop, with groups such as California's La Miranda Symphony and San Antonio's Sagebrush Symphony. Performing in 1995 with a symphony orchestra at the Copper Mountain Resort in Colorado before an audience of 15,000, Jeffries stole the show from the better-known contemporary singers there, such as Mary Chapin Carpenter.

Note

1. This article was based on interviews with Jeffries conducted by the author.

9

Musical Traditions of Twentieth-Century African American Cowboys

ALAN GOVENAR

Determining the musical traditions of black cowboys has been a neglected and somewhat difficult task. In this chapter, musicologist and folklore specialist Alan Govenar points out how the music of black cowboys varied from the pattern of white cowboy movies and songs; Govenar learned that blacks were more likely to sing blues and church songs than the traditional cowboy songs. One songster, Alfred Johnson, found himself influenced by bluesman Mance Lipscomb. African American rancher A. J. Walker hosted zydeco dances along with his rodeos. Vincent Jacobs composed a song that ended with the refrain "ride along black cowgirl, ride." According to a few of Govenar's sources, contrary to a popular notion, black cowboys did not sing to the herds in the evening as long as they were peaceful. As Govenar puts it, "The musical repertory of African American cowboys in Texas varied from ranch to ranch and often reflected, not only the cultural backgrounds of the cowboys themselves, but the taste of their ranch bosses."

While the importance of African Americans in Texas ranching before and after the Civil War has been recognized, the musical traditions of the cowboys themselves have remained virtually undocumented. John Lomax in his book *Adventures of a Ballad Hunter* recalled that African American ranch hands were more reluctant to sing for him, but that "two or three Negro cowboys sang lustily" when he got them away from the crowd. Unfortunately, Lomax does not discuss the songs that these cowboys performed, although he does describe his

Originally published as Alan Govenar, "Musical Traditions of Twentieth-Century African-American Cowboys," in *Juneteenth Texas: Essays in African-American Folklore*, edited by Francis Abernethy et al. (Denton: University of North Texas Press, 1996), 195–206. Reprinted with permission of the Texas Folklore Society.

encounter with another black cowboy, whom he learned about from a German saloonkeeper in San Antonio, Texas, in 1908. "He directed me to another drink dispenser, a Negro, who ran a place down near the Southern Pacific depot out on a scrubby mesquite grove," Lomax writes, explaining that the man had been a trail cook for years and apparently knew a "world of cowboy songs." Lomax, however, only recounts one of his songs, "Home on the Range," which he recorded and later concluded that, after the music was "set down" and "touched up here and there, has since won a high place as a typical Western folk tune." Regrettably, Lomax was somewhat ethnocentric in his approach to collecting cowboy songs and seemed to neglect those tunes that didn't fit his preconceived notions, formulated from his knowledge of Anglo-American balladry and published sheet music.[1]

Moses Asch and Alan Lomax include two cowboy songs in *The Leadbelly Songbook* that Leadbelly recalled from his days working on farms and ranches in East Texas: "Come Along All You Cowboys" and "Cow Cow Yicky Yicky Yea." However, Asch and Lomax do not explore the natural context in which these songs were originally performed, or how they related to other songs in Leadbelly's repertory.[2]

From contemporary oral accounts and anecdotal evidence, it appears that, although black cowboys did sing some Anglo-American folk songs for collectors, their musical traditions among themselves were somewhat different than among their white counterparts. According to Alfred Johnson, who worked as a ranch hand in the 1920s and '30s, black cowboys sang blues and church songs rather than what are thought of as "cowboy songs."[3]

Johnson was born in 1913 in Cedar Creek, Texas, the son of Frank and Pearl Lee Johnson, who were sharecroppers on a farm and ranch owned by a man only remembered as "Mr. Yost." Johnson's memories of his childhood are sketchy, though he says that he often felt unwanted and that around the age of fifteen he went to work on another of Mr. Yost's ranches near Manchaca in Bastrop County. "They give me to them," he says. "They'd feed me, you know, shoe me and clothe me. And I did horseback riding, taking care of the cattle, herding the cattle, and farming. Everybody sang the blues in them days. Black cowboys sang blues. They didn't sing cowboy songs. They sang them blues and some church songs. All through this country now, if you go down there, and if you hear them singing, they're singing the blues."

Johnson learned about music by listening and watching. "All of my peoples," he says,

played some. My daddy was a fiddler and he played blues on the fiddle. My uncle, named Will Johnson, played guitar all the time. I couldn't get to play too much, because I wasn't over twelve or thirteen years old. That's when they gave me the nickname "Snuff" because I started using snuff around that time. Well, they'd let me pick up the guitar every once in a while. And I'd be paying attention to what my uncle was doing, how he was playing. And I would get to play a little bit. And then it would probably be a week or two weeks before I could get a chance to pick up another one. But I kept at it in my mind what he was doing and I wanted to be a guitar picker and play like the way he did. He stayed down there at Cedar Creek, and we'd always go to the country ball, because he'd always have one.

Those country balls were good. The people weren't like they are now. People would associate with one another. Maybe they'd have a country ball over to this place, maybe they have a country ball over to that place. It'd be just a house. That was every Friday and Saturday night. They'd have fiddle, guitar, and then we didn't have no drums. They'd get out there and slow drag, you know, and dance. They wouldn't get out there bopping and jumping and picking and kicking. They wouldn't do that. They just slow dance, mile-long slow dance. And we'd go because it was within walking distance. They would play country music, blues, just like I play now. Oh, Lord, they'd have some of all kinds. "Blues in the Bottle," "Goin' Downtown," "Black Gal." It was sorta like Mance Lipscomb.

I didn't know Mance Lipscomb personally. I knew of him a few times. I got to see him a few times. And then he would be playing. He mostly went on horseback or in the wagon. I guess I was about fourteen or fifteen. He was well known all around Cedar Creek. He was well known all the way through Bastrop, Elgin, Taylor, La Grange. He was from Navasota in Grimes County. Cedar Creek's in Bastrop County, seven miles out of Bastrop.

The influence of Mance Lipscomb is apparent in Johnson's playing, especially in his use of a strong thumb on the bass string, almost like the drum in a dance tune. About this, Johnson says, "That's right, when I be playing, I carry my bass with me. You can't find too many guitar pickers who can play and carry a bass."

In addition to playing a distinctive style of what might be called "black cowboy" blues at house parties and country balls, Johnson has also performed in his church. "It'd be with the sermon," Johnson says. "I get up there and play while the people are singing and I play along with them."

Many of the songs Johnson performs are remembered in bits and pieces and combine traditional lyrics with those he improvises as he goes along. He sings with a deep, almost moaning tone, accompanying himself on guitar and sometimes humming. "While you're humming," he smiles, "it gives you the thoughts of what verses to place in with your singing." Overall, Johnson's memory of his songs is inexact. His versions of "Hey, Little Girl" and "The Good Book Told Me," for example, are essentially guitar instrumentals that incorporate humming with the repetition of what seems to be a truncated lyric of a longer song that might have been forgotten or never learned. When asked about these, he says that "blues" of this kind was sung by people at leisure and at work. "They sang the blues when they were sitting or walking, sometimes when they were herding cattle or riding down the road. The blues comes from worries, and to sing the blues gives relief."

In some respects, American music specialist Kip Lornell suggests, Johnson's performance style is reminiscent of the black southern banjo/song/string band tradition that "could be found throughout the south, but especially in the southeastern United States during the teens and 1920s, and perhaps even earlier."[4] Moreover, many of the lyrics in Johnson's blues or blues-like songs, such as in "Good Morning Blues," consist of recompositions of familiar tunes.

Johnson's religious singing is largely indicative of the post–gospel camp meeting era. Such well-known gospel hymns as "Old Time Religion" and "Going Back to Jesus" typify the songs of the period from roughly the 1870s to the early part of the twentieth century. In addition to gospel hymns, Johnson draws upon the earlier African American spiritual tradition.

In many ways, Johnson's style of performance typifies the repertory of the

African American cowboy songsters of his generation. However, within Texas, there are some regional variations. Tony Lott, born in 1905 on bottomland near the San Antonio River in southeast Texas, recalled that his father often sang while he worked and that the lyrics were often spiritual in nature: "My dad used to sing 'Time Has Made a Change' when we were little. He used to sing that song and we'd walk right behind him. And he'd sing that song when riding on a horse or watching them cows. Another one was 'The Word of God Is Right, Hallelujah to His Name.' He'd sing that song when he was working in the field. We were picking cotton."[5]

When asked about blues, Lott replied that his parents were "church going people" and that they didn't sing secular songs, although he did remember one tune called "Angelina." "It was an old song," he said. "I don't know where he (my dad) got that from, and all I know is part of it":

> Miss Angelina, I sure love you, I sure love you
> There's no other one so good and true, so good and true
> Miss Angelina, oh, my black baby's you
> She's a daisy, run me crazy
> Miss Angelina, oh, my black baby's you.

Cowboys, Lott maintained, didn't do much singing while they were herding cattle. "They did a little hoop and hollering—we'd do that at night when we'd be cutting out yearlings from the herd. And the boys had to keep them yearlings from going back. That's when we'd be hollering, something like that."

At night, however, Lott said, "We had to calm the herd. Well, we'd sing 'Whoo-oo–oo, doggie, whoo-oo-oo, doggie. We'd sing the same verse over and over. That would calm them down. And then, sometimes, we'd have to hoop and holler to get them going again."

Given the relatively flat terrain of the coastal plains region where Lott worked, "calming the herd" was a fairly common practice at night on the range. Sudden and loud noises, like a gun shot or thunder and lightning, might cause the herd to stampede. In southeast Texas, in the area between Beaumont and Houston, the land was marshy and overgrown and, consequently, driving cattle was considerably more difficult.

Elton Laday, whose father owned a fifty-acre ranch in Cheeks, Texas (near Beaumont), said,

I wasn't too much of a singer, but I used to holler and squall, "Yeeeea, Yeeeea, hurry cattle, hurry, hurry," and they'd just come on. They start walking up. And sometimes we had to go behind them and pop the whip. You know what I mean, just sling a whip, and then we'd drive them out of these marshes and stuff. And if they got bogged down, you'd have to squall and jump off your horse and keep your horse from kicking you. But we'd manage to get far enough away. We had long reins and held onto them, and drag on out, and the horse and them cattle would come across."[6]

Often, by dusk, Laday recalled, the cattle were "tired out" and rarely ever had to be calmed. "They didn't get agitated. When you finally got them together, they'd all stay together. You had to ride around them on your horse a little bit. That was about it. You'd have to keep them from riding away in the bottom of the marshes. So, you'd throw a few squalls, and them old cows were pretty well-trained. They knew when you got to squalling, they'd come on out."

Laday was born in 1920 in Ville Platte, Louisiana, but moved with his family to Texas, near Beaumont, when he was two years old. He grew up baling hay and working as a cowhand on trail drives for the family-owned ranches in the area. Each year, Laday remembered, about fifteen cowboys drove approximately three hundred to four hundred head of cattle from Cottonwood, where the herd fed on native grass during the spring and summer months, across the intercoastal canal to Port Bolivar, where they were able to feed on salt grass from October to March or April, when they were brought back.

In southeast Texas, there was a greater concentration of black-owned ranches, some of which were started by freed slaves after the Civil War. Others were acquired by families, like the Ladays, who migrated from southwestern Louisiana and were slowly able to buy acreage.

A. J. Walker, born in 1930 in Opelousas, Louisiana, moved with his parents to Raywood, Texas, east of Houston.[7] His father, Tom Walker, was a rodeo promoter who, after several years of work as a cowhand, was able to purchase forty acres near Raywood in 1941. There, he established the Circle 6 Ranch and began hosting his own rodeos. Today, A. J. Walker continues to operate the ranch with the help of his sons, raising his own livestock and training and breaking horses. From March to October, Walker promotes rodeos on a monthly basis at his ranch. He coordinates his efforts with the other members of the Anahuac

Saltgrass Cowboy Association, who also organize ranch rodeos. The Anahuac Saltgrass Cowboy Association is principally comprised of African Americans and currently has about four hundred members.

In addition to promoting ranch rodeos, A. J. Walker organizes zydeco dances, which attract a cross section of the African American community in the region, especially those who have mixed French and Creole ancestry. Walker said that some of the working cowboys he knew as a child spoke and sang in French, although English has now become the principal language. French, however, is preserved among the zydeco bands, most of which travel from southwestern Louisiana, performing at the Circle 6 Ranch, as well as at clubs and dance halls in the small towns between Beaumont and Houston.

Vincent Jacobs, born in 1932 to parents of mixed Indian and African ancestry in Huffman, Texas, has worked as both a ranch and rodeo cowboy but has also performed as a singer in rhythm and blues bands.[8] Growing up, Jacobs remembered hearing the older cowboys singing blues and church songs, but his personal interest in music derived more from what he heard on radio and in movies.

"When I was a boy," Jacobs said, "I used to go to them old westerns at the movie theaters in Crosby and Barrett Station. The theater in Barrett Station was owned by a black man, James Thomas, but the one in Crosby was segregated. If you were black, you had sit up in the balcony. And I never saw any black cowboys in them movies, but I did see Gene Autry and Tex Ritter. The black folks were doing the washing, the cooking, and working out in the fields."

Jacobs, however, was unaware of the "Negro singing westerns" produced in the late 1930s when he was a child. The first of these was *Harlem on the Prairie* (1937), produced and directed by Jed Buell and starring Herbert Jeffrey. Jeffrey, who was originally from Detroit, used the stage name Herb Jeffries and got his start as a singer for Earl Hines and his big band in 1933. After touring with Hines, he became a vocalist for the Duke Ellington Orchestra, and by the time he started making westerns he was well known as a singing emcee.

Harlem on the Prairie was a genre film and, despite its billing as the "first all-colored" western musical, the plot and music were not distinctively African American. It included such songs as "Old Folks at Home" and "Romance in the Rain," which were performed with a jazzy sentimentality, common in the popular music of the day. Nonetheless, *Harlem on the Prairie* was relatively successful and inspired Richard C. Kahn, another white Hollywood producer, director, and writer, to make three other black westerns featuring Herb Jeffries: *Two-Gun Man from Harlem* (1938), *The Bronze Buckaroo* (1939), and *Harlem Rides the Range* (1939). In sum, these movies, film historian Thomas Cripps maintains, "suffered from a reluctance to explore the realities of black life on the frontier. Instead they chose to mirror the most gimmicky white musical horse operas."[9]

Distribution for black musical westerns was limited to black theaters around the country, most of which were concentrated in urban areas. Consequently, these films were barely accessible to African Americans like Vincent Jacobs, who lived in a rural ranching community. As a ranch hand, Jacobs recalled hearing the old black cowboys humming some of the songs he heard in the movies, but they rarely sang the lyrics. "They'd hum songs like 'Back in the Saddle Again' and 'Home on the Range,' but they hardly ever seemed to want to sing the words."

In response to the apparent lack of a distinctive repertory of black cowboy songs, Jacobs wrote one of his own, adapting the tune from "Ghost Riders in the Sky" and creating his own lyrics.[10]

> An old black cowboy riding along one dark and windy day
> He rides along the devil herd as they ride on their way
> If you want to ride forever, riding in the sky
> Ride along, black cowboy, ride
> The horse was shining black with sweat as they ride on their way
> They've been riding at them for a month
> They haven't caught them yet
> If you want to ride forever, riding in the sky
> Ride along, black cowboy, ride
> Yippee, yi-o
> Yippee, yi-ay
> Ride along, black cowgirl, ride

Jacobs wrote the song when he was nine or ten years old and has continued to sing it upon request for his fellow cowboys. "Sometimes," Jacobs said, "we'll be just sitting around, taking a break, in between events at the rodeo, or maybe after, when we get together to party or dance." For a brief period, during the 1960s and 1970s, Jacobs played an organ and was a singer in Pete Mayes's rhythm and blues band. Mayes's uncle Manuel River owned a dance hall in Double Bayou, Texas, which was frequented by cowboys and African Americans in general in the region.

At the Double Bayou Dance Hall, Rivers presented not only rhythm and blues but zydeco bands as well. According to Cleveland Walters, who has worked as a cowboy with Jacobs over the years, "They didn't call the French music zydeco in the old days. They called it 'La-la,' and usually they'd have an accordion and a rub board [*frottoir*] or sometimes just a fiddle and a rub board."[11]

Walters, who was born in 1925 in Liberty, Texas, said that his father was a dance fiddler and that his brother played accordion, but that he preferred the harmonica. "I was raised up on the farm and we didn't have much of anything. And at Christmas, we got an apple, an orange, and a choice of either a cap pistol or a ten-cent harmonica, and I always picked the harmonica."

Like Jacobs, Walters's early influences were the western movies that he saw on Saturday afternoons when he was growing up. "I liked Tex Ritter and I'd try to figure out the songs on the harmonica, songs like 'Riding old pink and leading old ball, Old Ball ain't good for nothing at all, Yippee, Ti Yi Yay, Yippee, Yippee, Yippee, Yay.'"

In addition to the popular songs he heard in westerns, Walters also plays some traditional blues and zydeco tunes, as well as a traditional "train song," which, he said, he altered to make it his own: "I took the song "Freight Train Boogie" and renamed it "Crawfish Train," adding some of my own words:

Crawfish train goes all around
Crawfish train goes town to town
Crawfish train goes all around
Crawfish train goes town to town
Crawfish train is moving on down the line
Crawfish train goes all around
Crawfish train goes town to town

In this song, the harmonica mimics the sound of the train as it "goes up and down and all around, bringing the crawfish from Louisiana to Texas." Overall, Walters's repertory on the harmonica is essentially traditional and is reflective of the musical styles popularized through ranch dances and other community gatherings.

Given the mobile, and sometimes transient, lifestyle of cowboys, the harmonica was a relatively easy instrument to carry and consequently, as Walters reported, was fairly common. Clearly, however, the musical repertory of African American cowboys in Texas varied from ranch to ranch and often reflected, not only the cultural backgrounds of the cowboys themselves, but the taste of their ranch bosses. Tony Lott said that "Mr. Welder [of the Welder Ranch] liked to hear us sing Christian songs. And if we wanted to sing anything else, we had to do it when he wasn't around." E. J. Garza, who worked with Lott on the O'Connor ranch, concurred with this view but added that African American cowboys were also influenced by the Mexican vaqueros.[12]

Garza was born in 1918 on the McFaddin Ranch in Victoria County. His mother was black and his father was Mexican. On the ranch, Garza said, many of the working cowboys were bilingual and had mixed racial ancestry. As a young man, Garza was known among his peers as the "singing cowboy." He played guitar and, like his contemporaries, performed the songs popularized by Tex Ritter and Roy Rogers, but his repertory also included "Allá en el Rancho Grande," popularized by the bilingual sheet music and the Mexican movie of the same name and other songs in the *ranchera* tunes.[13]

In sum, the musical traditions of black cowboys in Texas are clearly varied, embodying not only the values of African American culture at large but the cross-pollination of musical styles—itself a result of the migratory patterns of blacks—as well as the impact of the recording industry and mass media commercialization. Not only is the black population of Texas less concentrated than that of other states in the South, but "black cowboy" music in Texas also evolved in proximity to other important musical traditions: the rural Anglo, the Cajun and Creole, and the Hispanic.

Notes

1. John A. Lomax, *Adventures of a Ballad Hunter* (New York: MacMillan, 1947), 46, 61.

2. Moses Asche and Alan Lomax, eds., *The Leadbelly Songbook* (New York: Oak, 1962).

3. Alfred Johnson, personal interviews, December 1 and 12, 1992, and March 15, 1994.

4. Kip Lornell, personal interview, March 16, 1994.

5. Tony Lott, personal interview, July 21, 1994.

6. Elton Laday, personal interview, March 14, 1993.

7. Alan Govenar, "A. J. Walker: Cowboy and Rodeo Organizer," in *Black Cowboys of*

Texas, ed. Sara R. Massey, 291–98 (College Station: Texas A&M University Press, 2000).

8. Vincent Jacobs, personal interviews, March 3, 1993, May 20, 1994, and November 11 and 23, 1994.

9. Thomas Cripps, *Slow Fade to Black: The Negro in American Film, 1900–1942* (New York: Oxford University Press, 1977), 336–37; see also Henry T. Sampson, *Blacks in Black and White: A Source Book on Black Films* (Metuchen, N.J.: Scarecrow Press, 1977).

10. "Ghost Riders in the Sky" was copyrighted by the Edmond H. Morris Company in 1949 with words and music by Stan Jones. The song was introduced by Burl Ives and was also a hit Victor recording by Vaughn Monroe. Gene Autry sang the song in the movie *Riders in the Sky*, and the song was revived in 1966 as "Ghost Riders in the Sky" by the Baja Marimba Band.

11. Cleveland Walters, personal interviews, April 27, 1994, and November 22, 1994.

12. Edward Jarrett "E. J." Garza, personal interview with author, ca. 1994.

13. John Lomax in *American Ballads and Folk Songs* (New York: MacMillan, 1934) identifies Silvano R. Ramos as the composer of "Allá en el Rancho Grande," with an Edward B. Marks publisher's copyright of 1927. Cataloged sheet music at the University of Texas, however, lists Emilio D. Uranga as composer and J. Del Moral as lyricist for a 1934 New York bilingual edition published by E. B. Marks. For more information on the musical traditions of Mexican *vaqueros*, see "14 Traditional Songs from Texas," transcribed by Gustavo Duran, *Music Series*, no. 4, April 1942.

❖

PART III

Outriders of the
Black Cowboys

10

Mary Fields's Road to Freedom

MIANTAE METCALF MCCONNELL

As mentioned in Cecilia Venable's chapter on Johana July, black women too had the skills of a cowhand. In Miantae Metcalf McConnell's contribution we see that Mary Fields was knowledgeable about and adept with horses, but we also learn of the many legends that grew up about Fields, most inaccurate or exaggerated. Fields, a former slave who took up residence in Montana Territory, hauled heavy loads of freight with her two-horse team and buckboard. Her reputation as a driver who prevailed against wilderness odds secured a new post—delivery of the U.S. mail. Unbeknownst to her, driving the prairie route would bring national recognition a century later when, in 2006, the U.S. Postal Service officially acknowledged Mary Fields as "the first known African American woman star route mail carrier in the United States." McConnell is also working on a literary nonfiction book about Mary Fields.

It was an act of love that compelled Mary Fields, a fifty-three-year-old African American woman, to board the night train in Toledo, Ohio, on March 18, 1885, and travel over fifteen hundred snow-laden miles to help her friend. A telegram had delivered the urgent plea for assistance, alerting nuns at the Convent of the Sacred Heart, the place of Mary's employment, that Mother Mary Amadeus, the facility's former Ursuline mother superior, had contracted pneumonia and was facing imminent death.[1]

One year earlier, on January 17, 1884, Mother Mary Amadeus had led a cadre of five nuns into the treacherous wilds of Montana Territory. Conflicts with native tribes had erupted—in particular, with Northern Cheyennes near the Tongue River. Lacking a reservation, the tribe defended its right to settle in southeastern Montana, where they had been sent by the U.S. government in 1881. White cattle ranchers demanded ownership of land the Cheyennes had filed for under the Indian Homestead Act of 1875. Threats escalated. Ursuline sisters worried that more Native American daughters would be killed, raped, or sold into prostitution. The founding charter of the Ursuline religious order, a Catholic sect, purposed its ministration to rescue innocent young women from such fates. Their charge was to house, educate, and provide means by which each pupil could manifest a moral Christian existence. Such was the nature of Mother Amadeus's mission.[2]

Satchels were packed within the hour. Mary Fields, the convent groundskeeper who had formed a bond with Mary Amadeus, was joined by Mother Stanislaus, the current Ursuline superior of Toledo, Sister Saint Rose, and Sister Mary of the Angels. They traveled west across seven states and debarked from the Northern Pacific at Helena, an emerging Montana city that afforded financial gain and political clout for the lucky few and profound disappointment to laborers, entrepreneurs, and gold seekers who had not struck it rich in the territory's mother lode of opportunity. From Helena, Mary and the nuns scrambled to find frontier transportation to take them seventy miles farther west to Saint Peter's Mission, located on the west side of the Continental Divide in a region called the Birdtail, named after a monolithic stone sculpture geologically carved into the shape of tail feathers. "Birdtail Rock" towered like a sentry or a crucifix, one thousand feet above the prairie floor. Saint Peter's Mission, situated in the southern section of the Birdtail, had been established by Jesuits in 1859. After Mother Amadeus and her Ursulines had arrived on October 30, 1884, the mission was governed by Jesuit brother and Ursuline sister communities operating as separate, independent religious orders yet functioning cooperatively, as determined by their superior officials and the Catholic bishop of Montana.[3]

The sight of two roughly hewn cabins identified by the Ohioans' driver as the Ursuline settlement must have drawn gasps from the passengers as they struggled to assimilate the state of the nuns' dilapidated shelter and its bleak perimeter: snow-swept isolation stretching from one mountain range to another; prairie, hills, and forest vast in all directions; sun glaring upon outcropped layers of rock nearby; and limitless lengths of daunting glacier peaks to the west, the legendary Rocky Mountains. Mother Amadeus had written in her Christmas letter dated December 19, 1884, "Think of me far away in the snowy mountains of an ice-bound savage land." The exhausted rescue party dismounted and rushed to a bedraggled and much-relieved congregation, who embraced them wholeheartedly. Mary Fields and the Ohio sisters were, at first, oblivious to the lack of heat, furnishings, and food, interested only in knowing that Mother Mary Amadeus, who lay before them on the frigid earth floor, was still alive. The newcomers attended to the purpose of their journey, helping the "Pioneer Nuns" care for their beloved superior general. They also assisted in the operations of two recently established boarding schools for girls (segregated Indian and white) as well as participating in an overwhelming number of mission chores.[4]

After Mother Amadeus and her sisters had come to Saint Peter's, they learned of further mandatory requirements in addition to rent and other prescribed fees; the mission washing, ironing, and mending of all clothes worn by *both* male and female mission occupants and the baking of bread for the same had been imposed upon them in order to retrieve the original promise of two hundred acres. Mother had also confided in her December missive, "Our Novitiate table is piled up with work that must be finished before Christmas— Jesuit cassocks, rabbis, birettas and shirts to be made: the Fathers and Brothers stockings to be knitted and stockings to be darned and all their clothes, even pants and coats, to be put in order. We have to wash, bake and mend for the Jesuit household; they believe in the law of compensation."[5]

As daily routines ensued, the Montana nuns disclosed that, not only had they labored for the Jesuits, they had managed with little food and no lodging for themselves other than a wagon. They had huddled in its box for a duration of several winter months and had survived numerous blizzards and painful frostbit limbs. Meanwhile, the sisters had delegated the clay-chinked, dirt-floor cabin built by the Jesuits twenty years earlier to serve as the white girls' school and dormitory. The Ursuline's first students, three daughters of local homesteaders, began attending classes on November 10, eleven days after the nuns' arrival. Eventually, miners had happened by and built the sisters a single-room log cabin, where they lived briefly before expediting its use to function as their Indian boarding school. Indoctrination of eleven female pupils transported from the Blackfeet reservation 112 miles northwest began on March 7, 1885— daughters whose safety had been entrusted by parents who called the white women wearing layers of black cloth "Black Robes."[6]

A small wood stove had been obtained. After school hours concluded, the nuns appropriated the space for work duties; at night they slept on its floor—a true luxury, they explained to their company, to retire in warm shelter after suffering through long durations of brutal cold. Disciplined, they rose before dawn, attended mass, and resumed their duties. Weeks later the collective agreed that Mother Amadeus had escaped the grips of death and was on the mend. Mary Fields knew that the superior should proceed with caution, given a weakened constitution and chronic stomach inflammation caused by previous lead poisoning. She also knew that the nun, piously driven, would not slow down. Having worked under Amadeus's tutelage in Toledo, Mary considered her own options: She could return to her work duties at Sacred Heart Convent and the affiliated parochial school, attending during off hours Toledo's cosmopolitan venues—musical and political events for which she had cultivated an enthusiasm. Or she could remain in the harsh but majestic hinterland with the doe-eyed assembly and a visionary leader who clearly could not accomplish all of the fundamental essentials alone—most important to Mary's mind, solutions for adequate food and shelter. She decided to stay on.[7]

Toledo nuns Mother Mary Stanislaus and Sister Saint Rose prepared to depart from the rustic facilities that would soon be designated as the Ursuline Motherhouse, the official headquarters and novitiate of the Ursuline order in Montana. Weathered by trailblazer experience, the sisters would, perhaps, as they headed home, entertain a new appreciation of their foundress, Saint Ursula, a princess who relinquished her title of royalty for vows of religious faith and embarked on a Holy Crusade guiding eleven women disciples across sixteenth-century Europe. Mary Stanislaus promised Mary Amadeus that she would dispatch whatever help she could, be it funding, postulants, or sisters recently professed, and granted Sister Mary of the Angels permission to remain with the frontier cloister.[8]

Mary Fields contributed physical strength and plantation expertise acquired from years working as a slave to complete the endeavors she had proposed. She staked a plot of land best suited for planting, then created and maintained a vegetable garden that fed the Ursulines and a growing population of Native American boarding students. Demonstrating skilled horsemanship, Mary routinely drove the mission horses and whatever vehicle was available—buckboard, buggy, or makeshift farm wagon—through terrain so rough it required an abundance of grit and knowledge to avoid or recover from any number of potential catastrophes known to have taken place on the thirty-four-mile trek from the mission to the nearest outpost and back. She hauled essential supplies: lumber, stone, hardware, tools, medicinals, dry goods, food, and the occasional passenger. Firearm proficiency, a useful advantage for freighters, has also been credited to Mary Fields's tally of skills, likely to have been further utilized hunting wild game to provide meat for her congregation. To those unfamiliar with the western wilderness, such excursions required stamina and courage.[9]

With Mother Amadeus's approval, Mary allocated enough of the precious locally planed lumber to construct her own vision: a hennery. By 1887, numbers of poultry exceeded four-hundred, the hens and ducks providing an alternate reliable source of meat and, equally important, eggs used for bread and other dietary staples needed by the Ursuline and Jesuit communities at Saint Peter's. In addition to freighting and managing the hennery, Mary contributed to Ursuline laundry duties, insisting on laundering Mother Amadeus's sacristy clothing (ornamental vestments worn in ceremony) herself. Until such time as the convent could afford hired hands, chores requiring manual labor such as tending livestock and repairing buildings were also passed on to Mary. Considering the Ursulines' significant reliance upon Mary Fields, it would be prudent to question whether the Birdtail Ursuline convent would have succeeded without her. It seems that no one else was available, willing, or able to contribute the substantial labor necessary to keep the cloister alive. Consequently, it is possible that the six Ursuline Montana missions established after the Saint Peter's Motherhouse may never have come to exist, if, indeed, Mary's labor had been the decisive factor. A nun's entry from the Saint Peter's Ursuline Annals stated, "She [Mary Fields] did everything that we couldn't."[10]

Each March at Saint Peter's Mission, the nuns organized what became an annual event to show their appreciation to Mary Fields. The Ursulines and all of their boarders, Indian and white, gathered to cheer "Happy Birthday, Mary," and present her with a cake and handmade gifts. One year, the mission girls began a new celebration, this time surprised by Mary Fields, who had organized an annual romp under the auspices of May Day. She led the young women on an excursion into meadows and hills where, after a picnic, participants spent the day gathering wildflowers that they bundled into May Day posies and distributed to Saint Peter's parishioners upon their return. Multiple records commend Mary's love for young people and her popularity with them. Perhaps she became a confidante-mother figure for the Native American girls, being the only woman on the compound who was neither white nor a nun and who was intimately familiar with the loss of personal freedom and her culture of origin.[11]

By July 1890, the number of Native American female boarders had grown to 113; the acreage needed for herb and vegetable gardens multiplied accordingly, as did Mary's frequent trips to town to obtain building materials used to construct larger schools and boarding facilities. These journeys were often perilous, and over the years Mary and her team of horses survived injuries from wolf attacks and wagon crashes and found themselves, more than once, alone in prairie darkness. They forged through squalls, subzero temperatures, and treacherous depths of ice and snow to get home, sometimes having spent the night staggering back and forth to keep from freezing to death. Still, Mary did not waiver in her dedication, which may have stemmed, at least in part, from the agreement made between herself and Mary Amadeus: she would remain with the Ursulines for the rest of her life. An integral member of the family, Mary had refused, more than once, to accept a salary for her work. Perhaps she saw no need, content that Saint Peter's would be her final home and resting place. Provided with room and board at the mission, Mary on occasion accepted freelance freight jobs that provided her with earnings and prevented further depletion of the nuns' limited resources.[12]

In the summer of 1894, nine years after Mary's arrival, the Right Reverend Bishop John Baptist Brondel, the first Catholic bishop of Montana, employed his position to circumvent Mother General Superior Amadeus's authority over her Montana Ursuline Motherhouse. Typically the bishop was not involved with Ursuline business unless requested by the foundress, who had by this time established eight missions in Montana and managed the operations with extraordinary efficiency. On July 26, Mother Amadeus and Mary Fields each received a letter from Reverend Bishop Brondel. Mother was instructed to dismiss Mary Fields immediately. In addition, Brondel decreed that Mary and the Ursulines were to sever all contact and that henceforth Fields was forbidden access to Saint Peter's Mission. He based his edict on allegations of Mary's unsavory hostility with no further explanation. Mary Fields's letter summoned her to the bishop's headquarters in Helena, a day's journey away. Ursuline annals reported, "Mary at first refused to go but was at length persuaded. Sister Philemona sat up all night to make her a dress." Mary left the following morning to confront the bishop, insistent that he prove his false claims. Ursuline annals report Mary's demand that he "bring witnesses to swear to what they [had] said against [her]." No testimony was supplied by the bishop and, unfortunately, no witnesses were privy to the conversation. Concurrent excerpts from the sisters' annals included "We should like to have an account of the interview between the Bishop and Black Mary" and "The community has determined to support her wherever she goes. It is hard for Mother to dismiss this faithful servant in her old age and one trembles to think of Mother's sorrow—and trouble in so doing, but the Bishop's orders are peremptory." Destitute, Mary left the haven she had helped to create.[13]

A woman experienced in both frontier and city living, Mary Fields had several options. As an American citizen, she had the right to homestead under the 1862 Homestead Act. Neighbors who lived between Cascade (the closest town) and Saint Peter's were homesteaders with whom she had had occasion to interact, gaining insight regarding the benefits and drawbacks of making a claim and "proving up." Plenty of land was available. Being a competent horsewoman, builder, and provider, she could homestead with relative ease. Or, she could relocate to a city where routine working hours would provide an easier lifestyle at the age of sixty-two. Great Falls, the Cascade County seat thirty miles away, offered a small yet thriving community of African Americans, if she desired the company of her race. Farther west, a large population of black citizens had gained notable political rights and opportunities in Seattle, an excellent choice if she desired the benefits of culture she had enjoyed previously.[14]

Well acquainted with Cascade and many of its residents after years working as a freighter, Mary knew that particular social and political elements within the fledgling town harbored racial hatreds that could strike like rattlers. She was also aware that ruffians of all persuasions periodically passed through or took refuge in outlying areas. Social dynamics became more complex as Southerners arrived via the Missouri River, which flanked the edge of town. Two years earlier, Fort Shaw, a military post, had been shut down and renovated into a new federal facility, a government-run "industrial" boarding school for Native American youth. Located twenty-two miles from Cascade, many citizens believed it was too close. The *Rising Sun* newspaper articulated an incident typical of those that confronted the region's frontier communities: "Execution of a Chicken Thief at Fort Shaw—No Trial or Hearing Whatever Allowed the Accused—Are Such Acts to be Allowed in a Civilized Country?" A lone black woman made an easy target. Mary's reputation as a sharpshooter would alleviate potential confrontation somewhat. She must have weighed the decision carefully before she moved into Cascade and became its one and only black resident. Eager to earn money, she worked as a laundress. Other than herself and the Chinese who ran the Hong Chong Steam Laundry, the Cascade population was entirely white. Though Mary maintained acquaintances made through freighting, it would take time to form friendships with locals. No doubt she missed the comradery she had shared with the sisters and the many children whose lives had become intertwined with hers. The rifle she had kept by her side as she drove the mission buckboard had been replaced by a .38 Smith & Wesson strapped in a holster beneath an apron tied taut around her gathered skirt.[15]

In the fall of 1894, Mary Fields rented a small plank house on the west side of Cascade, from which she operated a laundry. After receiving unexpected reparation from Mother Amadeus, she opened a café where she cooked, cleaned, and served the locals, including cowboys and sheepherders who often could not pay their bills. Because of this generosity, she was forced to close the establishment nine months later. Soon after, she discovered an opportunity advertised in the *Rising Sun*:

> Mail Routes. The advertisement of the post office department inviting proposals for carrying the mails from July 1, 1895 to June 30, 1899, is out. Proposals will be received up to 4 p.m. May 21st, and the decisions will be announced on or before. Following are routes for which contracts will be let, in which Sun River and northern Montana are interested.

> Cascade to Saint Peter's Mission, every day except Sunday,
> 17 miles.

> Fort Shaw, by Florence and Augusta, to Cecil, 43 miles,
> three times weekly.

> Sun River to Choteau, 30 miles, three times a week.[16]

These routes were classified by the U.S. Post Office Department as star routes; accordingly, drivers were official star route mail carriers. A star route mail carrier transported mail from one post office to another, in contrast to rural mail carriers who delivered mail on routes that began and ended at the same post office. Though mail carriers in the Birdtail region had always been men, no one could dispute Mary Fields's ability to maneuver any kind of load or her previous experience driving the Saint Peter's Mission Road for close to a decade. She got the job, and though she may not have known it she had become the first African American woman star route mail carrier in the United States.[17]

A 1959 *Ebony* article by Gary Cooper, as well as subsequent accounts, claimed, "Mother Amadeus went to the government . . . and asked that Mary be given the mail route." This is unlikely, because the Post Office Department did not hire or employ mail carriers for star routes; it awarded star route contracts to persons who proposed the lowest qualified bids, and who in accordance with the Department's application process posted bonds and sureties to substantiate their ability to finance the route. Once a contract was obtained, the contractor could then drive the route themselves, sublet the route, or hire an experienced driver. Some individuals obtained multiple star route contracts and conducted the operations as a business. Mother Amadeus would have had to invest considerable time to acquire and manage a mail route; she may have supplied the route's contract holder with a recommendation on Mary Fields's behalf. The Postal Service reports that the whereabouts of contract records from the Cascade-Mission star route have not, as of yet, been located. It is unknown whether Mary acted as a subcontractor or an employee. Claims that Mary Fields was "the first African American woman hired by the U.S. Postal Service," or "the second woman in United States history to be given a postal route," or "the second woman and the first black woman to have a mail route in America" can be laid to rest. The Postal Service has, after receiving documentation supplied by me in 2006, recognized Mary Fields as the first known African American woman star route mail carrier in the United States.[18]

Mary's wagon route across the Birdtail landscape was perpetually challenged by extreme weather fluctuations: dry summer heat that sucked and burned, cold that froze flesh to bone, and blizzards that blinded—elemental forces known to give and take indifferently. Good mail carriers recognized signs and sounds of the seasons; they could detect danger and determine the right moment for action or reaction. Mary worked to fine-tune her operation as she groomed her steadfast hay burners, conditioned harnesses, and serviced the singletree and its rig. In winter, when horse or wagon passage proved impossible, she threw the U.S. mail sack over her shoulder and huffed the thirty-four-mile roundtrip on snowshoes. When her first four-year contract expired she accepted another. Nothing deterred her sense of duty. Homesteaders relied on Mary for postal delivery and for news; not everyone had transportation or opportunity for a trip to town. From the time Mary had become a Cascade resident in 1894, and particularly during the years of her mail delivery route, she utilized an original and practical avenue for her protection: socializing in Cascade saloons. Jawing with the local men, then stepping back to play a game of patience such as solitaire, she could acquire information—learn who was planning what, get the low-down on newcomers to the area and assorted versions of the latest goings-on—details that could impact her safety on the road and in town.[19]

At the age of seventy-one, in June 1903, Mary's eight-year star route career came to an end. She hung up the harness and began full-time residency in Cascade, relying on her laundry business to pay her way. She scrubbed, starched, and ironed and in her free time gardened, producing prolific quantities of vegetables and flowers. Chronicles state that she placed bouquets upon the small Catholic altar at the end of town each week during the growing season. Her friend Mother Mary Amadeus had gone to California to rehabilitate from injuries sustained in a train wreck, and Mary saw little of her from that time forward. Since moving to town she had also routinely lavished attentions upon the local boys and girls, many of whom she babysat regularly. Parents had requested that Cascade School close its doors for a half-day every March 15 so that the Mary Fields birthday tradition, initiated by the Ursulines, could continue. It was not long before Cascade had claimed the celebration as its own annual event. Earl Monroe, one of her charges, recalled during an interview in his ninety-seventh year, "She was a second mother to all of the school kids. . . . I remember she would always have hard candies and fruit that she would give to us children." Earl could still remember the location, explaining, "When you walk in her house, there was an icebox on the left, just inside, and she would keep the fruit and candy up there. . . . I remember sitting on her lap. She used to hum songs, and sing songs to me with a deep voice."[20]

Although Mary Fields was appreciated for specific contributions to her community, there is no record of her involvement in social circles other than the limited rapport found at the saloons. Membership in auxiliaries, societies, or guilds, such as the "Ladies' Aid," was not available to her. The white community, aware of their racial advantage, determined to what degree the black "old-timer" would be included or shunned. Such decisions were heavily influenced by familial variables, denominational affiliations, pressure to conform or control, superstition, fear of ostracism, and the need to maintain one's place in a structured pecking order. Genuine friendship with Mary would have been fostered in the privacy of homes. In 1910, Mary's male friends invited her to become the "official mascot" for their newly formed baseball team, the Cascade Cubs. A high-profile venture, it is probable that she considered potential repercussions before giving her answer. Undercurrents of hostility toward her person had been on the rise, and certain individuals would regard her presence on the team as a blemish impeding the success of the burgeoning community they had primed for economic advancement. The request to serve as official mascot epitomized a complex relationship. Some early twentieth-century mascots were "recognized" persons thought to bring good luck; other mascots, specifically Indians and blacks, or those who were deformed or disabled, became popular good-luck charms often employed by baseball leagues. Southerners had begun a tradition of rubbing a black mascot's head for luck. Animals, jesters, and costumed mascots were not used to endorse teams or products until mid-twentieth century. Mary's legendary status was a viable commodity generated by the attached moniker, "Stagecoach Mary," that had originated as an over-exaggeration of mail carrier—the Negress crack shot freighter galloping and gallivanting across the Birdtail, rifle in hand—and alluded to a trivialized, reactive, and ludicrous characterization that minimized her actual achievements. For whites in Cascade, acquisition of Mary's status was a comfortable arrangement—a perfect modus to keep "their" black resident within the confines of a lower social standing while providing desired notoriety for the Cubs. Because either representation of mascot could be claimed to encourage Mary's commitment, and either result—respect or degradation—could be rendered by the public, acceptance of the venture as a talisman batboy was problematic. A long-time survivor and sports enthusiast, the centrifugal force of those rough-and-ready legends, she agreed to do it, aware of the risks involved.[21]

The Cubs required that she oil the bats, care for the equipment, and stand in the dugout and cheer the team on, aware that this might, at times, cause trouble for her. Aside from the good-luck personifications, acceptance of a mascot position based upon and valued due to the erroneous legend meant that Mary had effectively become an objectified icon. The community's intentional withholding of acceptance that had permeated the town for years would now grow stronger. Mary took the game seriously, patriotically attending each Cascade Cub practice and competitive game. Her post as the official mascot did provide an integral, albeit not equal, place on the baseball field. Leader of cheers and diligent bat holder, she designed a second means for the team to stand out—handmade boutonnieres pinned to each player's uniform proudly worn at every tournament—fashioned by her from flowers grown in her garden. She also presented flower arrangements to Cubs who hit homers and awarded a victory bouquet to the winning team. The odd comradery lasted several years, a mutually beneficial arrangement despite the inevitable social repercussions for Mary. She took care of the Cubs and the Cubs protected her, true to their promise to punch anyone who dared antagonize their mascot.[22]

Town fathers applied for and received incorporation approval from state offices, Montana having been admitted to the Union in 1889. As a result, Cascade was elevated from town to city status in January 1911 and, thus, gained the right to administer its first election. Caucus nominations for mayor and six aldermen representing the Citizens' Party were confirmed and placed on one bipartisan ticket. On February 14, fifty-two men cast their ballots. To no one's surprise, the Citizens' candidates celebrated a landslide victory. The city's first mayor, Harvey D. Hall, wasted no time; he directed his council to predicate statutes that would regulate commerce and prescribe the moral character of their city. Among ordinances passed was one indited with specific categorical intent, purported to say "No member of the female sex has the right to smoke or drink liquor in a public place. No woman of any race will be allowed to enter any drinking establishment in Cascade for any purpose, from this time forward." This was one of two ordinances that were *not* published in the *Cascade Courier*. Complete texts of thirteen other statutes that were quickly drafted, approved, and ordained into law by the council between February 24 and May 5 were published in the *Courier*. Accounts from locals claim that, though the unpublished saloon ordinance applied to all females, it had been legislated solely to eliminate Mary Fields's access to the saloons. Ordinance number eight prohibited concealed weapons, including "knives, daggers, razors, dirks and slingshots" within city limits, except for authorized individuals. Though the statute proffered safer city streets, it also deprived Mary of her handgun.[23]

Ladies of the night who had previously relied on the saloons could steer clientele elsewhere with relative ease. Mary Fields's options were limited, and she was essentially forced into isolation. Her access to social exchange in group settings had been exclusive to the Cascade saloons; her fact-finding quests had been effectively terminated. It must have been grievous for Mary Fields, realizing that opportunity for human contact and companionship had been reduced to minimal levels—social discourse to be obtained during brief interactions with merchants and opportunities while babysitting. Weather permitting in summer months, she could join a conversation outdoors, though much of the population would be preoccupied with agricultural work. Mary would probably have agreed with sentiments voiced by Helena resident J. B. Bass, African American editor and publisher of the *Montana Plaindealer*, who had been denied a caucus nomination previously promised to secure his candidacy to run for the Montana House of Representatives. Bass's front-page exposé editorialized: "The Colored voters of Montana received a solar plexis [*sic*] blow from the Grand Old Party . . . to displace a colored man who won out on his merits, and was defeated by trickery—a slap at the race. . . . We are not surprised at anything that would happen in this country which is boss ridden."[24]

Mary persevered through yet another year governed by Mayor H. D. Hall that concluded, for her, with grounds to celebrate. Democratic candidates who had launched an enthusiastic campaign against the incumbent Citizens' won the second Cascade city election on April 7, 1913, claiming a two-to-one ballot count victory. Mary had reason to whoop encores of cheer, for the new mayor elect, David W. Monroe (D.W.), along with his wife Hattie and their three boys, had become Mary's closest Cascade friends. Resolutions proclaimed by the Democrats included, " We believe in equal rights, and justice to all," and they demonstrated their sincerity by amending the discriminatory ordinance that had caused such angst, composing an addendum to state that one woman, and one woman only, Mary Fields, was from that day forward allowed access to all Cascade saloons. At some point in 1913, D. W. Monroe purchased the Silver Dollar Saloon. It became a safe haven where Mary Fields could relax unchallenged. Free to patronize establishments of choice, she exercised a rekindled freedom until eighteen months later when she fell ill in mid-November 1914. The diagnosis was twofold: dropsy—swelling caused by an accumulation of fluids, a condition known to accompany heart failure, kidney failure, or diabetes; and asthma—bronchial distress more likely to have been pneumonia, since winter temperatures had eliminated most airborne allergens. Earl Monroe recalled, "When Nigger Mary got sick at the end of her life, we kids found her and my mother and father took her in the train to Great Falls, to the hospital." Journals report that Mary did not want to leave her home.[25]

Mary Fields died in Columbus Hospital days later at 6:00 p.m., December 5, 1914. Cascade had no funeral parlor or Catholic church, so arrangements were made for her funeral to take place in the newly constructed Pastime Theater. A Jesuit father from Saint Peter's Mission officiated the services on December 8. Floral arrangements were in abundance. A renowned soprano sang several hymns. The *Cascade Echo* reported, "Many were the friends and neighbors who gathered to pay homage to her [Mary] who was one of the most loyal citizens." Six prominent Cascade businessmen, including Mayor Monroe and R. B. Glover (the Cubs manager), served as pallbearers. Mary Fields was buried at Hillside Cemetery just outside Cascade on Saint Peter's Mission Road. A small tin cross, unmarked, headed her grave. It was *not* inscribed "Mary Fields 1832–1914," the epitaph engraved on a rugged granite boulder that would replace the cross years later—a heartfelt tribute from Earl Monroe.[26]

Social etiquette required attendance at Mary's funeral. Many of those present embraced loving memories of Mary Fields and felt sorrow at her passing; others did not. Obituaries from Cascade's two newspapers reported activities from Mary's life history and attested to her love for children—the gifting of candies and stories and picnics. The *Cascade Echo* closed by stating, "[Mary] succumbed to the Inveitable [*sic*] and answered the call of *her* God." Inference of a separate God is indicated by departure from time-period memorial prose such as "*Our* Divine Creator of the universe has seen fit to remove from the sphere of his earthly labors *our well-beloved*." What the newspaper narratives lacked was testimony to Mary's character—her humor, generosity, and zest for life. During a twenty-nine-year span of active enterprise and cooperative ventures in the Birdtail, there was no mention of Mary in any newspaper until 1910, when an anecdotal birthday tribute surfaced. "Mary Fields, Well Known Old Timer Who Is Known All over the State," recounted a pre-Montana legendary story citing Mary's presence on the Mississippi River steamboat *Robert E. Lee* the day it triumphed in a famous race against the *Natchez*. The reporter quoted Mary recalling, "It was so hot. . . . It was expected that the boilers would burst," and finalized the brief article with a commendation of Mary's past and present ability "to do much hard labor." It appears as though the purpose of the article was, at least in part, to promote Cascade under the guise of Mary Fields legends rather than to acknowledge Mary's contributory achievements as a member of the community.[27]

Events that *did* involve Mary directly were not chronicled. When her house, located just blocks from the *Cascade Courier* office, burned down during Mayor Hall's term of office, it apparently did not meet editor "Scoop" Tierney's criteria for publication. Other significant news remained unreported: Mary Fields's 1910–14 position as official mascot with the Cascade Cubs, the City of Cascade's controversial 1911 segregation ordinance, and the second City Council's 1913 ordinance amendment. Though in-depth coverage of baseball games reliably filled the *Courier* front page year after year, the chronicles failed to mention boutonnieres, bouquets, or Mary Fields, though play-by-play details extolling the hits, runs, steals, pitches, and tags made by each Cub player were colorfully recounted. These omissions of Mary Fields's presence indicate intention to ignore, or eliminate evidence of, her existence. Unspoken agreements that wove the dynamics of Cascade's cooperative racial web had, primarily, been shaped by Mary and the town's white male hierarchy. They had allowed her entry into their private social arenas; she allowed them to treat her as a privileged side-kick who accepted, or appeared to accept, the quantified limits. She divined the delicate balance needed to remain in their favor, constantly adjusting to fluctuating attitudes and changes in power. In earlier years, she had befriended the nuns, postal patrons, and customers from her café; as a Cascade resident, she continued to ingratiate herself by providing fundamental labor for services desired by the community at large: laundry and child care. These contributions also happened to fit within prescribed parameters of racial-gender imposed boundaries. She did so on terms that met her criteria as an entrepreneur—not as an employee.[28]

After Mary Fields's death, the *Cascade Courier* stated, "A large attendance of friends and acquaintances . . . left nothing undone to make the services complete in every respect for one of the oldest land-marks in Cascade." The funeral for the "land-mark" (a renowned object) may have manifested for some an inverse need to disclaim their racism by overcompensating with bountiful memorial offerings. It would be the children Mary had cared for who, as the last living residents of the time period, would provide credible stories about their babysitter and second mother. They imparted vivid personal remembrances in contrast to what became, as time passed, a communal preamble chorused to explain: "Mary Fields was six feet tall," and "she [weighed] over two hundred pounds," and "her face was as black as burnt over prairie." A "crack shot with rifle and revolver," she "drove the stagecoach" and was reputed "to be a match for any *two* men in the Montana Territory." "She was our mascot." This final ditty deserves thoughtful reconsideration.[29]

Mary Fields's road to freedom began on a Tennessee plantation where she was born in the spring of 1832. She had already lived a lifetime as a slave prior to emancipation. Her pivotal decision to stay in Montana sparked a new begin-ning. Perhaps the broad expanse of open prairie spirited her will and determi-nation as she devised liberated milestones along the way.[30]

Notes

1. Letter from P. F. Quigley (pastor of Saint Francis de Sales Church, Toledo, Ohio) sent from Saint Mary's Seminary, Cleveland, Ohio, to Reverend Mother Sacred Heart in Miles City, Montana, March 21, 1885, Ursuline Centre Archives, Great Falls, Montana; Lelia Mahoney, ed., *A Tree in the Valley: The Highlights of the Annals, 1884–1979* (Toledo, Ohio: Kalmbacher Bookbinding, c. 1980), 47; Irene Mahoney, *Lady Blackrobes: Missionaries in the Heart of Indian Country* (Golden, Colo.: Fulcrum, 2006), 54.

2. Mother Angela Lincoln, ed., *Life of the Reverend Mother Amadeus of the Heart of Jesus, Foundress of the Ursuline Missions of Montana and Alaska* (New York: Paulist Press, 1923), 61–64, 29, 35, 37, 42; Suzanne H. Schrems, *Uncommon Women Unmarked Trails: The Courageous Journey of Catholic Missionary Sisters in Frontier Montana* (Norman, Okla.: Horse Creek, 2012), 58; letter from Joseph Bandini to Mother Amadeus, June 1884, Jesuit Oregon Province Archives, Gonzaga University, Spokane, Washington; Sister Genevieve McBride, *The Bird Tail* (New York: Vantage Press, 1992), 25–37; "Explore the Homesteading Timeline," U.S. Department of Interior, Bureau of Land Management, "Northern Cheyenne Reservation Timeline," Northern Cheyenne Tribe, Indian Education Montana Office of Public Instruction (March 2010); Northern Cheyenne Tribe, ed., "The Northern Cheyenne Tribe and Its Reservation," *A Report to the U.S. Bureau of Land Management and the State of Montana Department of Natural Resources and Conservation* (April 2002), chap. 2, 14–17; Christina Gish Berndt, "Kinship as Strategic Political Action: The Northern Cheyenne Response to the Imposition of the Nation-State," (Ph.D. dissertation, University of Minnesota, 2008), 149–54.

3. Interview, Sister Kathleen Padden, Archivist, Ursuline Convent of the Sacred Heart, Toledo, Ohio, with author, September 18, 2014; Mahoney, *Tree in the Valley,* 47; Mahoney, *Lady Blackrobes,* 52; Lincoln, *Life of the Reverend Mother Amadeus,* 92, 98; L. B. Palladino, *Indian and White in the Northwest* (Lancaster, Pa.: Wickersham, 1922), 184, 188; McBride, *Bird Tail,* 68–69.

4. E. W. J. Lindesmith, Chaplain, U.S. Army, "Father Lindesmith's Diary of 1887" August 15, 1887, entry, "History of Mission," Ursuline Centre Archives. Sister Genevieve McBride, "Mary Fields," in *Mountains and Meadows: A Pioneer History of Montana Cascade, Chestnut Valley, Hardy, St. Peter's Mission, and Castner Falls 1805–1925,* ed. Jean Conrad Rowe (Great Falls, Mont.: Blue Print and Letter, 1970), 62, contradicts the Lindesmith account, citing accommodations as adjoined cabins built by Jesuits in 1860s, with chapel attached. Letter from Mother Amadeus, St. Peter's Mission, to Mother Stanislaus, Convent of the Sacred Heart, Toledo, December 19, 1884, Toledo Convent Archives. Wrote Lindesmith, "Father Lindesmith's Diary of 1887," "Even at this late date let me tell you one instance of hardship of the nuns at Saint Peters viz ever since they came here and now yet they sleep every night on the bare floor wrapped up in a blanket." Father Lindesmith called them "Pioneer Nuns"

in the same diary; Lincoln, ed., *Life of the Reverend Mother Amadeus*, 94.

5. Mahoney, *Lady Blackrobes*, 75; letter from Mother Amadeus, St. Peter's Mission, to Mother Stanislaus, Convent of the Sacred Heart, Toledo, December 19, 1884.

6. Lindesmith, "History of the Mission"; McBride, "Mary Fields," 63. On the white school, see McBride, *Bird Tail*, 71; Saint Peter's Ursuline Annals, Ursuline Centre Archives.

7. Letters from Mother Amadeus dated March 29, April 2, and April 20, 1885, to Mother Stanislaus, Toledo, copies in author's possession; Lincoln, *Life of the Reverend Mother Amadeus*, 44–45; Fields's employment records 1884–1885, Sacred Heart Convent Archives; Mahoney, *Tree in the Valley*, 47.

8. Mahoney, *Lady Blackrobes*, 54–55.

9. Lindesmith, "History of the Mission"; "'Nigger Mary' Fields, Early Day Resident of Cascade, One of State's Noted Characters," *Great Falls Tribune*, May 22, 1939, 10; Saint Peter's Ursuline Annals, Ursuline Centre Archives.

10. Lindesmith, "History of the Mission"; Saint Peter's Ursuline Annals, July 27, 1894, Ursuline Centre Archives; M. McBride, "'Black Mary' Labored Long at Old St. Peter's Mission," Montana Newspaper Association, August 7, 1939; Mahoney, *Tree in the Valley*, 45.

11. "Death of Mary Fields," *Cascade Echo* 3, no. 5 (December 13, 1914), front page.

12. Saint Peter's Annals, Ursuline Centre Archives, November 21, 1893, April 26, 1894, July 27, 1894, October 11, 1898; McBride, *Bird Tail*, 111, 152, 173; "Heroic Woman of Montana Protected Catholic School and Carried U.S. Mail," *Negro Digest*, August 1950, 86.

13. Mahoney, *Tree in the Valley*, 45; St. Peter's Ursuline Annals, Ursuline Centre Archives, state that Fields and a hired hand "touched rifles" during an argument, and nothing became of the altercation. According to McBride, *Bird Tail*, 173, the annals report that trouble arose between Fields and a ranch foreman, Mr. Burns, after a horse broke loose from its harness while transporting Saint Peter's personnel. McBride recounts that Fields and Burns argued over a new and old harness and that Burns made a "grimace" at Mary, who threw a stone, hitting him—the quarrel ended when Father Andreis told Burns to go back to work.

14. Homestead Act of 1862, 37th Congress, Session II, 1862, approved May 20, 1862; Barbara Carol Behan, "African Americans in the Montana Territory 1864–1889," *Journal of African American History* 91 (Winter 2006): 33–34; Quintard Taylor, "The Emergence of Black Communities in the Pacific Northwest: 1865–1910," *Journal of Negro History* 64, no. 4 (Autumn 1979): 342–54.

15. John T. Greer, "A Brief History of Indian Education at the Fort Shaw Industrial School" (Master's thesis, Montana State College, 1958), 39–40; Superintendent Fred Campbell in *Native American* 22, no. 21 (1921): 252; Sun River Historical Society, *Pictorial History of the Sun River Valley* (Shelby, Mont.: Promoter Publications,

February, 1989), 158; *Rising Sun*, June 12, 1889; Rowe, *Mountains and Meadows*, 41; anon., "Mary Fields," typewritten account, Montana Historical Society Archives.

16. From *Cascade County Gazetteer* 1896–1897 (business directory): "Fields Mary, laundry," 210; Rowe, *Mountains and Meadows*, 41; McBride, "Mary Fields," 158; *Rising Sun*, 1895.

17. Marshall Henry Cushing, *The Story of Our Post Office, the Greatest Government Department in All Its Phases* (Boston Mass.: A. M. Thayer, 1893), 23.

18. Gary Cooper, as told to Marc Crawford, "Stage Coach Mary, Gun-Toting Montanan Delivered U.S. Mail," *Ebony*, October 1959, 97; McBride, "Mary Fields," 158; Cushing, *Story of Our Post Office*, 25–28. For "the first African American woman hired by the U.S. Postal Service," see "'Stagecoach' Mary Fields (1832–1914)," *Chicago Tribune*, Section 8, March 3, 2004; for "the second woman in United States history to be given a postal route," see Sanjay Talwani, "Frontierswoman and Former Slave Was a Mission Character," *Great Falls Tribune*, Parade section, January 30, 2000; for "the second woman and the first black woman to have a mail route in America," see Eunice Boeve, "Past Times, Mary Fields: The Tough, Tender Legend of Cascade," *Montana Magazine*, January/February 2001, 70–74. USPS archive historian Jennifer Lynch established Mary Fields's standing as the "first known African American woman United States star route mail carrier" in 2006.

19. Card games for one player were called games of patience.

20. *Cascade County Directory 1903*, "Fields Miss Mary, exp." (Expressman), 381; *Cascade County Directory 1906*, "Fields Mary, laundry," 380; *Cascade County Directory 1908–1909*, "Fields Mary, laundry," 383; Interview, Earl Monroe, nonagenarian born in 1909, last living resident acquainted with Mary Fields and son of Cascade's second mayor, D. W. Monroe, May 13, 2006, transcript in author's possession; "'Nigger Mary' Fields, Early Day Resident of Cascade, One of State's Noted Characters," *Great Falls Tribune*, May 22, 1939, 10; E. R. Jones (Birdtail native), "The Cowboy's Corner, 'Mary Fields,'" *Cascade Courier*, July 6, 1944, reported, "She always cared for the altar in the Wedsworth Hall."

21. Rowe, *Mountains and Meadows*, 49; Jones, "Cowboy's Corner, 'Mary Fields,'" includes photograph, "The Old Cascade Ball Club That Made Real History"; Frank Fitzpatrick, "The Disturbing History of Baseball's Mascots," *Inquirer*, June 23, 2014; Cooper, as told to Crawford, "Stage Coach Mary, Gun-Toting Montanan Delivered U.S. Mail," *Ebony*, October 1959, 97–100; Jennifer Dwyer, "The Legend of Stagecoach Mary," *Toledo Blade*, June 7, 1981, 16; "Mary Field, Well Known Old Timer Who Is Known All over the State," *Cascade Courier*, March 18, 1910; Mahoney, *Tree in the Valley*, 48; "Cubs" photograph, circa 1910, in "'Nigger Mary' Fields, Early Day Resident of Cascade, One of State's Noted Characters," *Great Falls Tribune*, May 22, 1939, 10.

22. Don Miller, "Mary Fields, Freight Hauler and Stage Driver," *True West*, August, 1982, 55; Mahoney, *Tree in the Valley*, 48; "'Nigger Mary' Fields, Early Day Resident

of Cascade, One of State's Noted Characters," *Great Falls Tribune*, May 22, 1939, 10.

23. *Cascade Courier*, January 27 and February 19, 1911. The whereabouts of original or copies of the segregation ordinance are unknown. Multiple sources state similar recollections of the ordinance text: Jones, "Cowboy's Corner, 'Mary Fields,'" states, "When Cascade became incorporated and Harvey Hall was voted its first mayor, he placed a ban on Mary entering a saloon"; Rowe, *Mountains and Meadows*, 158, states, "It almost broke her [Mary Fields's] heart when a ruling was passed that women would not be allowed in the saloons"; *Cascade Courier*, May 5, 1911.

24. "Repudiated! Republicans Deny Their Loyal Ally the Colored Voter Any Recognition Whatever in the Distribution of Patronage. The Colored Voters of the State Are Righteously Indignant at This Unfair Deal," *(Helena) Montana Plaindealer*, January 11, 1907, front page.

25. *Cascade Courier*, February 7 and March 28, 1913, April 11, 1914; Rowe, *Mountains and Meadows*, 43; "Death of Mary Fields," *Cascade Echo* 3, no. 5 (December 13, 1914), front page; "Old Timer Passes Away," *Cascade Courier*, no. 47 (December 11, 1914), front page; Monroe interview, May 13, 2006.

26. "Old Timer Passes Away," *Cascade Courier*, no. 47 (December 11, 1914), front page; "Death of Mary Fields," *Cascade Echo* 3, no. 5 (December 13, 1914), front page; Monroe interview, May 13, 2006.

27. "Old Timer Passes Away," *Cascade Courier*, no. 47 (December 11, 1914), front page; "Death of Mary Fields," *Cascade Echo* 3, no. 5 (December 13, 1914), front page; "Mary Field, Well Known Old Timer Who Is Known All over the State," *Cascade Courier*, March 18, 1910.

28. *Cascade Courier*, June 23, 1911, April 26, 1912, May 30 and September 19, 1913, May 1 and May 22, 1914.

29. "Old Timer Passes Away," *Cascade Courier*, no. 47 (December 11, 1914), front page; "Death of Mary Fields," *Cascade Echo* 3, no. 5 (December 13, 1914), front page; Monroe interview, May 13, 2006; for "Mary Fields was six feet tall," see Mahoney, *Tree in the Valley*, 47; William Loren Katz, *The Black West*, rev. ed. (Harlem Moon, Broadway Books, 1971), and most magazine articles written about Mary Fields. For "she [weighed] over two hundred pounds," see Charles W. Hutton, "Tales of School on the Prairie in Days When Montana Was Young," *Great Falls Tribune*, November 29, 1936. Hutton, former Cascade school teacher, recounts pupil Allie Whitcomb's essay from 1880, "Nigger Mary." Whitcomb wrote, "Her face is as black as burnt over prairie." See also McBride, "Mary Fields," 158; George Everett, "Ex-slave Mary Fields Felt at Home in Montana, whether Working in a Convent or Managing a Mail Route," *Wild West Magazine*, February 1996, 32; Miller, "Mary Fields, Freight Hauler and Stage Driver," 54; Jones, "Cowboy's Corner, 'Mary Fields.'"

30. 1910 Federal Census, Montana, Cascade County; Montana, Cascade County Records, 1888–1945, Census records and Vital Statistics.

II

"No Less a Man"

Blacks in Cow Town Dodge City, 1876–1886

C. ROBERT HAYWOOD

During the days of escorting cattle from Texas to the north, black cowboys as well as black settlers arrived at cattle trading centers, including Dodge City, Kansas. As C. Robert Haywood reports here, black cowboys just off the range found life in Dodge City to be as entertaining and exciting as did white cowhands, but not always in the same location. At the same time they expected and received better treatment than black residents of Dodge City. Even though they were used to some discrimination on the job, particularly with extra shifts and harsher work, they were respected for their ability and knowledge. Haywood discovered that well-known blacks visited, and even stayed for a time, in Dodge City; that list includes Nat Love, Ben Hodges, and Jim Kelly. As Haywood notes, "In the most important occupation, cattle herding, blacks and whites shared the same food, the same living accommodations, and the same pay."

In an age when blacks were stereotyped as either foolish or primitive and where their opportunities to advance, either socially or economically, were limited, ranch-related jobs offered more dignity and more opportunity for self-expression than any other employment available. Whites in the ranching business realized the importance of the contributions of all cowboys—black, white, or Mexican—and adjusted their prejudices accordingly. While on the trail north with the year's profit in their care, the success of the venture depended on each man performing his assigned duties. The mutual interdependence left little room for arrogant displays of racial superiority or overt discrimination,

Originally published as C. Robert Haywood, "'No Less a Man': Blacks in Cow Town Dodge City, 1876–1886," *Western Historical Quarterly* 19, no. 2 (May 1988): 161–82. Reprinted with permission of the Western History Association and the author.

no matter how ingrained. Nor was there room for feelings of oppression or resentment. The intimacy of the job, the living conditions (where men slept or where they ate), and the long hours spent in each other's company precluded the presence of the usual white-black attitudes. Once the herd reached the final destination, the weeks of shared toil, dangers, and good times could not be easily ignored by those who had made the journey.[1]

But what of the cattle towns, their ultimate destination? Did the leveling experience of the trail drive continue to alter significantly race relations in the end-of-trail towns? However comforting an unconditional affirmative answer would be, reality forces a more cautious assessment. Economic self-interest and black and white cowboy expectations did moderate town residents' action, and perhaps to a lesser degree racial attitudes toward the black trail-crew members. Permanent black residents and the temporary camp followers shared some of this goodwill and felt less discrimination than they would have in other parts of the United States. However, the white business, professional, and laboring people of the community were themselves only recent arrivals who brought with them the intellectual baggage and social convictions of mainstream America. Bigotry did not end overnight. Prejudices were muted but not abandoned. The result was an ambivalence of feelings and action marked by selective segregation and a mixture of racial intolerance and personal acceptance. The economic importance of blacks in the towns was not questioned; their "place" in the rest of the life of the community remained undefined and largely dependent on each person's reaction to specific situations. Once the economic impact of the trail herds was removed, these ambivalences were replaced by the standards and attitudes prevalent in the rest of the United States.

Each of the cattle towns was unique, but a review of Dodge City—one of the most publicized, if not the most familiar, of these towns—can serve as a case study and perhaps a model for other western frontier settlements. Dodge City became a cattle town after the Atchison, Topeka, and Santa Fe Railroad Company built a small stockyard there in the winter of 1875–1876. For the next decade, cattle were a major concern of the city's citizens who catered to the summer trade of cowboys, ranch owners, and cattle buyers. The life this preoccupation spawned ended in 1886, when Kansas ceased to be a major shipping point for Texas herds.

Although original sources dealing with blacks during this period are scarce, and secondary references all but nonexistent, there is enough material, especially in the newspapers—which were a kind of social barometer of community convictions—to reveal much about the role blacks played and the interaction that took place between the races. The handiest source of information on any group in nineteenth-century Dodge City is the census reports. This is as true for blacks as any other category of residents. Easy access, however, does not necessarily mean great accuracy of detail.[2] The alternative contemporary narrative accounts and extant remembrances were written by whites who tended to ignore blacks. If somewhat flawed, the census docs offer a needed, less-biased overview.

As would be expected, the 1880 census reveals that the percentage of blacks in western Kansas was lower than in the more settled sections. Blacks represented 4.3 percent of the total Kansas population in 1880, while the forty-two individuals recorded by the enumerator as either "Negro" or "Mulatto" represented only 3.3 percent of Dodge City's population.[3] There were seven discernible family households. In four of these, the wives did not work outside the home and two of the six children listed were in school. Only one adult woman, not counting the homemakers, was not employed. With but one exception, all of the seventeen males and fourteen females who were gainfully employed worked in the most poorly paid service occupations. The cold statistics indicate little upward mobility. The highest position any achieved was that of cook. Apparently, the pay was sufficient to maintain a family, since three of the five male cooks were the sole support of their families; one other male cook was single, and a single woman, Elizabeth Harris, cooked at one of the hotels. Hotels, in fact, used the services of black men more than any other business. Nine found work there as porters, cooks, dishwashers, or waiters. Five other males listed themselves as laborers, and two had some job involved with driving horses; one of these may have been a cowboy.

Servants, black and white, represented 11.4 percent of the total work force and could always find a position on Front Street or in the homes of the more prosperous businessmen. In one line of personal service, laundry, blacks had a near monopoly and at one point exercised a bit of economic exclusiveness of their own by complaining of "Chinese . . . wash Tub artists" threatening to take over.[4]

Since domestic servants earned less than $3.00 per week and laborers about $1.25 per day, life for most blacks was at the subsistence level. Unemployment, however, was rare. Twelve of the women were servants, a job much in demand, as reflected in the advertisements in the newspapers specifically requesting black female servants. As one citizen of Dodge told prospective black immigrants: "Many thousands of industrious men and women . . . could find employment at fair wages [in Kansas]. The labor of competent unmarried female house servants is especially in demand at high wages."[5]

The demand for labor remained high until the late 1880s; the black population responded to the new job openings, resulting in a steady increase in population of about 6 percent per year, roughly the same rate as the increase of permanent white residents. By the time the Kansas census of 1885 was taken, the census enumerator's count increased to sixty-eight. This census was less carefully taken and is less informative than the decennial count. But with all the census's shortcomings, it revealed a number of insights into the lives of the black residents.

The available jobs in 1885 remain roughly the same as in 1880—thirteen men were listed as laborers, two as cooks, and four as porters. For the men, there was more variety in the job market than there was for women; listings included a stone mason, a merchant, a farmer, a cowboy, and a telegraph messenger. Dodge was enjoying a building boom in 1885, which accounts for the increased number of laborers and the stone mason. No occupation for the women was included in this census, but it does not stretch historical construction too far to suggest that the six unrelated, single women between the ages of twenty-one and thirty-one who lived in one abode with an unmarried male would have been listed under the occupation of "sporting" by the earlier, franker enumerator.[6]

Surprisingly, only two names were listed in both censuses. Clearly, young, single blacks (twenty individuals in 1880 over the age of nineteen were listed as single), like their white counterparts in the same age bracket, considered Dodge only a temporary haven. If freedom of movement is interpreted to mean the right to "move on," blacks clearly felt no restraint. As was true of the western frontier generally, young people were on the move, seeking ever greater opportunities.[7]

The number of family units was growing (eleven in 1885 compared to seven in the five previous years), but even these were permanent residents only in a restricted sense. For blacks, life in Dodge was undoubtedly better than it had been in their past experience. Even with the handicap of minority status, there were enough individuals of assorted ages to give some feeling of community. Housing, always in short supply in cow town Dodge, was not a serious problem for the single servants and laborers who "lived-in." Houses available for families were small and inadequate, but they were gradually improved after 1885 when blacks began buying lots close together in Shinn's Addition south of the Arkansas River, a move which enhanced the cohesiveness of the community.[8] But even before that, the sense of a community did exist.

Black residents tended to take care of their own—a trait admired and respected by the whites: "A colored woman recently from Leavenworth died last Wednesday. She was a poor woman, but was decently buried by the colored people here."[9] This is in contrast to the fate of William Davis, a well-known barber on Front Street. Davis became ill while on an east-bound train, got off at Spearville, and staggered into G. A. W. Boedecker's hotel where he died during the night. He was diagnosed first as suffering from "bad whiskey and exposure," but since the townspeople did not know him they came to fear the worst when a rumor began to circulate that he died of smallpox. This story caused great consternation, and Boedecker, with an unwanted, possibly contagious corpse on his hands, sought advice from the county attorney, James T. Whitelaw, as to his responsibilities and what he should do. Whitelaw recommended a quick burial. But by the time the hotel keeper decided to act, a group of white towns- men had panicked and assumed the undertaker's chores. They moved the body to an isolated barn a mile from town. Over the protests of many townspeople, Boedecker recovered the body and buried it in the Spearville cemetery. The *Dodge City Globe* praised him for his humane action in taking in the sick man, "even if he was a colored man," and condemned the Spearville citizens "who do not think one man's carcass is as good as another."[10]

As was true of the white community in Dodge, the blacks separated them- selves into a Front Street crowd and a respectable class. The "better" element held religious services in homes and occasionally supported revival meetings "across the dead line." The Union Church which catered to any and all congre- gations, and for that matter, any itinerant evangelist, also served the blacks.[11]

Dancing was one activity all blacks shared, and as was true of the white community some of the balls were quite elaborate. The *Globe*, January 22, 1878, covered one such affair, "The Colored Masquerade," with a reference to "soul" music that has a contemporary ring to it:

> The colored people of Dodge City had a masque ball last Wednesday evening at the house of Nancy Jones, they done the thing up in good style and like any undertakings in Dodge City, it was a success. Goddess

of Liberty, schoolgirl, cowboy, ballet girl, Sioux squaw, red and white Turks, school mistress, women in white—were among the many characters represented. Big Eph was there and got the bound for using language unbecoming to a gentleman, and being a nuisance generally.

Some "white trash" were there as spectators. The music was furnished by Huston Ross' string band, the "Arkansas Traveller," and "Bonnie Blue Flag" had "the soul of music shed" into them in a style never before equalled.

Occasionally, high spirits got the best of the participants. The *Times* noted that the ball given by Mrs. Sallie Doke on Washington Street was "festive and greatly inclined to hilarity . . . except [for] a mild unpleasantness between two of the gentlemen, everything passed off in grand style." The "unpleasantness" was not always caused by the blacks; the *Globe* described another such "pleasant affair . . . undisturbed by bad white boys who heretofore have been in the habit of distrursing [*sic*] cayenne pepper on such occasions."[12]

Unpleasantness within and without the community occasionally led to violence. One such affair grew out of a dispute between two neighbors. John Alexander, a messenger at the telegraph office, and his wife had a quarrel. Mrs. Alexander sought shelter with the Boltens, another black couple. Alexander saw Bolten walking near the telegraph office, words were exchanged, and Alexander shot Bolten three times, seriously wounding him. Bolten returned the fire, slightly wounding Alexander, who tried to run away but was caught, arrested, and put in jail. About six weeks later, Alexander and eight other men escaped jail and fled the county. Bolten eventually recovered.[13]

There were other brushes with the law, but the record of blacks in Dodge is fairly clean. Billy Davis, before his death in Spearville, along with "Handsome Ike," engaged in the same kind of rowdy activities as the "festive cowboy" and other whites in the Front Street sporting crowd. Their names appear in the papers frequently, but they seem to have escaped arrest, or at least jail.[14] If the case involved bona fide crimes, blacks were treated as other criminals, certainly no more severely. An anonymous "colored man" was fined $25.00 and costs for carrying a concealed weapon; and Buck Green, a black convicted of horse stealing, was sentenced to two years and six months in prison. Both were typical sentences for such violations.[15] At least one black man was confident enough in the fairness of the court system to refuse the opportunity to escape jail and to elect to stand trial.

The courts, if not totally color blind, were willing at least to treat each accused person as an individual and citizen. Community reaction was not as consistent and impartial. Nicholas "Nick" Klaine of the *Times*, in reporting the Bolten-Alexander affair, apparently after little or no investigation used the typical, stereotyped explanation of black troubles arising from "marital infidelity." "The shooting scrape," he wrote, "occasioned no excitement."[16] The other two papers found Bolten to be a hard-working, sober person and both continued sympathetic coverage. Klaine's automatic reaction and the cayenne pepper incident indicate considerable racism. However, once the respectability of an individual was demonstrated, a black generally was treated as a person and not merely as a member of a race.

The few people who lived on isolated ranches and farms in the rural areas around Dodge were part of the larger black community. They came as independent homesteaders or ranchers and frequented Dodge City because it was the major trade center for southwestern Kansas. Willis Peoples was one such rancher who became something of a local folk hero when he destroyed a cunning wolf, "Old Two Toes," the leader of a marauding pack preying on Ford and Meade County stock.[17]

The number of black farmers in the area increased considerably when, as a kind of Turnerian safety valve for relieving social and economic oppression of the ex-slave, colonization projects in the West were begun in the 1870s. The town boosters' desire to attract people to their community sometimes led to a temporary tolerance of these minority settlements. Dodge City shared little of such false liberality.[18] When the blacks arrived in neighboring Hodgeman County, Dodge kept a nervous eye on the development and gave no encouragement to other black colonies to settle in Ford County.

A number of the Hodgeman colonists eventually moved to Dodge. Lillard Sanders operated a large hog farm two miles north of town. He had been born a slave, had run away during the Civil War, and eventually had joined the Union Army. In Dodge, he became a well-known figure, marching in every patriotic parade in his old uniform, proudly displaying his decorations and medals, and frequently holding forth on a street corner as a fire-and-brimstone preacher.[19] Auntie Standsfield, who first settled in Hodgeman County, was even more widely known than Sanders. Her daughter-in-law, Maggie, was to be one of the first to find employment in Dodge as a domestic servant. Eventually her mother joined her in a small house in town. As a staunch Baptist, Auntie Standsfield was not only a faithful, confessing Christian, but one who took her obligation for "good works" seriously. Bringing flowers to the ill and giving cornbread to the children ("It's better for you than candy!"), she was welcome in any house in Dodge, black or white.[20]

An interesting anomaly in status was Sallie Frasier. It is not certain when she came to Dodge, but as early as 1878 one editor indicated that she was "one of the landmarks of the frontier." Other Dodge Citians thought that in her "veins flowed the blood of several races" and considered her part of the black community; but she claimed she was born in the Indian Territory in 1814, the daughter of an Indian chief, and listed herself as the only Indian in the Dodge City census of 1880. Whatever her race, her restaurant was one of the respectable places blacks could meet. She was also the only woman listed by the census as a business owner. This gave her a special place in both the white and black communities. She lived with an adopted black daughter, Whila Duck, and employed blacks in her restaurant adjacent to the Green Front Dance Hall on Front Street.[21]

Aunt Sallie's place was one of the most popular in town, patronized by cowboys, freighters, homesteaders, train passengers, and dance hall girls as well as the "respectable" citizens of Dodge. Her restaurant was one of several places—the skating rink, the circuses, political rallies, and certain of the entertainment halls—where all of society could rub elbows. Her establishment was free of profanity, boisterous language, drinking, and fighting. Enforcement of the rules came by Sallie's own will, strongly supported by all factions who came there to eat. Her independence of spirit brought her into several conflicts which could be settled only in court. Her biggest case came when she engaged E. H. Borton to sue the Atchison, Topeka, and Santa Fe Railroad for $10,000. Apparently, the case was settled out of court.[22]

A major disturbance, which reflects the ambivalent limits of feelings of the white community, occurred when her black cook married a white woman. Charles S. Hungerford, referred to as the "ex-Rev." in the *Globe's* report, but who was in fact the operator of the butcher shop a few doors down from the restaurant, presided at the affairs. Harry Gryden, the legal counselor and friend of every underdog in Dodge, and Deputy Sheriff William Duffey also participated in the ceremony. The newspaper reported that "Rev. Hungerford performed the sacred Marriage ceremony with the gravity and wisdom of an owl in his most sanctimonious mood, uniting the African and the American without the least apparent reluctance." The pair were later greeted with a "shower of rotten eggs." Given the Front Street proclivity for charades and practical jokes, this may or may not have been intended as a legal, binding ceremony. Later, when the *Kansas City Journal* reported that Dodge Citians had whipped a white woman for living with a black man, the *Globe* was quick to deny the charge. Throwing rotten eggs and defending a mixed marriage reflect, again, the disparity of white racial attitudes. But whether it was a prank or a legal ceremony, Dodge Citians of that day apparently saw little damage done to community morals by "The Blending of the Races" (the title of the article describing the affair in the *Globe*).[23]

If Dodge Citians were not of one settled mind in dealing with the permanent black residents, there is also little to indicate unanimity of action or attitude toward the black transients who arrived with the summer trail herds. The transient population, black and white, frequently outnumbered the permanent residents when summer season brought cattlemen and cowboys to town. These men, in turn, attracted gamblers, prostitutes, entertainers, and other camp followers. This was as true for blacks as for whites.

There is no way of accurately determining the number of black cowboys who came to Dodge or were there at any one time. George W. Saunders of the Trail Drivers Association, as valid an authority as there is, estimated that about 25 percent of all cowhands were black.[24] Estimates made at the time indicated that there were usually around 1,550 cattlemen and cowboys in Dodge during the summer-trail season. Of these, about 1,300 were cowboys.[25] This would mean that as many as 325 black men were in or near the town from June through August. Allowing for error as great as 50 percent, black cowboys, with the same dollars in their pockets as their white compeers, represent a significant factor in Dodge's economy.

Although subject to some of the same attitudes and customs as the permanent black residents, the black cowboys expected and received better treatment. The freedom and equality of range life had conditioned them to a more integrated relationship. As Kenneth Porter observed, "Actually firsthand accounts of ranch and cattle-trail life indicated about as much segregation as prevailed on Huckleberry Finn's and the 'Nigger Jim's' raft before the appearance of 'The King' and 'The Duke.'"[26]

Since "The King" and "The Duke" represented to Huck all the worst features of civilization (sham, duplicity, education, and nonsense), the allegory has comparable significance for Dodge City. As the cow town grew in population, it also became more "civilized"; that is, it came closer to the rest of the nation's prevailing philosophical and racial attitudes. But as long as Dodge was a raw, open cow town, the black cowboy felt nearly as comfortable there as he did on the range or trail. Just how relaxed a black, trail-herd cowboy, a cook, for instance, could be is illustrated by Colonel Jack Potter's description of the arrival of a cattle crew when "old Ab Blocker's colored cook, Gordon Davis, marched into Dodge City, mounted on the back of his left wheel oxen, with fiddle in hand, playing 'Buffalo Girls Can't You Come Out Tonight.'"[27]

Few, if any, of the early hotels, bars, and restaurants were segregated. J. A. Comstock recalled his own error in trying to exclude "a young mulatto cowboy" from the Dodge House where Comstock was clerk. After the cowboy had checked in, Comstock assigned a drunken white cowboy to share the extra bed in the same room. The black didn't mind sharing the room, but not with a raucous inebriate. When he ordered the drunk out of the room at pistol point, the man fled. Because of his action, Comstock's boss told him not to accept the black cowboy the next night. But when the clerk told him there were no rooms, the cowboy drew his pistol and waved it in Comstock's face, saying, "You are a liar!" The clerk quickly rechecked his roster and found a suitable room.[28]

Nat Love, "the Deadwood Kid," one of the West's most notorious, or at least most publicized, black cowboys, remembered Dodge as the place where all cowboys tried to drink all the "bad whiskey" and staggered to the task of painting the town a "deep red."[29] This did not necessarily mean that the celebrating and carousing were done in the same bars and brothels along Front Street that catered to the white trade. By 1880 the black population was large enough to furnish its own distractions for the black cowboy. The weekly newspapers mention black-owned "bawdy houses" and "a sort of boarding house and dance hall." There were also respectable establishments where blacks were welcome, such as Aunt Sallie's Restaurant, and parties and dances blacks could attend.[30] The result was that the black cowboy just off the range found Dodge as entertaining as his white coworker, although not always in the same surroundings.

Considering the rarity of clashes between blacks and whites recorded in contemporary sources, the relationship must have been fairly smooth, a condition encouraged by most of the white community. Although tradition has it that the first man killed in Dodge City was a black named Tex, an innocent observer of a gambler's quarrel, there is little evidence of violence committed against blacks during Dodge's cattle town era.[31] The economic cost, if not a more tolerant conscience, was too great to allow much harassment. In Dodge there were fewer sanctions imposed against blacks generally and fewer still for those who helped create the industry that supported the town.

Then too, the white residents of Dodge were appreciative of the role the cowboy played and were well acquainted with the hazards and discomforts of a cattle drive. Any cattleman or cowboy was only too willing to expand on the theme in the Long Branch or Dodge House. The listeners were made aware that the black cowboys had "held point," ate the dust of "the drag," shared the night shift, helped hold off marauding Indians, and braved the dangers of river crossings. Years after the trail drives were only memories, white participants recalled their gratitude for some past favor or aid that came through a black companion's effort.

Charlie Siringo, the "cowboy detective" who spent considerable time in Dodge, wrote of many pleasant experiences on the trail with black riders. He was especially grateful for these companions who saved him when he was thrown and dragged by a runaway horse and when he was in other serious trouble.[32] Print Olive, one of Dodge City's toughest ranchers, who had killed both white and black cattle thieves, had more reason for gratitude than Siringo. His employee and constant companion, James Kelly, was at the saloon the night Print was shot by Jim Kennedy, the son of Miflin Kennedy, well-known cattleman from Corpus Christi. As Kennedy stood over Olive preparing to empty his gun into the wounded rancher, Kelly, from an awkward sitting position, fired one shot that brought Kennedy down and saved his friend's life.[33] Jim Kelly was also among the black cowboys who had "seen the elephant and heard the owl holler" during an unwinding fling in Dodge City. Print Olive and eleven men, including black hands Jim Kelly and Uncle Willy Teaball, brought a large herd from Texas by way of Fort Griffin to Dodge in the spring of 1876. They stopped long enough in Dodge to stock up on supplies and "let off steam" before moving on to the Platte. When Print had to leave his son Ira in charge of the Platte operation, he ordered Jim to stay with him as a mitigating influence on Ira's "overbearing [ways] with Negroes and Mexicans."[34]

Coming to the aid of a trail-drive companion was a two-way street. When a celebrating cowhand filled with Dodge City whiskey began abusing a black cook, a white member of the same outfit took on the bully and whipped him in a bare knuckles fight.[35] There are, however, few recorded clashes between whites and blacks in town, but the necessity for a white man to defend a black did occasionally occur. There were only one or two known instances of a white killing a black cowboy in or around Dodge. One such incident involved a white boy who was suspected of killing Jack King in a camp south of Dodge. King had worked for Henry Beverley in Dodge, and his death was considered a great tragedy. The body was found in camp and the boy and a horse were missing. The exact circumstances of King's death were never determined, but it was assumed that the boy had killed him.[36]

Black violence against black was far more common. Henry Hilton, a black man who owned a small ranch and some cattle south of Dodge, was involved in the death of both a black and a white man. When he killed the white cowboy, Hilton was supported by other cowboys who saw it as a clear case of self-defense. The killing occurred when the white cowboy was threatening to lasso Hilton and the black man warned him to stop. The "horse play" continued in an even more threatening manner, and Hilton drew his gun and shot his tormentor. In October 1883, Hilton was at a black dance hall south of the railroad tracks in Dodge when he and "Negro Bill" Smith quarreled over the affections of a girl. The two men exchanged shots and both were killed. Editor Klaine used the incident to suggest that times were changing in Dodge, since everyone viewed the slaying not as sensationalism, but as a tragedy.[37]

An interesting twist to such affairs is the murder of a white cowboy by William Allen in a "cow camp" south of Dodge on the Cimarron River. In the preliminary hearing before Dodge City's justice of the peace, R. G. Cook, witnesses testified both for and against Allen, although "the evidence for the defence tended strongly to justification of the homicide." However, since the evidence was divided, Allen was bound over to the next session of the district court.[38] Allen was defended by Harry Gryden and prosecuted by district attorney Michael Sutton, one of the cleverest and most tenacious attorneys to fill the position. Gryden secured a continuance and Allen continued to languish in jail. While waiting trial, two white prisoners broke jail and tried to persuade Allen to join them. He refused, preferring to take his chances with the legal system. Gryden secured another continuance in January 1881 and finally secured his release, although it was a close call when Allen was found guilty of murder in the third degree.[39]

When it came to horses, that most essential tool of the cowboy's trade, the

color of a man's skin attracted little attention in trading, racing, roping, breaking, and driving. Charlie Siringo and J. M. Hawkins remembered frequent pur-
chases and trades with black cowboys. As for breaking horses, Porter attested
that "the prowess of . . . Negro riders, horsebreakers, and horse trainers, was so
outstanding as to contribute to the commonly held belief of the time that there
was some natural affinity between Negroes and horses."[40] The exploits of black
horsemen such as Frank Smith, who worked for Ab Blocker, one of Texas's
legendary cattle kings, were frequently the subject of high praise in cattlemen's
conversations in Dodge saloons. Smith was so good at his trade that he "didn't
work with the herd at night like the rest of the boys; he just did the roping."[41]

Some of the cattlemen developed special relationships with black cowboys.
Kelly left Print Olive's service after his boss's imprisonment, but, by the time
the Olive family had settled in Dodge City, Jim had been replaced by Sam
Johnson. This lanky, taciturn black man accompanied Print on all his business
trips and worked closely with him at his ranch on the Sawlog. "There were
few secrets between Print and Sam," according to Harry Chrisman, and, on
occasion, the boss "poured out his plans to the colored man."[42] John Slaughter's
hand, John Battavia "Old Bat" Hinnaut, played a similar role of confidant and
bodyguard.[43] George Bolds had firsthand knowledge of another such relationship when, as a young man newly come to Dodge, he bedded down in the same
room of the Dodge House with Colonel Draper and his black companion
Zeke, "the biggest Negro I had ever seen." Zeke stuck a knife in a doorjamb
and another in the floor alongside a package which, Draper explained, contained $5,000. With these precautions Draper said to his hand, "Goodnight,
Zeke," and to Bolds, "Put out the lamp, sonny."[44] Bolds did as he was told but
spent a sleepless night conjuring up visions of bloody mayhem at the hands of
what he considered two dangerous men. Frank Smith, a black cowhand who
frequently followed a herd to Dodge City, was far more than a cook, reaching
what amounted to partnership status with Ab Blocker. At one point, when
his boss was sorely pinched for funds, Smith loaned Blocker $4,000, which
Blocker let ride at 10 percent interest year after year as he moved cattle up the
Western Trail until a large fund had been accumulated. When Smith bought
supplies for Blocker's outfit in Wright, Beverley & Company's store, the bill of
lading was made out to "Smith & Blocker."[45]

Unfortunately, the total picture of black-white range and trail relationships
was not always amicable. Even though shared hazards modified the natural,

society-bred bigotry, there still remained a considerable gulf between the races. There are many instances of both physical and mental cruelty. Some old cowhands remembered that black cowboys were called on for extra shifts on cold or rainy nights and received the more dangerous stations in crossing swollen streams. An incident that became folklore in Dodge reflects the undercurrent of racial ambivalence generated by the complicating presence of black cowboys. A trail boss quarreled with a cook on C. C. Pepperd's ranch south of Dodge in Comanche County. The trail boss settled the matter by putting a bullet between the eyes of the offending black cook. The Negro was given a decent burial and it might have ended as another violent incident if Pepperd had not decided that justice in this case, even though the victim was black, needed to be served. He rode to Dodge City to report the murder and to get the sheriff to issue a warrant. The sheriff refused to act since, he said, there was no proof of death, "no corpus delicti." Infuriated that his word had been questioned, Pepperd rode back and exhumed the body to bring in the evidence. But in the summer heat, the body was in a state of advanced decomposition, so the rancher chopped off the head, put it in a gunny sack, and returned to Dodge. The next day he rode into town and rolled the head out on the table in front of the startled sheriff. The sheriff still wouldn't act, and the justice of the peace sided with him. There followed what the local paper called "a 'serio-comical funeral' for the severed head placed at rest some 60 miles from the torso."[46]

The treatment of death on the range, especially that of a stranger, was usually quick and informal, but the callousness displayed by this black man's death went beyond the necessity of prompt action. Most contemporaries treated the incident as a humorous, if somewhat ghoulish, affair. The dignity of the victim mattered little. It is certain that if a white man had been the murdered man all those involved—sheriff, Pepperd, and burial party—would have behaved in a different manner. Pepperd's crude attempt at justice and the town's treatment of it as a joke reflect the conflict of emotions aroused in the town, even for the more favored cattle-range black.

The same mixture of humorous tolerance and assumed superiority was present in the town's attitude toward one of the West's greatest con artists. Ben Hodges arrived in Dodge as a member of a trail-herd crew and remained on as a handyman working for various people.[47] Ben was the roving son of a San Antonio black and Mexican union. According to Robert M. Wright, Dodge City's leading political and business figure, Ben's spectacular career in Dodge began as "just a joke" when two local businessmen, in teasing the down-on-his-luck drifter, "a genuine negro, with a squeaky voice," asked if he was a descendant of the Spanish grandee who, the newspapers reported, still had claim to large acreages in the West. Ben naturally, and in all modesty, answered "yes."[48] After a quick trip to Texas, he returned with documented proof of his noble ancestry. A number of prominent men supported the claim with money and legal advice. Hodges made the most of the hoax by extending his credit as the matter worked its leisurely way through the justice system.

In the midst of that scheme, Ben launched another by paying taxes on large blocks of Gray County land whose true ownership couldn't be proven because the legal papers had been destroyed in Wright, Beverley & Company's fire. With the tax receipts which indicated ownership of the land, he bargained for thousands of head of range cattle and sought funds from eastern bankers. By the time all three schemes had fallen through, Ben was a well-known figure in cattle, financial, and railroad circles from San Antonio to Kansas City.

Dodge Citians, given to extravagant practical jokes and elaborate charades, found Ben's escapades more amusing than immoral. Robert Wright marveled at how "an ignorant darkey could make such a stir out of nothing." Wright gave Ben all the aid he could because he enjoyed watching a good confidence man at work. In one of Hodges's cattle-stealing trials, Wright worked behind the scenes to convince the judge that Ben would be served best as his own lawyer. The result was all Wright had hoped for: "Sometimes he would have the jury laughing until the Judge would have to stop them, and again, he would have the jury in deep thought. They were only out a little while, when they brought in a verdict of not guilty." Wright thought it the best show in town.[49]

In later years, when Ben was totally unmasked and reduced to poverty, the old-time Dodge Citians furnished him a shack and, as a reminder of the good old days, willingly let him perpetuate small swindles on them in the purchase of geese and garden produce he raised on his small plot and loans he cadged with marvelous stories of how they were to be repaid. When Ben died, they made certain his funeral reflected his flamboyant life, and he was buried among the early-day cattlemen who had preceded him. "We buried Ben [in Maple Grove Cemetery] for a good reason," one of his pallbearers is reported to have wryly observed. "We wanted him where we could keep an eye on him."[50]

Dodge's reaction to Ben was that of disbelieving respect for his larcenous talents. Generally treated as an audacious buffoon who gulled the greenhorns and other easy marks, he was kept on by the white cattlemen as a kind of western-style court jester. For Ben, his white benefactors expressed great fondness, but little in the way of personal acceptance, even when they followed the hearse to their shared graveyard. In this town of legendary violence, discrimination took the form not of a love-hate relationship but of a respectful distance based on societal custom and the vestiges of lingering stereotypes, modified by personal loyalties and a practical appreciation of black contributions. Because of the black cowboy's economic value to the community, he was given a heightened status, but there was still a strong undercurrent of racism rippling just beneath the surface and occasionally becoming visible. Deacon Klaine couldn't always restrain his bigotry even in the case of the cowboy. When "Big Ear" rode into town from Texas in the spring of 1878, Klaine noted his arrival with one of his crudest racist statements.[51]

The concessions made by white residents to the black cowboy were not necessarily extended to other members of the race. This was certainly true of black prostitutes attracted to Dodge by the influx of cowboys. One consequence of catering to the desires of the cowboy was a number of bordellos, which became increasingly recognized by the permanent residents as a liability. When Dodge moved into the calmer, less exciting role of a granger's trade center, one of the first things to pass was open prostitution.

Unfortunately for women, both black and white, the most prominent profession in the frontier boomtowns—in the sense of visibility and newspaper coverage—was prostitution. In Dodge City, there was great demand for "soiled doves" during the summer cattle drive season, and some of the women remained the year around. They were established in brothels, dance halls, and independent residences. Gamblers and prostitutes floated between Mobeetie, Tascosa [Texas], and Dodge City. J. Wright Mooar reported that they "just made a grand circuit down there. Any number of those women at Tascosa were Dodge City women."[52] Nicholas Klaine, so prim and proper most folks called him Deacon, believed there were around forty prostitutes plying their trade in Dodge in 1878. Other estimates tended to be higher. Whatever the exact figure, the business was lucrative enough for Dodge, like other cow towns, to use fines levied on the trade as a major source of revenue in financing local government. Dodge City fined the prostitutes and brothel keepers at a higher rate than most towns: $5 to $100 for the latter and $5 to $50 for the women.

The only documented all-black house of prostitution recorded was that of Henry Forrester, where six women were listed in the 1885 Kansas census; but black prostitutes and pimps had been present from the beginning and remained to the end of the cattle town era. Blacks in the business did not escape the long arm of the revenue collectors, although some claimed that the police judge favored them and charged only court costs and forgot the fines. In July 1883, "Wm. Smith, colored, was arrested, charged with keeping a bawdy house." The fine and court costs totaled $41.50, and the three girls were charged $5.50 each. These fines were nondiscriminatory, being typical of those charged against whites.[53]

One consequence of the revenue acts was that black prostitutes and their procurers were prominent in the courts and the newspapers. Even greater notoriety came when the girls engaged in a fight. Frontier communities always found the spectacle of women brawling an especially humorous sight. The Dodge City papers reported such instances with considerable exaggeration and unrestrained hyperbole. When black women were involved, racist comments were added, apparently to heighten the humor reporters and white readers found in these accounts. Phrases such as "fullgrown male courtesan," "razors flashed," "hair-pulling fair octoroon," and "soiled dove of color" sprinkled these stories.[54]

When such cases reached the courts, as some of them did, the candid legal language is less entertaining, but certainly no less revealing: "Sallie Doke defendant arrested on the complaint of Annie Lewis charging that on the 7th day of April A.D. 1877 at the said City of Dodge City, the said defendant Sallie Coke called affiant a dirty bitch, a Whore, and that the affiant was afflicted with the clap, all of which was done in a loud and boisterous manner, contrary to an ordinance made and provided."[55]

More frequent than fights between the prostitutes was the violence meted out by a pimp or customer, which resulted in a charge of disturbance of the peace and an appearance before a judge. One of the more blatantly racist accounts appeared in the August 11, 1877 *Times*, involving the beating of a black prostitute by a black client, Monroe Henderson. "Miss Carrie looked 'the last rose of summer all faded and gone to—.' Her starboard eye was closed, and a lump like a bisquit ornamented her forehead." The story noted that "the idol of her affection" had "kicked the stuffing generally out of Miss Carrie" until she "procured a hollow ground razor." The prosecuting attorney spent his time, the reporter added, describing "the heinousness of a strong giant man smiting a frail woman." Both Henderson and Carrie were fined $5.00 and costs plus "an eighteen-dollar moral lecture," delivered to Carrie, who was guilty of carrying a concealed weapon.[56]

The court carried a far more prosaic statement indicating that Henderson had "conducted himself in a riotous and disorderly manner and did beat, wound and bruise this deposant against the peace and disquiet of the city and contrary to the provision of Sect. II of ordinance no. 16."[57] The newspaper accounts were not intended or understood at the time to be factual reporting but were, in the words of Joseph Snell, "the eruptions of humorous journalese." Frontier humor tended to be broad and, in this instance, was both racist and sexist. The bigoted language in a paper seeking public subscriptions indicates common acceptance of derogatory name-calling and insensitive stereotyping. Klaine had condemned prostitution on many occasions, but when presented a specific case he did little to call attention to the dangers and meanness of the prostitute's life. The courts, at least, treated the victim as an offended person. The small nonpunitive fine, however, was nearer to Klaine's assessment. In all fairness, the Dodge City papers treated accounts of white prostitutes with the same callousness, minus the racial slurs. The implication was that the soiled doves got what they deserved and were considered only as objects of derision.

The case of Andrew Paine, "an energetic colored gentleman," was treated with the same levity when he was fined "for the slugology administered his dusky partner."[58] In at least one instance, the consequence could not be treated lightly, even by Deacon Klaine. A black prostitute, Keziah Morse, familiarly known as "Kasock" or "Keezock," who supplemented her earnings by taking in washing, was brutally murdered by Henry Chambers, also black. Klaine used the occasion to remind his readers of the "wages of sin": "The old, old story is repeated in details of this murder. Whiskey and lust bring misery, ruin, and death." Apparently the brutality of the act incensed many in town. W. F. Petillon reported: "The talk of lynching him was boosh. Vigilantes may as well tumble to the fact that no Ford County sheriff ever had or ever will have a prisoner taken away by strangers." In fact, the only lynching in the Dodge City region (an innocent white man) had taken place before law and order came with the cattle trade. Chambers eventually was convicted of second-degree murder.[59]

Occasionally, a prostitute appeared before the courts for other than disturbing the peace or plying her trade. Fannie Nash, "a soiled dove of color, who has been in the habit of giving Ben Daniels [assistant marshal] a little chin music was caught up by him . . . and put in the jug." It never paid to insult the representatives of law and order. Marshal Dave Mather pursued two girls to Emporia, brought them back to Dodge, and held them for trial because they had stolen a customer's watch.[60] Such arrests were rare.

Other more legitimate, that is, socially acceptable, entertainers were given a far different reception. Entertainment in Dodge City ranged from grand opera and violin concerts to trained bears and sword swallowers. Front Street's tastes were less refined and favored the farcical, crude, and cruel variety. Cock fighting was available, and Dodge proudly boasted that it was "especially distinguished as the only town in the state, or the whole United States, for that matter, that ever conducted a bull fight."[61] Dodge's attitude toward violent entertainment was about the same as its stand on lawlessness: toleration as long as it did not threaten the cattlemen or their willingness to come to Dodge on business. Considering the level of danger and brutality in the everyday life of a cowboy, this gave considerable latitude.

Boxing matches, better described as "slug fests," were well supported; even the boxing exhibitions at the Opera House brought large crowds, while a program demonstrating the more subtle Greco-Roman style wrestling was sparsely attended.[62] Occasionally, blacks were involved in brutal sports and were, if not well paid, at least paid. Whites, of course, engaged in fights every bit as brutal as those in which blacks participated. The headline "Bloody Prize Fight in Dodge City" set the tone of one such fight. By comparison, a brief story in the *Globe* read: "Two French gentlemen of African descent indulged in a slugging match last Sunday. Both received varnished countenances."[63] There was at least one interracial bout between "'Piano Bill' [white], a slugger of no mean pretensions . . . and the big 'coon' that works for Singer and Lahey." The *Democrat* carried a round-by-round description of the fight, which went to the black man after he knocked down his opponent twice. The purse was $11.00.[64]

"A shade worse than the prize fights," according to one Dodge City official, was a duel with whips, referred to as a "lap-Jacket contest" witnessed by a Front Street crowd. This "African national game," as the white author called the exhibition, pitted two men with bull whips toeing a mark and whipping each other for the championship and fifty-cent prize money. "Blood flowed and dust flew and the crowd cheered until Policeman Joe Mason came along and suspended the cheerful exercise.[65] To charge the black men with responsibility for such a brutalizing display because of their African origin was an obvious attempt to shift the onus for the local popularity of vicious sports. Robert M. Wright, who reported the incident, did so long after such exhibitions ceased to be accept-able to the community. Even the term "jacketing" as a colloquial expression for beating had long since gone out of style. But at the time, public acceptance of, or at least indifference toward, specific instances of brutality—the Pepperd affair, the lap-jacket duel, and the prostitutes' trials—placed black individuals in a different, less protected posture from white citizens. The press, apparently supported by the community, settled for a detached tone of humor or scorn. In these instances, the participants were not considered as individuals, but only as indistinguishable members of their race, which is, of course, the genesis and essence of racism.

Not all black entertainment was of a violent nature. Minstrel shows were particularly popular, even the "cowboy minstrel show."[66] Many of these shows were black-face white companies traveling the West, but some were all-black troupes who played at the Opera House. The Billy Kersand Company ("all are genuine colored folks") and the Callender Minstrels were well received; the latter, it was said, "took the town by storm." The Great Boston Double Uncle Tom's Cabin Company of "ten colored plantation singers," and Dave McCoy, "celebrated magician and Ethiopian comic performer," were applauded enthu-siastically.[67] These were family performances, requiring the bar to be closed during the show. "Dick Brown and his banjo, with the two angels (without wings) who sit between him and the colored pussons are a full hand that's hard to beat," was intended for a more boisterous audience.[68]

Life in Dodge City as a frontier cattle town was sometimes exciting and dangerous, often dull and laborious. The sun and heat of a western Kansas summer could make life miserable; the wind and cold of winter could be life threatening; and, in between the extremes, it was certainly not the garden spot of the world that town boosters claimed. Blacks were a part of it all. Although less prejudice existed in the early period than would have been encountered in most sections of the country, the white Dodge Citians who controlled the financial, political, and social life of the town were guided by a disconcerting ambivalence in dealing with and thinking about the blacks they met on Front Street or employed in their homes and businesses. Blacks accepted, suffered, or used this imprecise frame of reference depending on their perception of it, their personality, and their past experience. The relationship was not fixed and was, certainly at best, awkward for both whites and blacks.

Discrimination was an ever-present condition of daily life; segregation was less apparent. Blacks and whites prayed to the same God, but only occasionally together. Black children attended public schools; black men voted in public elections, sat as jurymen trying white men for crimes (even capital offenses) against other white men, testified in trials against white men, helped white men carry their dead to the cemetery, and were locked in the same cells with white prisoners. In the most important occupation, cattle herding, blacks and whites shared the same food, the same living accommodations, and the same pay.

The census of 1880 lists two black children in school, and white and black children intermingled off the playground, as noted by the paper when the new flag pole was said to "have been a great curiousity to small boys of the town, both black and white."[69] A. B. Webster—businessman, onetime mayor, a leading light in most affairs of the town—was served by eight pall bearers, two of whom were black, long-time employees.[70] Testimony of a white man indicated cryptically that a "colored man . . . was persuaded to vote."[71] John Sheridan, a white gambler booked as a vagrant, refused to pay a fine and court costs until he discovered he would be placed in a cell "with a darkey," yet eight other white men and John Alexander, a convicted black, joined in escaping that same jail.[72] On the jury hearing the case of Ben Daniels, who had killed, in cold blood, another white businessman, sat "Jas. Robb (colored)."[73] A. P. George, instrumental in establishing a number of white Methodist churches in southwestern Kansas, preached to blacks in Mrs. Dolley Gaskin's home, and both blacks and whites shared the Union Church building—separately.[74] Aunt Sallie, whose real name was Sallie Frazier, hired a white lawyer to sue the most powerful economic force in Dodge City, and her homemade biscuits were prized by all who came to her integrated and respectable restaurant. Nicholas Klaine, who used his paper to advance church services, prohibition, and anti-prostitution legislation, repeatedly published, in the same paper, racial slurs and every "darkey joke" that came along. Robert Wright, mayor and state representative, conspired with a judge to get a black confidence man freed because he enjoyed seeing someone, to whom he felt vastly superior, swindle other whites who had the same feelings of superiority.

White Dodge Citians did not quite find the proper "place" in their society for the black men and women who shared their town. Black cowboys commanded respect, and close associates earned it. Dodge City, as one of the last bastions of free and easy individualism, felt both resentment and acceptance of the idea of "place." But there it was, an apparently inescapable part of their heritage and education. In spite of public expressions of blatant racism that demanded "place," there was the conflicting awareness that the whole concept of "place" had no merit in a town given to avoiding proper form and decorum.

Even Deacon Klaine, for all his public callousness, was aware of the shared human predicament of both races. In a listing of recent deaths, he concluded: "Another less known, but no less a man, though of a dark skin, also passed in his chips, and called the turn. Wm. Davis, the colored barber, died."[75] The *Globe* editor, Daniel M. Frost, always more aware of the shared humanity of blacks and whites, expressed his convictions when he wrote of the tragic circumstances of a mixed marriage involving a man charged with murder:

> Added to all this, the murderer was a man who had but few friends in the community, being ostracised by all who considered themselves decent and respectable, because he was married to a woman whom the Creator had seen fit to cover with a motley skin. It is not definitely known whether or not Webb has Negro blood in his veins. [He did not.] He was born and raised in the south, his father being quite an extensive planter and slave owner. During his long confinement, awaiting his trial, the prisoner possessed not the sympathy of a single individual except that of his Negro wife, who was a constant and patient laborer in his behalf. There is really nothing strange in the fidelity of this colored woman to the father of her two children. Despised though she may be, she is human, and a mother.[76]

The ambivalence reflected in Klaine's reactions is important, for he was the spokesman for the community standards that eventually were to prevail. By 1886, Dodge had left behind its wayward, reckless lifestyle as a cow town to settle for the Victorian respectability of a rural mercantile center. Both discrimination and segregation were to keep pace with the change. One of the casualties, along with demon rum, was that feeling of ambivalence that had haunted blacks and whites in the cowboy mecca. In its stead came a less awkward and less humane, but clearer, understanding of "place."

Notes

1. Kenneth W. Porter, *The Negro on the American Frontier* (New York: Arno Press, 1971), 521–22; William Loren Katz, *The Black West: A Documentary and Pictorial History of the African American Role in the Westward Expansion of the United States* (New York: Doubleday, 1971), xi.

2. U.S. Census of 1880, Ford County, Kansas. See C. Robert Haywood, "The Dodge City Census of 1880: Historians' Tool or Stumbling Block?" *Kansas History* 8 (Summer 1985): 95–109.

3. Carroll D. Clark and Roy L. Roberts, *People of Kansas: A Demographic and Sociological Study* (Topeka: Kansas State Planning Board, 1936), 50.

4. *Dodge City Ford County Globe*, June 10, 1879; hereafter cited as *Globe*.

5. See the ad of Robert M. Wright, *Dodge City Times*, August 16, 1883; hereafter cited as *Times*; quote from *Times*, May 20, 1879.

6. Three of these women had been arrested for disturbing the peace the previous year. *Dodge City Democrat*, May 31, 1884; hereafter cited as *Democrat*.

7. Absence or opportunity, real or perceived, was a major motivation for western frontier mobility. See Robert A. Burchell, "Opportunity and the Frontier: Wealth-Holding in Twenty-Six Northern Californian Counties, 1848–1880," *Western Historical Quarterly* 18 (April 1987): 177–96.

8. *Globe*, February 24, 1885.

9. *Globe*, November 8, 1881. See also a note on the death of a cook by the name of Moore in which "all the colored population turned out for the funeral"; *Globe*, February 10, 1885.

10. *Globe*, February 13, 1883; *Times*, February 15, 1883.

11. See, for example, *Times*, March 16 1879, October 4, 1883.

12. *Times*, March 9, 1878; *Globe*, October 22, 1878.

13. *Democrat*, December 12, 1885, February 6, 1886. Of the three newspapers, the *Democrat*, edited by W. F. Pelillon, was the most sympathetic to the black, the *Globe*, under Daniel Frost, generally so. Klaine in the *Times* was by far the most racist and bigoted in his reporting.

14. See Klaine's remarks, *Times*, March 9, and July 27, 1878.

15. *Times*, October 23, 1884; *Democrat*, August 16, 1884.

16. *Times*, December 10, 1885.

17. Harry E. Chrisman, *Lost Trails of the Cimarron* (Denver: Sage, 1961), 97–99.

18. Craig Miner, *West of Wichita: Settling the High Plains of Kansas, 1865–1890* (Lawrence: University Press of Kansas, 1986), 101–102, found the same to be true in other west-

ern Kansas cattle towns.

19. Heinie Schmidt, "Site of a Hodgeman County Ghost Town Recalls Unfulfilled Dream of Pioneer," *High Plains Journal,* January 10, 1952.

20. Census of 1880, Ford County, Kansas; Heinie Schmidt, "Auntie Standsfield Corn Bread," *High Plains Journal,* April 20, 1950.

21. *Globe,* April 9, 1878; *Dodge City Journal,* May 20, 1948.

22. *Times,* June 30, 1877; *Democrat,* March 8 and November 22, 1884; *Dodge City Kansas Cowboy,* November 27, 1884; *Frost & Wood v. Frazier,* District Court Cases, Civil Case No. 55, Ms. Roll 806, and *Sallie Frazier v. A. T. & S. F. Ry. Co.,* District Court Cases, Civil Case, Unnumbered, Ms. Roll 808, Archives Department, Kansas State Historical Society, Topeka.

23. *Globe,* September 2, 16, and 23, 1879.

24. J. Marvin Hunter, ed., *The Trail Drivers of Texas* (Austin: University of Texas Press, 1985), 453.

25. *Globe,* May 7, 1878.

26. Porter, *Negro on the American* Frontier, 515.

27. Jack M. Potter, *Cattle Trails of the Old West* (Clayton, N.Mex.: Laura R. Krehbiel, 1939), 75.

28.   J. A. Comstock recalled the incident years later to Heinie Schmidt; *Dodge City Daily Globe,* July 28, 1933.

29. Nat Love, *The Life and Adventures of Nat Love, Better Known in the Cattle Country as "Deadwood Dick"* (Los Angeles, Calif., 1907), 54.

30. *Globe,* September 2 and January 22, 1878, October 9, 1883; *Times,* July 12 and October 11, 1883.

31. Robert M. Wright, *Dodge City: The Cowboy Capital of The Great Southwest* (Wichita, Kans.: Wichita Eagle Press, 1913), 169.

32. Philip Durham and Everett L. Jones, *The Negro Cowboys* (New York: Dodd, Mead, 1965), 27–31, 27–31; Charles A. Siringo, *Riata and Spurs* (Boston: Houghton Mifflin, 1927), 17–18, 28.

33. Harry E. Chrisman, *The Ladder of Rivers: The Story of I. P. (Print) Olive* (Denver: Sage, 1962), 122.

34. Richard Crabb, *Empire on the Platte* (Cleveland, World Publishing, 1967), 129.

35. Porter, *Negro on the American Frontier,* 517.

36. *Times,* August 18, 1881.

37. *Times,* October 11, 1883; *Globe,* October 9, 1883; Wright, *Dodge City,* 178.

38. *Times,* September 4 and 11, 1880; *Globe,* September 7, 1880.

39. *Globe,* January 25, 1881; *Times,* September 11, 1880.

40. Hunter, *Trail Drivers,* 112; Porter, *Negro on the American Frontier,* 501.

41. Edward Seymour Nichols, *Ed Nichols Rode a Horse,* ed. and comp. Ruby Nichols Cutburth ([Austin]: Texas Folklore Society, 1943), 8–9; James C. Shaw, *North from Texas: Incidents in the Early Love of a Range Cowman in Texas, Dakota and Wyoming, 1852–1883* (Evanston, Ill.: Branding Iron Press, 1952), 19.

42. Chrisman, *Ladder of Rivers,* 122, 321, 359, 367.

43. Allen A. Erwin, *The Southwest of John H. Slaughter, 1841–1922* (Glendale, Calif.: A. H. Clark, 1965), 147–50.

44. James D. Horan, *Across the Cimarron* (New York: Crown, 1956), 48–49.

45. J. Frank Dobie, *Cow People* (Boston: Little, Brown, 1964), 142.

46. Wright, *Dodge City,* 180–81; C. Robert Haywood, "Comanche County Cowboy: A Case Study of a Kansas Rancher," *Kansas History* 4 (Autumn 1981): 185–86.

47. Ida Ellen Rath, *The Rath Trail* (Wichita, Kans.: McCormick-Armstrong, 1961), 152.

48. *Times,* December 25, 1884; *Democrat,* December 20, 1884.

49. *Democrat,* December 20, 1884; *State v. Benjamin Hodges,* Ford County District Court Cases, Criminal Cases, Case No. 709, Ms. Roll 809, Archives Department, Kansas State Historical Society, Topeka; Wright, *Dodge City,* 273–80.

50. David Kay Strate, *Up from the Prairie* (Dodge City, Kans.: Cultural Heritage and Arts Center, 1974), 60–61; Chrisman, *Lost Trails,* 179–80.

51. *Times,* June 29, 1878.

52. Hervey E. Chesley, *Adventuring with the Oldtimers: Trails Traveled—Tales Told,* ed. Byron Price (Midland, Tex.: Nita Stewart Haley Memorial Library, 1979), 48.

53. *Globe,* August 23, 1883; *Times,* August 10 and 17, 1878.

54. *Dodge City Kansas Cowboys,* September 6, 1884; *Times,* March 24 and August 25, 1877.

55. *The City of Dodge City v. Sallie Doke,* Ford County District Court Case (Kansas), Ms. Roll 799, Archives Department, Kansas State Historical Society, Topeka. The quotation taken from Police Court file when Doke appealed the case to the District Court.

56. Nyle H. Miller and Joseph W. Snell, *Great Gunfighters of the Kansas Cowtowns, 1867–1886* (Lincoln: University of Nebraska Press, 1967), 172. To present-day thinking, the extent of the racism is most clearly revealed in the strange sensibility of a "family paper" that required blanking out the word "hell" in the same story that used the terms "coon" and "niggus."

57. *City of Dodge City v. Monroe Henderson,* Selected Court Cases, Ms. Box 799, Archives Department, Kansas State Historical Society, Topeka.

58. *Times,* March 16, 1878.

59.   *Times*, February 21, 1884; *Democrat*, February 23, 1884; *Globe*, March 4, 1884.

60.   *Dodge City Kansas Cowboy*, May 16, 1885: *Times*, December 13, 1883.

61.   Wright, *Dodge City*, 239.

62.   See, for example, Mr. James Elliott's show, which included a $2,500 prize for any man who could successfully stand against him; *Globe*, February 20, 1883. For the Greco-Roman failure, see the *Democrat*, May 1, 1886.

63.   *Times*, June 16, 1877; *Globe*, August 5, 1879.

64.   *Democrat*, May 31, 1884.

65.   Wright, *Dodge City*, 242.

66.   *Globe*, May 8, 1883.

67.   *Democrat*, August 2, 1884, April 13 and August 29, 1885.

68.   *Globe*, June 11, 1879.

69.   *Globe*, April 29, 1879.

70.   Heinie Schmidt, *Ashes of My Campfire* (Dodge City, Kans.: Journal, 1952), 55.

71.   *R. W. Tarbox v. P. E. Sughrue*, Kansas Supreme Court Case No. 3940, Series II, Archives Department, Kansas State Historical Society, Topeka.

72.   *Globe*, September 25, 1883; *Democrat*, February 6, 1886.

73.   *Globe*, November 23, 1886.

74.   *Times*, October 4, 1883, February 14, 1884.

75.   *Times*, February 1, 1883.

76.   *Globe*, January 13, 1880.

12

Charley Willis

A Singing Cowboy

JIM CHILCOTE

Some black cowboys developed musical traditions of their own and subsequently acted in movies and wrote their autobiographies. Jim Chilcote provides us with details about the career of a black cowboy who, though not necessarily an excellent singer, did, as did most cowboys on the long trails of the late nineteenth century, sing to the cattle to keep them from stampeding or even straying. One such black cowboy, Charley Willis, returned from a trail drive singing the song "Goodbye Old Paint." Likely he authored the song.

A number of years ago I was asked to sing for a convention of physicians at an evening "Wild West Show." Present were a number of rodeo cowboys, ropers, bulldoggers, bronc riders, and several bull riders. While we waited behind the chutes, the cowboys stretched out, unkinked ropes, resined rigs, checked cinching, and talked rodeo. Despite the fact that several of them had just met, they became a tight-knit group within minutes, for what bound them had little to do with where they were from, where they had attended school, or from what social strata they had originated. They were all cowboys, talking stock, spurs, horses, rigs, and bruises.

Just before the end of the rodeo, after the calves had been roped, the broncs busted, and the songs sung, the arena lights went out—a blown breaker no doubt. With the bulls yet to be ridden, I wondered how the master of ceremonies would deal with the disappointed crowd. Within moments, however, the bull riders bounded into the middle of the dark arena for a quick meeting.

Originally published as Jim Chilcote, "Charley Willis: A Singing Cowboy," in *Black Cowboys of Texas*, edited by Sara R. Massey (College Station: Texas A&M University Press, 2000), 173–78. Reprinted with permission of Texas A&M University Press.

They had come to ride bulls and were not about to get cheated out of the fun. Immediately, cowhands sprang to their trucks, arranged them at one end of the arena, and turned on their headlights in an attempt to illuminate the scene. That evening, to the deafening cheers of the dazzled audience, by the dim, striated, and woefully inadequate light, three cowboys made the most daring bull rides I've ever seen. All three bull riders were African American cowboys. What those cowboys had done that night spoke volumes about pride, spirit, guts, and the cultural history of being a cowboy. Later, I happened to make the acquaintance of Will Arthur (Artie) Morris, an accomplished country singer, who told me of his great-grandfather, Charley Willis, a black cowboy who went "up the trail" in 1871. Remembering those bull riders, I decided to learn his story.

Charley Willis was born in 1850 in Milam County, Texas. After the Civil War, Charley was freed, and he went to work for E. J. Morris on the Morris Ranch near Bartlett, Texas, in Bell County. He continued to work off and on at the ranch for over twenty years, breaking horses and doing all the other jobs of cowboys.[1] It is believed that his wife, Laura, was part Seminole and probably migrated to Texas from Mexico with other Black Seminoles during the Civil War.[2]

The 1880 census lists Charles Willis in Milam County with wife Laura, age twenty-six, and four children: Andrew, age ten; Magdalene, age eight; Joshua, age six; and Clemmer, age two. The birth dates given are Laura, 1854; Andrew, 1870; Magdalene, 1872; Joshua, 1874; and Clemmer, 1878. A census error listed Clemmer, or "Bud" as he was later called, as a daughter rather than a son.[3]

In 1871, Charley Willis at twenty-one took to the trail with one of ten herds driven north to Wyoming by the Snyder brothers, well-known cattle drovers from Georgetown, Texas.[4] This drive, terminating in Cheyenne, was roughly two thousand miles round-trip on horseback and would have taken several months to complete with all the dangers inherent in herding cattle a long distance. The year that Charley went up the trail marked the all-time peak of trail activity for the era. Cattle drive figures for the years 1868 through 1885 show that 1871 was the bumper year, with over 600,000 head of cattle being driven on the trails.[5] That Charley was an accomplished cowboy seems beyond question, given the length of his employment with E. J. Morris, as well as his hiring on with the Snyder brothers for the trail drive. It was a common practice at that time for cowboys to hire on with other ranchers for the long trail drives. His job of breaking horses was not for the soft or fainthearted. Breaking horses was reserved for the best and toughest cowhands, and, given the investment involved in a large-scale trail drive, cattle ranchers wanted to procure the most experienced cowboys obtainable. Charley's photograph suggests that he was rather small and wiry, a favorable combination for working green saddle stock.

During his trek with the Snyder herds up to Wyoming, Charley was exposed to all aspects of trail driving along with the sweat and dangers. One element of cowboy life Willis certainly experienced was "singing to the herds." As cattle drovers were quick to discover, longhorns were prone to stampede at the slightest provocation unless within earshot of the human voice, hence the phenomenon of the singing cowboy. In fact, "some cattle drovers, realizing the value of music to a trail herd actually hired singers to take part in the drives."[6]

Some trail bosses didn't like to hire a fellow who couldn't sing. We boys would consider it a dull day's drive if we didn't add at least one verse. On bad, dark nights the cowboy who could keep up the most racket was the pet of the bunch. We called him the bellwether, and he always brought up his side of the herd. . . . When the trail hand gargled his throat . . . he usually had a practical purpose. In threatening weather, when the cattle began to drift and showing signs of stampeding, a hymn or a ballad might quiet them. . . . Songs were the best antidote to rumbling in the sky or the howl of a lobo wolf on a distant hill. . . . the cowboy puncher who could sing better than the average had an advantage. In his long days in the saddle, songs helped to speed the hours and to keep him from growing lonesome. In the evening around the campfire, they gave a bit of diversion before the tired men hit their bedrolls. The hands on night guard used songs not only to keep the cattle quiet but to keep themselves awake.[7]

"What you would hear as you passed your partner on guard would be a kind of low hum or whistle, and you wouldn't know what it was. Just some old hymn tune, likely as not—something to kill time and not bad enough to make the herd want to get up and run. . . . The cowboy hardly ever knew what tune he was singing his song to, just some old, old tune that he had heard and known as a boy." While the repertoire of the cowboys was anything but high brow, it was likely to include "hymns, bawdy ditties, familiar ballads, cowboy songs of communal authorship, popular songs of the day, and poems that had been put to music with either original or borrowed tunes." "Methodist hymns were popular . . . although good old-fashioned Negro minstrel songs have been found equally effective in soothing the breast of the wild Texas steer. . . . after the men had sung a few lullabies to the steers, they (the steers) all lay down and started snoring."[8]

Charley must have had an ear and an aptitude for music, because he returned to Texas singing some of the trail tunes endemic of the cowboy. "Horses, which play an essential and intimate part in the daily life of the trail hand, were the heroes of many of his (the cowboy's) songs."[9] On one trip Charley returned singing the oldest traceable version of the song "Goodbye Old Paint." Family tradition suggests that he authored the song, which is possible. No one knows if Charley had a horse named "Ol' Paint," as most cowboys did not own horses,[10] but the song continued into history.

Sometime around 1885 when Charley was breaking horses for E. J. Morris, he taught the song "Ol' Paint" to E.J.'s son Jesse, replete with a Jew's harp accompaniment. Jesse Morris, later to become an accomplished cowboy himself, received his first lessons on the fiddle from another black cowboy on the Morris Ranch, Jerry Neely, and continued playing Charley Willis's version of "Ol' Paint" throughout his life. In 1947, at the request of folk musicologist John Lomax, Jesse Morris recorded "Goodbye Old Paint" for the Library of Congress. The preservation of the song was commented on by the director of the repository at the time: "Morris . . . has the oldest known version: he traces it to the point of first origin, Charley (Willis)."[11]

Jim Bob Tinsley says, "Credit for saving it from obscurity must be given to three Texans: a black cowboy (Willis) who sang it on the trail drives, a cowboy who remembered it (Morris), and a college professor who put it down on paper (Lomax)." "Goodbye Old Paint," as sung by Charley Willis:

Goodbye Old Paint

My foot's in the stirrup, my pony won't stand,
Goodbye Old Paint, I'm off to Montan'.

[Repeating chorus:]
Old Paint, Old Paint, I'm a-leavin' Cheyenne,
Goodbye Old Paint, I'm a-leavin' Cheyenne.

Old Paint's a good pony, he paces when he can,
Goodbye little doney, I'm off to Montan'.

Go hitch up your horses and feed 'em some hay,
An' set yourself by me as long as you'll stay.

We spread down the blanket on the green grassy ground,
While the horses and cattle were a-grazin' around.

My horses ain't hungry, they won't eat your hay,
My wagon is loaded and rollin' away.

My foot's in the stirrup, my bridle's in hand,
Goodbye little Annie, my horses won't stand.

The last time I saw her was late in the fall,
She was ridin' Old Paint and a-leadin' Ol' Ball.[12]

Cowboys rarely had good singing voices. "If he had one to start with, he always lost it bawling at cattle, or sleeping out in the open, or tellin' the judge he didn't steal that horse. . . . Cowboy songs were always song by one person, never by a group."[13] Charley, like most cowboys, probably didn't have a trained voice, but the song he conceived someplace on the trail drive is now an enduring cowboy ballad.

Sometime after his return from Wyoming, Charley and Laura took up residence in DaVilla, Texas, some fifteen miles southwest of Cameron in Milam County. The family homestead, approximately six acres, is situated adjacent to the DaVilla Cemetery, near the school and Baptist church. The family home no longer exists, but a walk on the site with Artie Morris turned up pottery shards, broken glass, and rusty remnants of pots and pans from the old homestead.

It is unclear when Charley died. Vyree Willis Moore, great-granddaughter of Charley and Laura, has no recollection of Charley, whereas she remembers Laura quite well. It is likely that Charley died about 1930. A walk through the DaVilla Cemetery with Vyree failed to confirm the location of Charley's grave, as a draw had widened over the years, eroding the earth and washing away many of the markers that Vyree remembered from her childhood.[14]

The legacy of Charley Willis and his wife Laura is substantial. In addition to the four children listed in the 1880 census, two more were born later, Victoria and Ruth. Two descendants carry on the Willis family tradition. "Goodbye Old Paint" continues to be sung by the Willis family and Artie Morris. Artie, a great-grandson of Charley, lives in Fischer, Texas, and is a singer of country and western music. He is a national performer who counts among his honors being invited backstage at the Grand Ole Opry in Nashville. Clarence Gonzales, another great-grandson of Willis, led a lengthy life as a rodeo cowboy from the late 1940s through the early 1970s. Living now in Richmond, Texas, Clarence used to compete in all events, but his forte was bull riding. He won honors in rodeos at such places as Madison Square Garden and the Boston Garden.

Today, hundreds of descendants participate in the Willis Connection, an organization founded by Willis descendant Franklin Willis of Los Angeles, California. Willis Connection members, as a means of celebrating their family heritage, continue to attend annual family reunions, correspond regularly, and support a newsletter.[15] The legacy of Charley Willis, an African American cowboy who drove cattle up the trail in the 1870s continues, not only in his descendants, but also in our country and western music today as we sing "Goodbye Old Paint."

Notes

1. Jim Bob Tinsley, *He Was Singin' This Song* (Orlando: University Presses of Florida, 1982), 124.

2. James Brown, telephone interview with Jim Chilcote, May 7, 1998.

3. U.S. Government, 1880 Census (Washington, D.C.: Department of Commerce, Division of Census).

4. Tinsley, *He Was Singin' This Song*, 124.

5. William Forbis, *The Cowboys* (New York: Time-Life Books, 1973), 162.

6. Tinsley, *He Was Singin' This Song*, 7.

7. Wayne Gard, *The Chisholm Trail* (Norman: University of Oklahoma Press, 1954), 243.

8. N. Howard "Jack" Thorp, *Songs of the Cowboys* ([1908] New York: Clarkson N. Potter, 1966), 16, 18–19; Tinsley, *He Was Singin' This Song*, 7; Gard, *Chisholm Trail*, 243.

9. Gard, *Chisholm Trail*, 244.

10. Joe A. Stout, "Cowboy," in *The Reader's Encyclopedia of the American West*, ed. Howard R. Lamar, 269 (New York: Thomas Y. Crowell, 1977).

11. Tinsley, *He Was Singin' This Song*, 7, 125; Duncan Emrich, *Cowboy Songs, Ballads, and Cattle Calls from Texas*, LP Record No. AAFS L28 ca. 1948 (Washington, D.C.: Archive of American Folk Song, Library of Congress, 1949); Duncan Emrich, *Folklore on the American Land* (Boston: Little, Brown, 1971), 489–92.

12. Tinsley, *He Was Singin' This Song*, 7, 122.

13. Thorp, *Songs of the Cowboys*, 16.

14. Vyree Willis Moore (great-granddaughter), interview with Jim Chilcote, Temple, Texas, March 31, 1998. James Brown, great-grandson of Charley Willis, supports the view that Charley Willis was interred at the DaVilla Cemetery; he reports having seen the marker sometime in the late 1970s during a pilgrimage to the Willis homestead.

15. For more information, contact Franklin Willis, Willis Connection, 594 South Cimarron, Los Angeles, CA 90047.

13

Bass Reeves

A Legendary Lawman of the Western Frontier

ART T. BURTON

Not all black cowboy types worked as cowboys, as Art T. Burton points out in this chapter. Bass Reeves was a fearless U.S. marshal, a large man, an excellent shot with his weapons, and a marshal for thirty-two years. As Burton reflects, Reeves was "one of the truly great American frontier heroes." Reeves patrolled a territory that included 75,000 square miles with outlaws who were murderers, bootleggers, or horse thieves. As William Loren Katz noted in *Black People Who Made the Old West* (1992), Reeves "faced some of the most desperate and treacherous men in the territory, and had handled himself with courage and success." We should add that he accomplished these feats successfully. Burton has also written a book-length biography of Reeves, *Black Gun, Silver Star* (2006), from which this chapter is drawn, and he discusses other black lawmen and outlaws in his *Black, Red, and Deadly* (1991). For other studies of the lives and careers of black lawmen, see Daniel F. Littlefield Jr. and Lonnie Underhill, "Negro Marshals in the Indian Territory" (1971), and Nudie Williams, "Black Men Who Wore the Star" (1981).

Bass Reeves was often called "one of the bravest men this country has ever known." "Invincible," others noted, "a Deputy U.S. Marshal whose devotion to duty was beyond reproach." He was honored posthumously with the National Cowboy Hall of Fame's "Great Westerner" at a Western Heritage Award program.

Reeves was born near Van Buren, Arkansas, in 1838 as a slave and grew up in North Texas. Reeves was hired by the U.S. marshal for Judge Isaac C. Parker federal court at Fort Smith in 1875 to track down criminals in western Arkansas

Originally published as Art T. Burton, "Bass Reeves: A Legendary Lawman of the Western Frontier," *Persimmon Hill* 20, no. 2 (Summer 1992): 45–48. Reprinted with permission of *Persimmon Hill* and the author.

and Indian Territory. This was a lawless and untamed region of Oklahoma that was an attractive refuge for criminals due to the territory's scarcity of towns and villages and the presence of so many Indians, who had jurisdiction only over themselves.

When Judge Parker assumed jurisdiction of the Fort Smith, Arkansas, court in 1875, he believed blacks would be good candidates for deputy U.S. marshals. Many Indians who lived in the territory had a distrust of white deputies, some of whom had abused their power, and the Indians often trusted blacks more than they did whites. There were former slaves known as Indian Freedmen in all the Five Civilized Tribes, and in some instances these African Americans were utilized as Indian policeman. They sat on governing councils, and some towns even had black judges and chiefs.

Parker considered Bass Reeves a good man for the tough job of a deputy U.S. marshal. Reeves had once boasted that he knew Indian Territory "like a cook knows her kitchen" and, as a result of his skill and his knowledge of the territory (gleaned in part from living among the Indians for a time), he was able to make substantial sums as a scout and tracker for peace officers. His service included enforcement of everything from petty misdemeanors to murder.

Believed to be one of the first African American deputy U.S. marshals commissioned west of the Mississippi River, Reeves served longer than any deputy U.S. marshal on record in Indian Territory, and during this thirty-five year tenure he acquired a reputation as "one of the best deputy marshals to ever work out of the Fort Smith Federal Court."

He was in fabled company. The Fort Smith court helped create reputations, not only for Bass Reeves and Judge Parker, but for such other noted deputy marshals as Heck Thomas, Grant Johnson, John Mershon, Heck Bruner, and Sam Sixkiller.

Bass Reeves was a big man—six feet two inches tall and weighing 180 pounds; he was an imposing figure, a lawman to be feared and a man who was legendary in the territory. A police chief once noted, "The veteran Negro deputy never quailed in facing any man." He had no fear of his master and once, when they got into an argument over a card game in the early 1860s, Reeves knocked his master out cold, an offense punishable by death for a slave. He fled into Indian Territory, finding refuge living with and fighting Civil War battles for the Union Seminoles and Creek Indians and eventually becoming close friends with Creek chief Opothleyaholo.

Everything about Bass Reeves seemed to invite legend. People said he always rode a large sorrel stallion with a white blazed face, or a large white horse. But he kept two good riding horses for pursuit, as well as a run-of-the-mill horse for undercover work. To outlaws, the sign of a superior pony was a tip-off that the rider was a deputy marshal.

Reeves always wore a large black hat with a straight brim that was slightly upturned in the front. And old-timers said he often carried his guns in many different ways. He was particularly noted for wearing two Colt revolvers, calibrated for the .45 cartridge, butt forward for a fast draw. It didn't matter that he was ambidextrous. Bass Reeves always got the job done. When the Colts weren't pressed into service, he used his fine Winchester rifle, chambered for the .44 cartridge. He was such an expert with pistols and rifles that later in his life he wasn't even allowed to compete in turkey shoots because his skill was far superior to any competition.

Given to using aliases, he also was known as a natty dresser, with his boots always polished to a gleaming shine. But most of the time, when he was in pursuit of an outlaw, he was a master of disguise. Sometimes he dressed as a preacher, drover, or a cowboy, other times as a farmer or a gunslinger. He even dressed as an outlaw when the occasion warranted that approach.

When Reeves began riding for Judge Parker, the jurisdiction covered more than 75,000 square miles. The deputies from Fort Smith rode to Fort Reno, Fort Sill, and Anadarko, a round trip of more than eight hundred miles. Whenever a deputy marshal left Fort Smith to capture outlaws in the territory, he took with him a wagon, a cook, a guard, and usually several possemen, depending on the temperament and reputation of the outlaws he was pursuing.

The Missouri, Kansas and Texas (MK&T) Railroad, running across the territory, marked the western fringe of civilization. Eighty miles west of Fort Smith was known as "the dead line," and whenever a deputy marshal from Fort Smith or Paris, Texas, crossed the "dead line" they could be killed. Outlaws left messages on cards nailed to trees and posts to threaten the deputies. To Bass Reeves, the "dead line" posed a thrilling challenge.

Reeves figured there were three principal classes of outlaws in the territory: murderers, horse thieves, and whiskey bootleggers. Added to the Indians and mixed Africans were the white outlaws, the biggest problem; many had fled from Texas, Arkansas, Kansas, and other states.

His reputation was praised often, and on November 19, 1909, the *Muskogee*

Times Democrat wrote: "In the early days when the Indian country was over-
ridden with outlaws, Reeves would herd into Fort Smith, often single handed,
bands of men charged with crimes from bootlegging to murder. He was paid
fees in those days that sometimes amounted to thousands of dollars for a single
trip . . . trips that sometimes lasted for months."

One of those trips found Reeves in pursuit of two young outlaws in the Red
River Valley of the Chickasaw Nation. Reeves studied the many ways in which
he might capture them and snare the $5,000 reward. When he heard they were
sequestered near the Texas border, he selected a posse and journeyed to the
vicinity where he felt the outlaws were hiding. He set up camp twenty-eight
miles from the suspected hideout so he could review the terrain and take his
time in planning their capture without creating any suspicions. He disguised
himself as a tramp. In doing so, he removed the heels from an old pair of shoes,
carried a cane, concealed his handcuffs, pistol, and badge under his clothes, and
wore a floppy old hat into which he had shot three bullet holes. Thus disguised,
Reeves started out on foot in the direction of the outlaws' probable hideout, the
home of their mother.

When she greeted Reeves at the door, he asked for a bite to eat and
lamented how much his feet hurt after walking such a long distance. Reeves
told her this was the first opportunity he had to stop after being pursued by a
posse that had put three bullet holes in his hat.

She invited Reeves into her home, gladly fed him and even proceeded to
tell him about her two outlaw sons. When Reeves finished eating, he feigned
weariness and asked to stay a while longer. She consented and said, "It would
be a good plan that you and my two boys join forces so you can be a protection
to one another."

After the sun had gone down and the night ruled supreme, Reeves heard
a sharp whistle from the nearby creek. The woman went outside and gave an
answer. Two riders rode up and had a lengthy conversation with her. When
they finally came into the house, she introduced Reeves to her sons as another
outlaw. The boys agreed the trio should join forces for theft and plunder.

When they prepared to go to bed, a place in a separate room was made
for Reeves. But he immediately suggested they all sleep in one room, saying,
"Something might happen, and if we are separated we couldn't be much protection to one another."

While in bed, Reeves kept a watchful eye on the boys. As soon as the out-laws were asleep, Reeves left his bed and managed to handcuff the pair without awaking them. He waited until early morning before he kicked the boys from their sleep and said, "Come on, boys, let's get going from here." When the two boys finally got the sleep out of their eyes, they realized they were in the hands of the law.

As Reeves started out with his prisoners, the mother followed him for three miles, cursing him and calling him all sorts of vile names. The boys were forced to walk the full twenty-eight miles to Reeves's camp, where all his possemen were waiting for him to deliver the outlaws and claim his reward.

By 1901, Reeves had arrested more than three thousand men and women in his service as a deputy U.S. marshal. But no manhunt was harder for Reeves than the one involving his own son. The incident occurred late in Reeves's career as a lawman. Upon delivering two prisoners to the federal jail in Muskogee, Reeves related another harrowing experience. He had nearly been killed when the three men he had warrants for ambushed him deep in the Creek Nation. He killed one in the ambush and got the other two to surrender. After deliver-ing his prisoners to U.S. marshal Leo Bennett, Reeves was looking forward to a well-deserved rest.

But there was yet another warrant to be served. Bennett had to break the news to Reeves that his own son was charged with the murder of his wife and was a fugitive somewhere in Indian Territory. Bennett wanted to bring young Reeves in alive if he could, and for two days the warrant lay on Bennett's desk, with all the deputies fearing they would be chosen for the unpleasant task.

Although Reeves was visibly shaken by this tragedy, he demanded to take the warrant. He told Bennett it was his responsibility to bring his son in even though he knew it would be the toughest, saddest manhunt he was ever involved in.

Reeves located the Muskogee house his son Bennie was in and arrested him without any incident. Bennie was turned over to Marshal Bennett and sent to Leavenworth Prison at the end of a trial. After thirteen years, a citizen's petition, and an exemplary prison record, Reeves's son was pardoned and lived the rest of his life as a model citizen.

When Reeves retired from federal service, he had numerous stories to tell his children and numerous grandchildren, nieces, and nephews. And he had in his possession a dozen of those cards that outlaws had posted on the "dead line." To Reeves, those cards were like badges of courage for a career that always found him living on the edge of danger and intrigue.

When Bass Reeves died, January 12, 1910, the *Muskogee Phoenix* wrote of the legendary lawman:

> Bass Reeves is dead. He passed away yesterday afternoon about three o'clock and in a short time news of his death had reached the federal courthouse where it recalled to the officers and clerks many incidents in the early days of the United States in which the old Negro deputy figured heroically.
>
> Bass Reeves had completed thirty-five years' service as a deputy marshal when, with the coming of statehood at the age of sixty-nine, he gave up his position. For about two years he then served on the Muskogee Police Force, a post he gave up about a year ago on account of sickness, from which he never fully recovered. . . .
>
> In the history of the early days of Eastern Oklahoma the name of Bass Reeves has a place in the front rank among those who cleansed out the old Indian Territory of outlaws and desperadoes. No story of the conflict of government's officers with those outlaws, which ended only a few years ago with the rapid filling up of the territory with people, can be complete without mention of the Negro who died yesterday.
>
> For thirty-five years, beginning way back in the seventies and ending in 1907, Bass Reeves was a Deputy United States Marshal. During that time he was sent to arrest some of the most desperate characters that ever infested Indian Territory and endangered life and peace in its borders. And he got his man as often as any of the deputies. At times he was unable to get them alive and so in the course of his long service he killed 14 men. But Bass Reeves always said that he never shot a man when it was not necessary for him to do so in the discharge of his duty to save his own life.
>
> Reeves served under seven United States marshals and all of them were more than satisfied with his services. Everybody who came in contact with the Negro deputy in an official capacity had a great deal of respect for him, and at the court house in Muskogee one can hear stories of his devotion to duty, his unflinching courage and his many

thrilling experiences. And although he could not write or read, he always took receipts and had his accounts in good shape. . . .

Reeves had many narrow escapes. At different times his belt was shot in two, a button shot off his coat, his hat brim shot off and the bridle rein which he held in his hand cut by a bullet. However, in spite of all these narrow escapes and the many conflicts in which he was engaged, Reeves was never wounded. And this, notwithstanding the fact that he never fired a shot until the desperado he was trying to arrest had started the shooting.

Nine decades after his death, Bass Reeves is still considered one of the truly great American frontier heroes. The legend of Bass Reeves will live as long as people recall stories of bravery and courage in the American West.

Concluding Overview
In Search of the Black Cowboy

MICHAEL N. SEARLES

In this final presentation, Michael Searles focuses his effort on the background and experiences of the multitude of blacks who became cowboys before and immediately after the Civil War, offering us numerous vignettes about African Americans who became black cowboys. Even after the end of the trail drives, he points out, blacks "found work on ranches, in feedlots, at horse auction barns, on the rodeo circuit, and as horse traders and trainers."

The words "black cowboys" are an oxymoron for much of the general public even with their inclusion in scholarly books, bibliographies, anthologies, and popular accounts generated over the past years.[1] The limited circulation of books on black cowboys may be one reason that a knowledgeable audience is so small. There are a great many Americans who have never seen a black man in the role of a cowboy in life or in literature. It has been only recently that western fiction has recognized black cowboys, and it was not until the 1950s that they were portrayed as legitimate characters on the silver screen.[2]

Selective black audiences were presented with a touch of the Old West in the late 1930s and early 1940s when Herb Jeffries blazed the trail in *Harlem on the Prairie*, *Harlem Rides the Range*, and *The Bronze Buckaroo*. These movies were big hits with African Americans; however, they had a surreal quality since all the characters were black. A West peopled with all black folk may have

---

Originally published as Michael N. Searles, "In Search of the Black Cowboy in Texas," in *The African American Experience in Texas*, edited by Bruce A. Glasrud and James M. Smallwood (Lubbock: Texas Tech University Press, 2007), 86–101. Reprinted by permission of Texas Tech University Press and the author.

given credence to a West peopled with no black folk, since an all-black West was not credible, even to a black audience.

The connection among black men, horses, and cattle began in Africa and spread to the Americas during the colonial period. Africans and Indians were often selected as cowboys in North and South America.[3] Peter H. Wood, who chronicled the history of blacks in South Carolina from 1670 to 1739, argues that African expertise developed the cattle industry in that state.[4] In South Carolina and Georgia, it became common practice to advertise and sell land, cattle, and a Negro with knowledge of tending cattle in a single package.

The history of black cattle tending in the New World has been explored by Richard W. Slatta and Terry G. Jordan. Both scholars supported the idea of active African involvement in cattle raising in the West Indies, South America, and Mexico. Concurrent with African participation in tending cattle was an expertise with horses. The ability with horses demonstrated by blacks caused some to believe that it was instinctual. Frederick Remington was neither the first nor the last to express this sentiment. In a turn-of-the-century magazine article, he stated that black cavalrymen carried on conversations with their horses and that it was perfectly apparent that the horses understood what they said.[5]

Black cowboys were found in states east and west of the Mississippi River; however, Texas claimed the largest concentration. In 1860, slaves and free blacks exceeded 30 percent of the Texas population with more than 83,000 people. Following the end of slavery, the numbers of African Americans in Texas continued to grow while steadily declining as a percentage of the total population. The large number of cattle in Texas offered opportunities for enterprising men to turn a profit. In selected Texas counties, the cattle to population ratio was higher than 40 to 1.[6] In those counties, especially in the southeast, black cowboys were the cowboys of choice for some ranchers.

A substantial number of slaves crossing the Red and Sabine Rivers were put into direct contact with cattle. In some cases, it was a first contact and for others it was a continuation of a tradition that extended back to Africa.[7] Sam Jones Washington, a slave of rancher Sam Young who lived along the Colorado River in Wharton County, Texas, spoke about cowboying as a slave and a freedman. Washington's words, a part of the Slave Narratives project of the Works Progress Administration (WPA), suggest that some blacks associated the cowboy life with freedom: "I first ran errands, and then massa larn me to ride, as soon as I could sit a horse. Then I stayed out with de cattle most of the time, and I was tickled. I sure liked to ride and rope those cattle, and massa always fixed me up with good clothes and a good horse and a good saddle. I stayed there till long after surrender."[8]

Like Sam Jones Washington, a number of other freedmen stayed on their former masters' ranches and farms after surrender and throughout the nineteenth century. Many of them did cattle work as long as it provided them with a living, but as the cattle business waned they turned to farming, sheep raising, service jobs, factory work, railroad work, and the military. Sam Jones Washington typifies those men who turned their hands to farming.

It is in the life of Washington that we confront the difficulty of finding the black cowboy. Many men labored for as many as twenty or more years as cowboys and then as a result of the economy, ill health, or age left cowboy work with little evidence of their involvement. While these cowboys had local notoriety, they were often ignored or forgotten when town, county, and regional histories were written.

Much of what we know about these nearly anonymous black cowboys comes from the biographical sketches collected by the WPA. Tom Mills spoke of his lifelong commitment to the cowboy life as follows: "When I got to workin' for myself, it was cow work. I done horse back work for fifty years. Many a year passed that I never missed a day bein' in the saddle. I stayed thirteen years on one ranch. The first place was right below Hondo City."[9]

In his years as a cowboy, he saw the trails and recounted many of the experiences reported by other black cowboys. He was expected to do his job well and when white cowboys fouled up to keep it to himself. Mills worked on other ranches delivering cattle down to the Rio Grande until he finally quit ranching and became a stock farmer.

Black cowboys were expected to do the roughest, most dangerous work and to do it without complaint. They often competed directly with white southerners who had little love for black men. Some whites had lost their land and possessions as a result of the Civil War, while others remembered that slavery had excluded them from the meanest work. The decision to make slavery the centerpiece of southern economy and life was not a choice made by the slave population, but the freedman was a visible reminder of white degradation.

There are a number of instances where black cowboys were run off by white southerners whose hatred for blacks was palpable. While black cowboys were given opportunities to work, it was often provided by cattlemen who once owned slaves. Former slave owners continued the patterns of paternalism that existed during the antebellum period. Owners, foremen, and trail bosses sometimes forced white cowboys to accept the presence of black cowboys and, while white cowboys were not generally free to shoot blacks, they made sure they did the meanest work.

In recollecting about black cowboys, John M. Hendricks, a well-established cattleman, made the following statement:

> They [black cowboys] did as much as possible to place themselves in the good graces of the [white] hands. This most often took the form of "topping," or taking the first pitch out of the rough horses of the outfit as they stood saddled, with backs humped, in the chill of the morning, while the [white] boys ate their breakfast. It was not unusual for one young negro to "top" a half a dozen hard-pitching horses before breakfast. . . . It was the negro hand who usually tried out the swimming water when a trailing herd came to a swollen stream, or if a fighting bull or steer was to be handled, he knew without being told it was his job.[10]

While more was expected of black cowboys, not every experience was a negative one. Some white cowboys formed friendships with black cowboys and, at least on the trail, worked and lived in relative equality.

Black cowboys seemed to enjoy life on the range, but it required a toughness of mind and spirit. One of the ways black cowboys tried to ensure themselves a job was to prove daily their worth to the boss and their fellow cowboys. In town after town in all regions of the West, black cowboys, bronco busters, and horse handlers gained reputations for being "the best cowboys to ever straddle a horse." Such stories were repeated in cowboy memoirs and by professional writers and prominent cattlemen of the West.

Upon hearing about the death of Bose Ikard, Charles Goodnight, whose name was synonymous with the cattle business in West Texas, had a monument erected with the following marker: "Served me four years on the Goodnight-Loving Trail, never shirked a duty or disobeyed an order, rode with me in many stampedes, participated in three engagements with Comanches, splendid behavior." Ikard was more than an average cowboy and was given many important responsibilities. According to J. Evetts Haley, Goodnight's biographer, Ikard served as Goodnight's detective, banker on the trail, and an all-around cowboy. Haley further states that Goodnight extolled Ikard's character with the extraordinary statement: "I have trusted him farther than any living man."[11]

Colonel Zack Miller lionized Bill Pickett, the man who invented the rodeo sport of bulldogging and brought fame and fortune to the Miller Brothers 101 Ranch Real Wild West Show. Colonel Miller wrote a poem eulogizing Pickett's virtues shortly after his death. The poem entitled "Old Bill Is Dead" paid Bill the supreme "compliment" of negating his color with the line "Bill's hide was black but his heart was white." Colonel Miller expressed his sentiment with great feeling and sincerity with no thought that his expression demeaned the man honored.[12]

George W. Littlefield, a prominent Texas cattleman, banker, and philanthropist, maintained a lifelong relationship with black cowboy Addison Jones. Old Add, or "Nigger Add," as he was generally known, cowboyed for the Littlefield Ranch most of his life and broke in many of the white and black cowboys who worked there. His ability handling horses, counting cattle, and identifying ear marks and brands prompted N. Howard (Jack) Throp, a cowboy and writer/songwriter, to memorialize Add with a poem entitled "Whose Old Cow?"[13]

The list of notable black cowboys does not end with Bose Ikard, Bill Pickett, and Addison Jones. Many white cattlemen and cowboys praised such black cowboys as Mathew "Bones" Hooks, Robert Lemmons, James Kelly, Jim Perry, Louis Powers, and Richard "Bubba" Walker.[14] In small towns and on ranches throughout the West, white cowboys recognized the skill and ability of black cowboys. Even today in small hamlets and towns far off the interstates, old men sit outside cafes and stores and talk about a particular black cowboy who could ride anything he could throw his legs over.

Joseph H. Proctor, Ol' Proc, was such a man. He began his life on a plantation in Burnett, Texas. He later trailed cattle from Texas to Wyoming and Montana. He decided, after several trips, to stay in Montana, where he worked for a number of ranches. His abilities with a lariat and with horses brought him great respect and admiration. When he died on July 19, 1938, the *Forsyth Time-Journal* wrote his memorial on its front page. The *Time-Journal* celebrated Proctor's life and made numerous references to his skills as a cowboy and his sterling character. It ended the lengthy tribute with words appropriate for any cattle baron or leading town citizen.[15]

Montana cowboy poet Wallace McRae wrote the poem "Ol' Proc" as a tribute to Joe Proctor, whose exploits were sung by McRae's grandfather and neighbors when Wallace was just a boy. The last stanza of his tribute poem indicates the presence and anonymity of black cowboys:

> I couldn't wait to meet Mr. Proc,
> Whose peers all praised his ways with stock.
> But when his calloused hand gripped mine, surprise hit me in waves.
> Those old cowboys who cut no slack
> Deemed it unimportant Proc was black,
> And wasn't worth a mention that Joe Proctor's folks were slaves.[16]

It was this anonymity, sometimes a result of courtesy and sometimes for other reasons, that kept black cowboys in the shadows. As the American West became symbolic of all that was good in the nation, there was a tendency to see a monochromatic landscape. The important figures who shaped the West were not red, brown, yellow, or black. In the history and literature of scholars and writers alike, the only color that mattered was white.[17] It was this lack of recognition that produced the popular notion that black cowboys did not exist.

Most black and white cowboys remained working men living from payday to payday throughout their lives. This was the case whether they continued to work as cowboys or made the transition to factory or other kinds of work. The rough and somewhat independent life on the range did not usually produce provident men with long-term goals of owning a spread of their own. There were some exceptions to this rule among white as well as black cowboys, but the transition was not an easy one. Sometimes, even when boys were of the same race and class, and were born in the same region, their accomplishments varied a great deal.

The coastal bend of Texas was the starting and sometimes the finishing place for a number of black cowboys. For some, however, the grass looked a great deal greener in West Texas. Jack Bess was born on Steve Bess's ranch near Goliad, Texas, in 1854. He lived his first eleven years as a slave and learned to like working horses and cattle. As was the case with other slaves, he continued in this pursuit throughout the Civil War and into freedom. Bess's recollections were preserved in the WPA Slave Narratives: "Our beds was pretty good when uses dem. . . . Our log huts was comfortable as we had some kind of floors in all of dem. . . . De eats we know was jes' good eats, lots of meat and vegetables and de like, 'possum and coon and beef and pork all cooked good. Our clothes was jes' home spun liked all de others."[18]

Some of the slave narratives were as short as a page, while others extended for five or six pages. Bess's eighty-plus years were described in just one-and-a-half typed pages. He spoke of hearing the news of freedom and going to work on a ranch in the old Ben Ficklin community in what became Tom Green County. Ben Ficklin is remembered in Texas history as a rival settlement to San Angelo and the county seat until 1882, when it was washed away by a flood.[19] Bess spoke of his working one ranch and then another in Ben Ficklin before the creation of San Angelo.

Daniel Webster Wallace was born September 15, 1860, in Victoria County, Texas. Webster lived with his mother, Mary Wallace, in what might be described as commodious quarters by slave standards. His mother was a house servant and wet nurse for Mrs. Mary O'Daniel. Mary Wallace received her freedom and decided to stay with the O'Daniels as Webster began his early life chopping weeds and plowing for about thirty cents a day. As with many other young boys of his day, the call of the trail and the cowboy life fueled his imagination.[20]

Neither Webster nor Jack Bess had much schooling, but they both treasured their dreams of becoming cowboys. The record does not indicate how Jack traveled from Goliad to Tom Green County, but Daniel Webster Wallace slipped away from his mother and joined a cattle drive heading for Coleman County. When Webster arrived in Coleman County, he was in the county adjoining where Jack Bess lived. Two black boys, formerly slaves, started new chapters in their otherwise fragmented lives as cowboys. It is not known whether the two boys knew each other, but that was unlikely. Yet they had begun their cowboy careers in close proximity and now once again were geographically connected in juxtaposed counties.

At this point, we can only speculate about the exploits and activities of Jack Bess. Daniel Wallace on the other hand would become the subject of a book, a master's thesis, an article in a West Texas yearbook, and a chapter in *Black Cowboys of Texas*.[21] Webster perfected his skills as a cowboy working for Sam Gholson, a buffalo hunter and Indian fighter, and the Nunn and Clay Mann outfits.[22] It was to be the Clay Mann brand, the numeral "80," that would forever be attached to his name: "80 John."

Daniel Webster Wallace was to shed Webster, his boyhood name, for "80 John," as he was to be known throughout Texas cattle country for the rest of his life. There was a certain irony in the fact that neither Webster nor 80 John was a name of his choosing. 80 John rode into Colorado City behind a dusty herd of Clay Mann's cattle but did more than "eat trail dust." He watched and listened to the actions and words of Mann as he learned the lessons that would later shape his life and career. 80 John came to know the value of keeping his word and the value of a dollar. He acquired good business sense and came to appreciate the value of education in a world of business and finance.

While most other cowboys spent and drank up their money as fast as they got it, 80 John had a portion of his salary withheld to acquire a nest egg for buying cattle and owning his own ranch. The element of trust that developed between Mann and Wallace was much like that of Bose Ikard and Charles Goodnight. In the days when transactions were often conducted with cash, cattlemen like Mann had large amounts of money that needed to be deposited in banks or transferred to a given rancher. Since cattle transactions were common knowledge, outlaws had a keen interest in large sums of money changing hands.

Mann's trust and faith in Wallace was demonstrated in his willingness to allow him to carry substantial cattle payments often many miles away. Wallace's experiences became a part of family conversations and may have been used by him to instill the same values in his children. The following story indicates the deep respect and friendship that existed between Mann and Wallace: "In those days, when banks were hundreds of miles away and cash was paid in all transactions, Mann sent thirty thousand dollars with 80 John in a wagon to the Cross Tie Ranch near Midland. This was a trip that required three days travel. 80 John delivered the money which he had carefully guarded, sleeping with it under his head at night."[23]

Evidence that Wallace was taking to heart the lessons he learned about saving money was seen in 1885, when he bought two sections of land in Mitchell County and started homesteading while still working for Mann.

Wallace, who decided at the age of twenty-five that he needed an education, traveled back to Navarro County in East Texas and enrolled in an elementary school. While studying his ABCs, he wooed and married Laura Dee Owens, a recent high school graduate who planned to become a teacher. Wallace and his new bride returned to Mitchell County and established a life for themselves on one of the Mann ranches.

It was shortly after Wallace's return that Clay Mann died in 1889. Wallace stayed on with the Mann outfit and extended his loyalty to Mrs. Mann, who died two years later. He now could become an independent rancher and develop a life out of the shadow of his employer of fourteen years. His standing in the community and his business acumen allowed him to secure a bank loan, purchase cows, and lease pasture land. He joined the Texas and Southwestern Cattle Raisers Association and acquired access to its brand records and new methods of ranching.

Like other ranchers, Wallace had to endure the vagaries of nature and business cycles. He weathered droughts, "die-ups" (massive death of cattle), and poor market conditions with an ability that often exceeded that of his white neighbors. His keen insight and, at times, loans from "banker-friends" allowed him to continue or sometimes start again when others were forced out of the cattle business. Wallace's good judgment was clearly demonstrated when his financial holdings were assessed at the end of his life. He had acquired fourteen and one half sections of land and six hundred head of cattle that he owned unencumbered by mortgage, loan, or taxes.

Wallace supported churches in his community as well as numerous charitable causes. He had a special interest in the education of young people and assisted some in meeting their college expenses. Most likely, it was the lack of opportunity to gain an education that sparked his interest in seeing others acquire what was denied him. Wallace's generosity and support of education encouraged the officials of Colorado City, Texas, to name a school for black children in his honor.

When Wallace died on March 28, 1939, many of his friends and fellow cattlemen brought or sent condolences to his family. He was recognized as a pioneer, a leading citizen of Mitchell County, and a man worthy of respect.

In most respects, the lives of the two black cowboys Jack Bess and Daniel Webster "80 John" Wallace were quite different in what they were able to accumulate and their positions in society. Yet, until recently, a search of the public record revealed very little about either Bess or Wallace. This lack of recognition began to change as Daniel Webster Wallace, the man known as "the most respected Negro ranchman in the Old West," received individual notation in the *Online Handbook of Texas*.

Bill Pickett, the most famous black cowboy of the old West, only recently regained some of the fame he had achieved in the halcyon days of the Miller Brothers 101 Ranch Real Wild West Show. In 1977, Colonel Bailey C. Hanes wrote a well-researched biography of Bill Pickett that introduced him to a general audience. In the foreword to *Bill Pickett, Bulldogger*, Bill Burchardt stated that Pickett's long and celebrated years as a rodeo star did not make him immune to obscurity: "It seems incredible that the story of a man of Bill Pickett's stature could virtually sink from sight in a single generation, yet it has. We are emerging from an era which has buried the stories of many Americans of minority races: Negro, Indian, and others. The Bill Pickett story easily could have been lost completely. It has been badly warped in a good many magazine articles written by pseudohistorians and bigots intent on propaganda."[24]

Pickett's life began, like that of many other black cowboys, as a child of slaves. According to his family, Willie Pickett was born on December 5, 1870, in Travis County, Texas. The Pickett family, like many other South Carolina and Georgia slaves, were experienced in the handling of cattle. In 1854, they left South Carolina with their slave masters, Dr. Welborn Barton and Colonel Alexander Barton, and moved to the Lone Star State. When the Picketts arrived in central Texas, they continued to work as cowboys and wranglers for their owners.

Bill was the second of thirteen children born to Thomas Jefferson and Mary Virginia Elizabeth (Gilbert) Pickett. Bill received little formal education and very early in his life devoted his time and energy to cow work. His cousins, Anderson Pickett and Jerry Barton, drove cattle up the Chisholm Trail when Bill was a young boy. Their stories of life on the trail provided Bill vicariously the hazards and excitement of encountering Indians, swollen rivers, and towns like Abilene, Kansas. Living around the cattle town of Austin also provided Bill ample opportunity to see cowboy life firsthand.

At a young age, Bill observed a technique that would bring him fame and fortune. The practice of using dogs to search out and catch cattle was popular with some ranchers. Bill observed a bulldog holding a cow by its upper lip. Once the bulldog had a firm grip on the cow's lip, the cow would stand perfectly still. This chance observation stuck in Bill's mind and later was used by him to thrill and amaze audiences.

Pickett perfected the "bite 'em down style" of bulldogging and began to exhibit his talent at county fairs and less formal gatherings. He passed his hat at these events and received whatever the audience was willing to give. Bill's "bite 'em down style" of catching and holding cattle also proved valuable in the mesquite brush of central Texas. Cowboys were expected to locate and bring half-wild cows out of the thickets where they would hide. In the heavy brush country where it was very difficult to use a lariat, Bill would jump off his horse and, by grabbing and twisting the cow's horns, bring the cow to a stop. He would then bite into its lip until the animal offered no resistance. This practice allowed a cow to be roped and dragged into a clear area and constrained until it was tame enough to stay with the herd.

By 1888, Thomas Pickett had moved his family to Taylor, Texas, where Bill and his brothers established a horse-breaking business. In December 1890, Bill married Maggie Turner and started his own family. With this new responsibility, Bill settled into the role of a responsible and respected member of the community. He worked on several ranches in the area, hunted, and picked cotton to make ends meet.

While Bill did exhibitions, his connection with promoters Lee Monroe and Dave McClure spread his fame across the state and the nation. Monroe, a rancher from Rockdale, Texas, arranged for Bill to perform in Houston, Dublin, and San Angelo as well as Forth Worth and Taylor. In 1903, McClure promoted Bill as the "Dusky Demon," a name that forever would be attached to him. Two of Pickett's biographers believed that McClure chose the "Dusky Demon" sobriquet to mask Bill's racial identity, since a variety of nationalities could presumably be dusky. The Demon reference may have been added to suggest that his talents had a supernatural origin.

While black cowboys had long established themselves as expert horse handlers and riders, during the first half of the twentieth century they generally were not permitted to compete in rodeo events with whites. In a segregated America, "the mixing of the races" was considered demeaning and against the law. The effort to introduce a less than candid portrait of Bill may have been an effort to shield his race until he gained enough fame to overcome it.[25]

In 1904, Pickett achieved national recognition when he performed at the Cheyenne Frontier Days. Cheyenne Frontier Days began in 1897 as a fair for excursion passengers on the Union Pacific Railroad and continued to attract visitors from throughout the United States and abroad. President Theodore Roosevelt and George Eastman of Kodak were two of the notables who visited Cheyenne Frontier Days during the early part of the twentieth century. While it was reported that Buffalo Bill's Wild West Show performed for a cheering crowd of six thousand in 1898, newspapers reported that over 20,000 spectators watched and admired Bill Pickett in 1904. The presence of the *Wyoming Times*, the *Denver Post*, and New York's *Harper's Weekly* also guaranteed perhaps millions of people not in attendance would learn about the fearless colored man from Taylor, Texas.

While each newspaper celebrated the courage and daring of Pickett, each in its own way wanted the reading public to know that bulldogging a steer had been performed by a black man. Each newspaper stated that Pickett was a Negro or a colored man, but the *Wyoming Times* also thought it was important that its readers know that he had "strong ivory teeth." The *Denver Post* devoted two sections essentially written in dialect apparently to authenticate that Bill was a real Negro. The *Post* also thought that it should mention the connection between Bill's teeth and the tusks of an African elephant: "The ivory adornments of that spacious opening in the colored man's face attest to the truthfulness of every word he uttered, for the teeth that remain are big and sharp and strong, but several are gone in part as the result of encounters with especially muscular steers, which refused to be humbled without a struggle."

The *Harper's Weekly* article made no reference to Bill's teeth and refrained from the use of dialect in describing his accomplishments. John Dicks Howe, *Harper's* special reporter, wrote a descriptive article without offensive appellations until the last sentence of his story. He then stated: "So great was the applause that the darkey again attacked the steer, which had staggered to its feet, and again threw it after a desperate struggle."

In 1905, Pickett's career would make another leap forward when he performed at the National Editors Association's convention in Oklahoma. The Miller brothers, Zack, George, and Joe, who were responsible for his coming to the convention a few years later, made him the premier act in their Ranch Wild West Show. The 101 Wild West Show toured the United States, Canada, Mexico, South America, and England, entertaining millions of adoring fans. With the trip to England in 1914, Bill had the opportunity to meet British royalty and perform before the royal family.[26]

Pickett originated the rodeo sport of steer wrestling and established himself as the most famous black cowboy of the American West. In 1971, he was the first black cowboy to be inducted into the National Cowboy Hall of Fame in Oklahoma City, and in 1989 he was inducted into the Pro Rodeo Hall of Fame in Colorado Springs, Colorado. His name was resurrected in 1984 when a black rodeo company adopted it in forming the Bill Pickett Invitational Rodeo. In 1987, the North Fort Worth Historical Society commissioned a bronze statue showing Pickett bulldogging a 1,000-pound longhorn. The life-like sculpture was unveiled on the grounds of the Cowtown Coliseum where Pickett had performed during its grand opening in 1908. Pickett received many other honors, including being selected for the 1994 stamp panel entitled Legends of the West.

Few cowboys, black or white, gained the renown of Bill Pickett, but black cowboys played their parts in transforming the West. They rode the lonely trails, branded and herded cattle, and continued to work cattle long after the long drives up the Shawnee, Chisholm, Western, and Goodnight-Loving Trails ended. They found work on ranches, in feedlots, at horse auction barns, on the rodeo circuit, and as horse traders and trainers. When new opportunity arose, some left their cowboy past and worked for the railroads or found jobs in cities. Some bought small ranches where they cowboyed on the weekend. Many left cowboy life and seemingly forgot that they once had worked on horseback.

The fragmented remembrance of black cowboy life and the scant written record would seem to evince the insignificance of the experience. Yet the lack of archival records and the relatively small numbers of black cowboys in some areas of the West do not tell the whole story. The black cowboy population had a dynamic impact on American life in several important areas. One of those areas was the music sung by cowboys as they sat around campfires and as they did night herding. Many of those songs were remembered and documented by working cowboys, song collectors, and folklorists. In the introduction of *Cowboy Songs and Other Frontier Ballads*, collected by J. A. and Alan Lomax, the following statement is found:

> Often the best of the singers were black cowboys, who brought their African and Afro-American heritage of hollers and herding songs to the Texas cattle country. Both Charles Siringo and Teddy Blue, two noted cowboy historians, said that the best singers and musical cattle handlers were black cowboys from whom they learned their trade in the early days. John Lomax took down many of his finest songs, including "Home on the Range" and "Sam Bass," from black trail bands. Truly this western tradition linked many trails.[27]

In a conversation with a friend some years ago, I was told a story of her experience in Montana. She and a friend, both of whom were white school teachers in Chicago, stopped in a small cafe and received some ribbing by local cowboys. The cowboys could not understand how they could stand to be around niggers. When a black cowboy entered the cafe, the cowboys went over and greeted him with what appeared to be genuine affection and respect. Once the black cowboy left, my friend asked why they had been so antagonistic to them while they related so well to the black cowboy. Their response was that he was not black, he was a cowboy.

There are still black cowboys who earn their living in places as widely separated as Florida and California. A comprehensive account of those twentieth-century experiences has yet to be written. Although black men remain a minority among cowboys, their stories are worth collecting, assessing, and integrating into the broader fabric of the western region. How did the West change those black men who became cowboys? How did black cowboys change the West? Did the experience of the black cowboys have an impact of the way we see the West? There is much to be researched about the black cowboy's quality of life, his working relations with other cowboys, and the manner in which he negotiated the uncertain racial terrain in the West.

Notes

1. See Philip Durham and Everett L. Jones, *The Negro Cowboy* (New York: Dodd, Mead, 1965; William Loren Katz, *The Black West: A Documentary and Pictorial History of the African American Role in the Westward Expansion of the United States* (New York: Doubleday, 1971); Kenneth Wiggins Porter, *The Negro on the American Frontier* (New York: Arno Press, 1971); W. Sherman Savage, *Blacks in the West* (Westport, Conn.: Greenwood Press, 1976). More recently additional books and bibliographies have been added, including Bruce A. Glasrud, ed., *African Americans in the West: A Bibliography of Secondary Sources* (Alpine, Tex.: Sul Ross State University Center for Big Bend Studies, 1998); Art Burton, *Black, Red, and Deadly: Black and Indian Gunfighters of the Indian Territories, 1870–1907* (Austin: Eakin Press, 1991); Cecil Johnson, *Guts: Legendary Black Rodeo Cowboy Bill Pickett* (Fort Worth, Tex.: Summit Group, 1994); Glenn Shirley, *Marauders of the Indian Nations: The Bill Cook Gang and Cherokee Bill* (Stillwater, Okla.: Barbed Wire Press, 1994); Alwyn Barr, *Black Texans: A History of African Americans in Texas, 1528–1995*, 2nd ed. (Norman: University of

Oklahoma Press, 1996); Quintard Taylor, *In Search of the Racial Frontier: African Americans in the American West, 1528–1990* (New York: W. W. Norton, 1998); Monroe Lee Billington and Roger D. Hardaway, eds., *African Americans on the Western Frontier* (Niwot: University Press of Colorado, 1998); and Sara R. Massey, ed., *Black Cowboys of Texas* (College Station: Texas A&M University Press, 2000).

2. Robert G. Athearn, *The Mythic West in the Twentieth Century* (Lawrence: University Press of Kansas, 1986).

3. Richard W. Slatta, *Cowboys of the Americas* (New Haven: Yale University Press, 1990), especially chap. 10, "Cowboy and Indians: Frontier Race Relations," 159–73; Peter Iverson, *When Indians Became Cowboys: Native Peoples and Cattle Ranching in the American West* (Norman: University of Oklahoma Press, 1994).

4. Peter H. Wood, *Black Majority: Negroes in Colonial South Carolina from 1670 through the Stono Rebellion* (New York: Knopf, 1972).

5. Slatta, *Cowboys;* Terry G. Jordan, *Trails to Texas: Southern Roots of Western Cattle Ranching* (Lincoln: University of Nebraska Press, 1981); Frederick Remington, "Vagabonding with the Tenth Horse," *Cosmopolitan* 22 (February 1897): 352.

6. Jordan, *Trails to Texas*, 127.

7. Wood, *Black Majority*.

8. Ron Tyler and Lawrence Murphy, eds., *The Slave Narratives of Texas* (Austin: State House Press, 1974), 56–57.

9. George P. Rawick, ed., *Texas Narratives*, Vol. 5, Part 4 of *The American Slave: A Composite Autobiography* (Westport, Conn.: Greenwood, 1972), 102–103.

10. John Hendricks, "Tribute Paid to Negro Cowmen," *Cattlemen* 22 (February 1936): 24.

11. J. Evetts Haley, *Charles Goodnight: Cowman and Plainsman* (Norman: University of Oklahoma Press, 1936), 243.

12. Johnson, *Guts*, xvii–xix.

13. Michael N. Searles, "Addison Jones: The Most Noted Negro Cowboy That Ever 'Topped Off' a Horse,'" in Massey, *Black Cowboys of Texas*, 193–205.

14. Massey, *Black Cowboys of Texas*.

15. *Forsyth (Montana) Time-Journal*, August 4, 1938.

16. Wallace McRae, *Cowboy Curmudgeon and Other Poems* (Salt Lake City: Gibbs Smith, 1992), 44–45.

17. Kenneth Wiggins Porter, *The Negro on the American Frontier* (New York: Arno Press, 1971); Jack Weston, *The Real American Cowboy* (New York: Amsterdam Books, 1985); Lawrence B. de Graff, "Recognition, Racism, and Reflections on the Writing of Western Black History," *Pacific Historical Review* 44, no. 1 (February 1975): 22–51; Patricia Nelson Limerick, *The Legacy of Conquest: The Unbroken Past of the American*

West (New York: W. W. Norton, 1987).

18. Rawick, *Texas Narratives*, Vol. 4, Part 1, 11–73.

19. Walter Prescott Webb, ed. *The Handbook of Texas*, Vol. 1 (Austin: State Historical Association, 1951), 539.

20. Joyce Gibson Roach, "Daniel Webster Wallace: A West Texas Cattleman," in Massey, *Black Cowboys of Texas*, 181–91.

21. Hettye Wallace Branch, *The Story of "80 John": A Biography of One of the Most Respected Negro Ranchmen in the Old West* (New York: Greenwich, 1960); Hertha Auburn Webb, "D. W. '80 John' Wallace—Black Cattleman, 1875–1939" (Master's thesis, Prairie View A&M College, 1957); R. C. Crane, "D. W. ('80 John') Wallace, a Negro Cattleman on the Texas Frontier," *West Texas Historical Association Yearbook* 28 (October 1952): 113–18.

22. Roach, "Daniel Webster Wallace," 183–84.

23. Branch, *Story of "80 John,"* 30.

24. Colonel Bailey C. Hanes, *Bill Pickett, Bulldogger: The Biography of a Black Cowboy* (Norman: University of Oklahoma Press, 1977), xi. The following review of Pickett is drawn from Hanes, *Bill Pickett*, 15–26, 40–46, and Mary Lou LeCompte, "Pickett, William," *Handbook of Texas Online*, http://www.tshaonline.org/handbook/online/articles/fpi04.

25. Along with Hanes, *Bill Pickett*, 40, see Johnson, *Guts*, 10.

26. Johnson, *Guts*, 113–21.

27. J. A. Lomax and Alan Lomax, *Cowboy Songs and Other Frontier Ballads* (New York: Colliers, 1938), xviii–xix.

Selected Bibliography

Acosta, Teresa Palomo. "Black Cowboys." *Handbook of Texas Online.* www.tshaonline. org/handbook/online/articles/arbo1. Texas State Historical Association.

Agogino, George. "The McJunkin Controversy: A Search for Answers at Wild Horse Arroyo." *New Mexico Magazine* 49 (May/June 1971): 41–43, 47.

Allmendinger, Blake. "African Americans and the Popular West." In *Updating the Literary West*, edited by Dan Flores, 916–20. Fort Worth: TCU Press, 1992.

———. "Deadwood Dick: The Black Cowboy as Cultural Timber." *Journal of American Culture* 16, no. 4 (Winter 1993): 79–89.

———. *Imagining the American West.* Lincoln: University of Nebraska Press, 2005.

———. "The White Open Spaces." In *Ten Most Wanted: The New Western Literature*, 17–31, 189–92. New York: Routledge, 1998.

Anderson, Burton. "The California Rodeo: A Central Coast Tradition." *Monterey County Historical Society* (1997). www.mchsmuseum.com/rodeo.html.

Anderson, Lavere. "The Cowboys." In *Saddles and Sabers: Black Men in the Old West*, 89–103. Champaign, Ill.: Garrard, 1975.

Behan, Barbara Carol. "Forgotten Heritage: African Americans in the Montana Territory, 1864–1889." *Journal of African American History* 91, no. 1 (Winter 2006): 23–40.

Bish, James D. "The Black Experience in Selected Nebraska Counties, 1854–1920." Master's thesis, University of Nebraska at Omaha, 1989.

Bloom, Sam. "Black Trailblazers and Cowboys." *Real West* 18 (March 1975): 30–34.

Bonner, Thomas D., ed. *Life and Adventures of James Beckwourth.* Lincoln: University of Nebraska Press, 1972.

Branch, Hettye Wallace. *The Story of "80 John": A Biography of One of the Most Respected Negro Ranchmen in the Old West.* New York: Greenwich Books, 1960.

Broussard, Albert S. "Cowboys." In *Expectations of Equality: A History of Black Westerners*, 46–48, 212–13. Wheeling, Ill.: Harlan Davidson, 2012.

Buchanan, Minor Ferris. *Holt Collier: His Life, His Roosevelt Hunts, and the Origin of the*

Teddy Bear. Jackson: Centennial Press of Mississippi, 2002.

Burton, Art T. "Bass Reeves: A Legendary Lawman of the Western Frontier." *Persimmon Hill* 20, no. 2 (Summer 1992): 45–48.

———. *Black, Buckskin, and Blue: African American Scouts and Soldiers*. Austin: Eakin Press, 1999.

———. *Black Gun, Silver Star: Bass Reeves*. Lincoln: University of Nebraska Press, 2006.

———. *Black, Red, and Deadly: Black and Indian Gunfighters of the Indian Territory, 1870–1907*. Austin: Eakin Press, 1991.

Clayton, Lawrence. "Bill 'Tige' Avery." In *Cowboys Who Rode Proudly*, edited by J. Evetts Haley. Midland, Tex.: Nita Stewart Haley Memorial Library, 1992.

———. "Nig London: Throckmorton County Cowman." *West Texas Historical Association Year Book* 67 (1991): 94–100.

Clayton, Lawrence, Jim Hoy, and Jerald Underwood. *Vaqueros, Cowboys, and Buckaroos*. Austin: University of Texas Press, 2001.

Cooper, Gary. "Stagecoach Mary." *Ebony* 14 (October 1959): 97–100.

Crane, R. C., ed. "D. W. Wallace ('80 John'): A Negro Cattleman on the Texas Frontier." *West Texas Historical Society Yearbook* 28 (1952): 113–17.

Crimm, Ana Carolina Castillo. "Mathew 'Bones' Hooks: A Pioneer of Honor." In *Black Cowboys of Texas*, edited by Sara R. Massey, 219–45. College Station: Texas A&M University Press, 2000.

Davis, Alvin G. "Black Cowboys and Ranchers in Texas." *Heritage* (Winter 1994): 10–12.

"Deadwood Dick and the Black Cowboys." *Journal of Blacks in Higher Education* 22 (Winter 1998/99): 30–31.

De Leon, Arnoldo. "Vamos Pa'Kiansis: Tejanos in the Nineteenth-Century Cattle Drives." *Journal of South Texas* 27, no. 2 (Fall 2014): 6–21.

Dempsey, Mary A. "The Bronze Buckaroo Rides Again: Herb Jeffries Is Still Keepin' On." *American Visions* 12 (August/September 1997): 22–26.

Drotning, Phillip T. "New Look at the Old Cowhand." In *Black Heroes in Our Nation's History: A Tribute to Those Who Helped Shape America*, 113–31. New York: Cowles, 1969.

Durham, David Anthony. *Gabriel's Story: A Novel*. New York: Doubleday, 2001.

Durham, Philip. "The Lost Cowboy." *Midwest Journal* 7 (1955): 176–82.

———. "The Negro Cowboy." *American Quarterly* 7 (Fall 1955): 291–302.

Durham, Philip, and Everett L. Jones. *The Adventures of the Negro Cowboys*. New York: Dodd, Mead, 1966.

———. "Negro Cowboys." *American West* 1 (Fall 1964): 26–31, 87.

———. *The Negro Cowboys*. Lincoln: University of Nebraska Press, 1983 [1965].

———. "Slaves on Horseback." *Pacific Historical Review* 33 (1964): 405–409.

Everett, Percival. *God's Country*. Boston: Beacon Press, 2003.

———. *Wounded*. St. Paul, Minn.: Graywolf, 2005.

Felton, Harold W. *Nat Love: Negro Cowboy*. New York: Dodd, Mead, 1969.

Flamming, Douglas. "The Cowboys." In *African Americans in the West*, 61–70, 90. Santa Barbara, Calif.: ABC-CLIO, 2009.

Folsom, Franklin. *Black Cowboy: The Life and Legend of George McJunkin*. Niwot, Colo.: Roberts Rinehart, 1992.

Fox, Charity. "Cowboys, Porters, and the Mythic West: Satire and Frontier Masculinity in *The Life and Adventures of Nat Love*." In *Fathers, Preachers, Rebels, Men: Black Masculinity in U.S. History and Literature*, edited by Peter Caster and Timothy R. Buckner, 184–202. Columbus: Ohio State University Press, 2011.

Franks, James A. *Mary Fields: The Story of Black Mary*. Santa Cruz, Calif.: Wild Goose Press, 2000.

Freedman, Russell. *In the Days of the Vaqueros: America's First True Cowboys*. New York: Clarion Books, 2001.

Gallaher, Bill. *High Rider*. Victoria, B.C.: TouchWood, 2015.

Gandy, S. Kay. "Legacy of the American West: Indian Cowboys, Black Cowboys, and Vaqueros." *Social Education* 72, no. 4 (2008): 189–93.

Garceau-Hagen, Dee. "Finding Mary Fields: Race, Gender, and the Construction of Memory." In *Portraits of Women in the American West*, edited by Dee Garceau-Hagen, 121–55. New York: Routledge, 2005.

Gill, Gale. "Texas Trail Ride: Negro Cowboys." *Ebony* 18 (May 1963): 115–22, 124.

Glasrud, Bruce A. "African Americans in the Wild, Wild West: Examples from Texas." *Journal of the Wild West History Association* 2, no. 6 (2009): 3–8.

———, ed. *African Americans in South Texas History*. College Station: Texas A&M University Press, 2011.

Glasrud, Bruce A., and Charles A. Braithwaite, eds. *African Americans on the Great Plains*. Lincoln: University of Nebraska Press, 2009.

Glasrud, Bruce A., Paul H. Carlson, with Tai D. Kreidler, eds. *Slavery to Integration: Black Americans in West Texas*. Abilene, Tex.: State House Press, 2007.

Glasrud, Bruce A., and Laurie Champion, eds. *The African American West: A Century of Short Stories*. Boulder: University Press of Colorado, 2000.

Glasrud, Bruce A., and Michael N. Searles, eds. *Buffalo Soldiers in the West*. College Station: Texas A&M University Press, 2007.

Glasrud, Bruce A., and Alan M. Smith, eds. *Promises to Keep: A Portrayal of Nonwhites in the United States*. Chicago: Rand McNally, 1972.

Govenar, Alan. "Musical Traditions of Twentieth-Century African-American Cowboys." In *Juneteenth Texas: Essays in African-American Folklore*, edited by Francis Abernethy et al., 195–206. Denton: University of North Texas Press, 1996.

Hales, Douglas. "Black Cowboy: Daniel Webster '80 John' Wallace." In *The Cowboy Way: An Exploration of History and Culture*, edited by Paul H. Carlson, 33–43. Lubbock: Texas Tech University Press, 2000.

Hancock, Sibyl. *Bill Pickett: First Black Rodeo Star*. New York: Harcourt Brace Jovanovich, 1977.

Hanes, Colonel Bailey C. *Bill Pickett, Bulldogger: The Biography of a Black Cowboy*. Norman: University of Oklahoma Press, 1977.

Hardaway, Roger D. "African American Cowboys on the Western Frontier." *Negro History Bulletin* 64 (January/December, 2001): 27–32.

———. "Cowboys." In *A Narrative Bibliography of the African American Frontier: Blacks in the Rocky Mountain West, 1535–1912*, 143–60. Lewiston, N.Y.: Edwin Mellen Press, 1995.

———. "Oklahoma's African American Rodeo Performers." *Chronicles of Oklahoma* 89, no. 2 (Summer 2011): 152–75.

Hardman, Peggy. "Bob Lemmons." *The New Handbook of Texas*, Vol. 4., edited by Ron Tyler et al. Austin: Texas State Historical Association, 1996.

Haywood, C. Robert. "'No Less a Man': Blacks in Cow Town Dodge City, 1876–1886." *Western Historical Quarterly* 19, no. 2 (May 1988): 161–82.

———. *Victorian West: Class and Culture in Kansas Cattle Towns*. Lawrence: University Press of Kansas, 1991.

Hendrix, John M. "Tribute Paid to Negro Cattlemen." *Cattleman* (February 1936): 24–26.

Hopkins, Seth, and Michael N. Searles, curators. *The Black West: Buffalo Soldiers, Black Cowboys, and Untold Stories*. Cartersville, Ga.: Booth Western Art Museum, 2009.

Hoy, Jim. "Black Cowboys." *Kansas* 18 (November 1986): 48–50.

Hundey, Ian. *John Ware: Cowboy*. Markham, Ont.: Fitzhenry and Whiteside, 2005.

"The Invisible Black Cowboys." *123HelpMe.com*. November 19, 2015. www.123HelpMe.com/view.asp?id=24166.

Jiles, Paulette. *The Color of Lightning: A Novel*. New York: William Morrow, 2009.

Johnson, Cecil. *Guts: Legendary Black Rodeo Cowboy Bill Pickett*. Fort Worth, Tex.: Summit Group, 1994.

Johnson, Michael K. *Black Masculinity and the Frontier Myth in American Literature*. Norman: University of Oklahoma Press, 2002.

———. *Hoo-Doo Cowboys and Bronze Buckaroos: Conceptions of the African American West*. Jackson: University Press of Mississippi, 2014.

Jordan, Terry G. *North American Cattle-Ranching Frontiers: Origins, Diffusion, and Differentiation*. Albuquerque: University of New Mexico Press, 1993.

———. *Trails to Texas: Southern Roots of Western Cattle Ranching*. Lincoln: University of Nebraska Press, 1981.

Katz, William Loren. *Black Indians: A Hidden Heritage*. New York: Atheneum, 1986.

———. *Black People Who Made the Old West*. Trenton, N.J.: Africa World Press, 1992.

———. *The Black West: A Documentary and Pictorial History of the African American Role in the Westward Expansion of the United States*. New York: Simon and Schuster, 1987 [1971].

————. *Black Women of the Old West*. New York: Atheneum Books, 1995.

Kelton, Elmer. *Wagontongue*. New York: Bantam Books, 1972.

Knox, Andrew P. "Before Hollywood Made the Myth: Negro Cowboys in the Old West." *Black World* 14 (September 1965): 80–83.

Lang, William. "The Nearly Forgotten Blacks on the Last Chance Gulch, 1900–1912." *Pacific Northwest Quarterly* 70, no. 2 (April 1979): 50–57.

Lape, Noreen Groover. *West of the Border: The Multicultural Literature of the Western American Frontiers*. Athens: Ohio University Press, 2000.

Lewis, Georgia. "The Black Ranchers of Lincoln County." *Nevadan*, July 18, 1971, 28–29.

Liles, Deborah M. "Slavery and Cattle in East and West Texas." *East Texas Historical Journal* 52, no. 2 (Fall 2014): 29–38.

————. "Southern Roots, Western Foundations: The Peculiar Institution and the Cattle Industry in Northwestern Texas." Ph.D. dissertation, University of North Texas, 2010.

————. *Southern Roots, Western Foundations: The Peculiar Institution and the Livestock Industry on the Northwestern Frontier of Texas, 1846–1864*. Baton Rouge: Louisiana State University Press, 2016.

Littlefield, Daniel F., Jr., and Lonnie Underhill. "Negro Marshals in the Indian Territory." *Journal of Negro History* 54, no. 2 (April 1971): 77–87.

Love, Nat. *The Life and Adventures of Nat Love, Better Known in the Cattle Country as "Deadwood Dick."* Lincoln: University of Nebraska Press, 1995 [1907].

MacEwan, Grant. *John Ware's Cow Country*. Vancouver, B.C.: Greystone Books, 1973.

Machado, Manuel A. *The North Mexican Cattle Industry, 1910–1975*. College Station: Texas A&M University Press, 1981.

Massey, Sara R., ed. *Black Cowboys of Texas*. College Station: Texas A&M University Press, 2000.

McKissack, Patricia C., and Fredrick L. McKissack Jr. *Best Shot in the West: The Adventures of Nat Love*. San Francisco: Chronicle Books, 2012.

Middleton, Stephen L. *The Black Laws in the Old Northwest*. Westport, Conn.: Greenwood, 1993.

Moos, Dan. *Outside America: Race, Ethnicity, and the Role of the American West in National Belonging*. Lebanon, N.H.: University Press of New England, 2005.

Mundis, Jerrold J. "He Took the Bull by the Horns." *American Heritage* 19 (December 1967): 50–55.

Myers, Walter Dean. *The Journal of Joshua Loper: A Black Cowboy*. New York: Scholastic, 1999.

Neri, G., and Jesse Joshua Watson. *Ghetto Cowboy*. New York: Candlewick, 2013.

Newgard, Thomas P., and William C. Sherman, eds. "Cattle and Ranching." In *African Americans in North Dakota: Sources and Assessments*, 48–52. Bismarck, N.Dak.: University of Mary Press, 1995.

Norton, Wesley. "Negro Trail-Driver, Jean Spence Perrault, and His Beaumont Descendants." *Texas Gulf Historical and Biographical Record* 19 (November 1983): 35–50.

Nugent, Walter. *Into the West: The Story of Its People.* New York: Alfred A. Knopf, 1999.

Pearson, Demetrius W. "Black in the Saddle: The Best Bull Rider You Never Saw." *African Studies* 3 (2009): 183–96.

———. Cowboys of Color: The Perceived Social and Cultural Significance of U2 Rodeo." *African Studies* 4 (2012): 63–76.

———. "Shadow Riders of the Subterranean Circuit: A Descriptive Account of Black Rodeo in the Texas Gulf Coast Region." *Journal of American Culture* 27, no. 2 (June 2004): 190–98.

Pelz, Ruth, and Leandro Della Piana. *Black Heroes of the Wild West.* Seattle: Open Hand, 1990.

Pinkney, Andrea, and Brian Pinkney. *Bill Pickett: Rodeo-Ridin' Cowboy.* San Diego: Harcourt Brace, 1996.

Porter, Kenneth Wiggins. "Cowkeeper Dynasty of the Seminole Nation." *Florida Historical Quarterly* 30 (1952): 341–49.

———. "Negro Labor in the Western Cattle Industry, 1866–1900." *Labor History* 10 (Summer 1969): 346–74.

———. *The Negro on the American Frontier.* New York: Arno Press, 1971.

Preece, Harold. "American Negro Cowboys." *Real West* 9 (January 1966): 26–30.

Ravage, John W. "Blacks in the American West." *History of Photography* 16 (Winter 1992): 392–96.

———. "Cowhands and Ranch Hands." In *Black Pioneers: Images of the Black Experience on the North American Frontier*, 51–55. Salt Lake City: University of Utah Press, 1997.

——— [Jack]. *Singletree.* Laramie, Wyo.: Jelm Mountain, 1990.

Reed, Ishmael. *Yellow Back Radio Broke-Down.* New York: Doubleday, 1969.

Resendes, Monica. "The Adventures of Deadwood Dick in the American West." *Historical Biographies*, May 2009.

Richardson, Barbara J. "Black Cowboys Also Rode." *Password* 31 (Spring 1986): 29–34, 41.

Rusco, Elmer R. "Farmers and Cowboys." In *"Good Time Coming?" Black Nevadans in the Nineteenth Century*, 142–46, 168. Westport, Conn.: Greenwood Press, 1975.

Sandler, Martin W. *Vaqueros: America's First Cowmen.* New York: Henry Holt, 2000.

Savage, W. Sherman. *Blacks in the West.* Westport, Conn.: Greenwood Press, 1976.

———. "The Negro Cowboys on the Texas Plains." *Negro History Bulletin* 24 (April 1961): 157–58, 163.

———. "The Negro in the Westward Movement." *Journal of Negro History* 25 (October 1940): 531–39.

———. "Negroes on the Cattleman's Frontier." *Midwest Journal* 6 (1954/1955): 35–48.

Scheckel, Susan. "Home on the Train: Race and Mobility in the *Life and Adventures of Nat Love.*" *American Literature* 74, no. 2 (June 2002): 219–50.

Schlissel, Lillian. *Black Frontiers: A History of African American Heroes in the Old West.* New York: Simon and Schuster, 1995.

Schrum, Keith. "Of Myth and Men: The Trail of the Black Cowboy." *Colorado Heritage,* Autumn 1998, 2–17.

Searles, Michael N. "Addison Jones: The Most Noted Negro Cowboy That Ever 'Topped Off' A Horse." In *Black Cowboys of Texas,* edited by Sara R. Massey, 193–205. College Station: Texas A&M University Press, 2000.

———. "The Black Cowboy—Yesterday and Today: A Hard Won Reputation." *Augusta Today Magazine* 4 (January/February 1997): 20–24.

———. "Buffalo Soldiers: Honed and Sharpened in the West." *Roundup Magazine* 22, no. 3 (February 2015): 8–14.

———. "In Search of the Black Cowboy in Texas." In *The African American Experience in Texas,* edited by Bruce A. Glasrud and James M. Smallwood, 86–101. Lubbock: Texas Tech University Press, 2007.

———. "Taking out the Buck and Putting in a Trick: The Black Working Cowboys Art of Breaking and Keeping a Good Cow Horse." *Journal of the West* 44 (Spring 2005): 53–60.

Slatta, Richard. *Cowboys of the Americas.* New Haven: Yale University Press, 1990.

Slotkin, Richard. *Gunfighter Nation: The Myth of the Frontier in Twentieth-Century America.* New York: Harper Perennial, 1993.

Sluyter, Andrew. *Black Ranching Frontiers: African Cattle Herders of the Atlantic World, 1500–1900.* New Haven: Yale University Press, 2012.

Speirs, Kenneth. "Writing Self (Effacingly): E-Race-D Presences in *The Life and Adventures of Nat Love.*" *Western American Literature* 40, no. 3 (Fall 2005): 301–20.

Stewart, Paul W., and Wallace Yvonne Ponce. *Black Cowboys.* Broomfield, Colo.: Phillips, 1986.

Taylor, Quintard. "Blacks in the West." *Western Journal of Black Studies* 1 (March 1977): 4–10.

———. *In Search of the Racial Frontier: African Americans in the American West, 1528–1990.* New York: W. W. Norton, 1998.

———. "Texas: The South Meets the West, the View through African American History." *Journal of the West* 48, no. 4 (Fall 2009): 56–64.

Todd, Bruce G. *Bones Hooks: Pioneer Negro Cowboy.* Gretna, La.: Pelican, 2005.

VanEpps-Taylor, Betti. "Cowboys and Ranchers of Western South Dakota." In *Forgotten Lives: African Americans in South Dakota.* Pierre: South Dakota State Historical Society Press, 2008.

Wagner, Tricia Martineau. *Black Cowboys of the Old West.* Guilford, Conn.: Globe

Pequot Press, 2011.

———. "A Force to Be Dealt With: Mary Fields." In *African American Women of the Old West*, 13–25. Helena, Mont.: TwoDot, 2007.

Watriss, Wendy. "The Soul Circuit." *Geo* 2 (December 1980): 134–50.

Wax, Darold D. "Robert Ball Anderson, Ex-slave, a Pioneer in Western Nebraska, 1884–1930." *Nebraska History* 64, no. 2 (Summer 1983): 163–85.

Webb, Hertha Auburn. "D. W. '80 John' Wallace: Black Cattleman, 1875–1939." Master's thesis, Prairie View A&M College, 1957.

Westermeier, Clifford P. "Black Rodeo Cowboys." *Red River Valley Historical Review* 3, no. 3 (Summer 1978): 4–27.

Wilder, Janeen. "Reins, Riggings, and Reatas: The Outfit of the Great Basin Buckaroo." *Oregon Historical Society* 104, no. 3 (2003): 366–93.

Williams, Brackette F. "Nat Love Rides into the Sunset of Slavery and Racism." In Nat Love, *The Life and Adventures of Nat Love*, vii–xviii. Lincoln: University of Nebraska Press, 1995.

Williams, Nudie. "Black Men Who Wore the Star." *Chronicles of Oklahoma* 59, no. 1 (Spring 1981): 83–90.

———. "Black Men Who Wore White Hats: Grant Johnson, United States Deputy Marshal." *Red River Valley Historical Review* 5 (Summer 1980): 4–13.

———. "A History of the American Southwest: Black United States Deputy Marshals in the Indian Territory, 1875–1907." Master's thesis, Oklahoma State University, 1973.

———. "United States vs. Bass Reeves: Black Lawman on Trial." *Chronicles of Oklahoma* 68 (1990): 154–67.

Wyman, Walker D., and John D. Hart. *The Legend of Charlie Glass*. River Falls, Wisc.: River Falls State University Press, 1970.

———. "The Legend of Charlie Glass." *Colorado Magazine* 46 (1969): 40–54.

Index

CPSIA information can be obtained
at www.ICGtesting.com
Printed in the USA
LVHW041153031120
670569LV00002B/161